The MAYA

Michael D. Coe

The MAYA

Fourth edition, fully revised

WITH 146 ILLUSTRATIONS

THAMES AND HUDSON

Ancient Peoples and Places
GENERAL EDITOR: GLYN DANIEL

Frontispiece: Wood carving of a Maya lord from Tabasco, Mexico. See ill. 48 for whole figure.

First published in Great Britain in 1966
by Thames and Hudson Ltd, London

Second edition published in the USA in 1980
by Thames and Hudson Inc., 500 Fifth Avenue,
New York, New York 10110
Third edition 1984
Fourth edition 1987

Library of Congress Catalog Card Number 86–51616

Printed and bound in Great Britain

Contents

Foreword   7

Chronological table   10

1 Introduction   11

The setting   13
Areas   21
Periods   21
Peoples and languages   24

2 The earliest Maya   29

Early hunters   29
Archaic collectors and cultivators   31
Early Preclassic villages   34
The Middle Preclassic expansion   38

3 The rise of Maya civilization   45

The birth of the calendar   47
Izapa and the Pacific Coast   51
Kaminaljuyú and the Maya highlands   54
The Petén and the Maya lowlands   61

4 Classic splendor: the Early period   67

The Esperanza culture   69
Tzakol culture in the Central Area   75
The Northern Area   83
The Cotzumalhuapa problem   84

5 Classic splendor: the Late period   89

Classic sites in the Central Area   93
Classic sites in the Northern Area:
    Río Bec, Chenes, and Cobá   112
Classic sites in the Northern Area: the Puuc   114

Art of the Late Classic 118
The end of Classic Maya civilization 126
The Putun Maya 128

6 **The Post-Classic** 131

The Toltec invasion and Toltec Chichén Itzá 131
The Itzá and the city of Mayapán 144
The independent states of Yucatán 147
The Central Area in the Post-Classic 148
Maya–Mexican dynasties in the Southern Area 149
The Spanish Conquest 153

7 **Maya life on the eve of the Conquest** 155

The farm and the chase 155
Industry and commerce 157
The life cycle 158
Society and politics 159

8 **Maya thought and culture** 161

The universe and the gods 164
The Classic Maya Underworld 166
Rites and ritual practitioners 169
Numbers and the calendar 173
The sun and the moon 175
The celestial wanderers and the stars 176
The nature of Maya writing 178
The content of Maya writing 182

Select bibliography 188

List of illustrations 194

Index 197

Foreword

This book was first conceived as a companion to *Mexico*, both volumes intended to present to the interested reader – including travelers and students – a concise and up-to-date introduction to the native civilizations of Mesoamerica. I first wrote *The Maya* because I believed that these fascinating people should be allowed to tell us about their own way of life and outlook on the universe. In the ensuing years, that goal has come far closer with the accelerating pace of decipherment of the hieroglyphic script: the ancient Maya can now speak to us across the void of time in their own words. They have now become the only truly historical people of the Pre-Columbian New World, as I hope that these pages will show.

The Maya first appeared in 1966. The past two decades have seen great advances in our knowledge of Maya civilization in both the Preclassic and Classic epochs, often in ways that earlier generations of scholars would not have approved. From a picture of the Maya that emphasized peaceful theocracies led by priest astronomers, ruling over relatively empty 'ceremonial centers', we now have highly warlike city-states led by grim dynasts obsessed with human sacrifice and the ritual letting of their own blood. Although traditional 'dirt' archaeology has contributed to our current view of the ancient Maya, the contributions of epigraphy and art history have been, in my opinion, truly revolutionary.

I would like to acknowledge my intellectual debt to the following scholars in the development of my knowledge of the Maya, which has resulted in the present edition: Yuri Knorosov, Floyd Lounsbury, Mary Miller, Linda Schele, Peter Mathews, Karl Taube, David Joralemon, Elizabeth P. Benson, David Stuart, Peter T. Furst, and Barbara and Dennis Tedlock; these are among the principal shapers of the new model of ancient Maya thought, although not the only ones. I would also willingly admit my deep obligation to some scholars who are now no longer with us, such as Tatiana Proskouriakoff, and particularly to my old friend the late Sir Eric Thompson, for whom I hope I am still the 'honorable opposition'.

In the preparation of this new edition, I have been greatly helped by the comments of three Mayanists for whom I have the greatest respect. Professor David Freidel and Dr David Pendergast, both notable field excavators, have made detailed suggestions to improve the previous edition; I have taken most of these into account, but of course they should not be held accountable for my sins of omission and commission. My friend Professor David Kelley encouraged me to include more of my own findings on Maya funerary ceramics which relate to iconography and religion, and stimulated me to take a less negative view of the possibility of trans-Pacific contact.

A few words should be said about the pronunciation of Maya names and words. The system of orthography comes to us from the early Spanish friars who were attempting to record the native language of Yucatán, so that most vowels and consonants are as in Spanish. However, the good priests were plagued by the fact that many Maya sounds were unknown to Europe and so had to devise new ways of writing them down. The letter *x* is used, as in sixteenth-century Spanish, to record a phoneme like English *sh*; *c* is hard, no matter which vowel follows it; *u* before *a, e, i,* and *o* is pronounced like English *w*. The Maya languages make an important distinction between glottalized and non-glottalized consonants, the former being enunciated with constricted throat. In the revised orthography of Yucatec Maya these would be as follows:

Non-glottalized	Glottalized
c	k
ch	ch'
tz	dz
p	pp
t	th

Glottal constrictions or stops may also occur between reduplicated vowels, although these are ignored in most dictionaries.

Some of the words relevant to this book are in Nahuatl, the national tongue of the Aztec state, which was used as a great trading *lingua franca* at the time of the Conquest. Nahuatl names were transcribed in Roman letters in terms of the language spoken by the *conquistadores* of the sixteenth century; they have not been accented here, since they are regularly stressed on the penultimate syllable, whereas Maya and Spanish names have been given their accents.

There have been important advances in the accurate correlation of dates derived from radiocarbon determinations with those of the Christian calendar. Dendrochronological studies of the bristlecone pine now suggest that before about 1000 BC there is an increasing deviation from 'true' dates back to a maximum of some 800 years at radiocarbon 4500 BC. No attempt has been made in this edition to calibrate prehistoric dates with the 'true' dates from bristlecone pine, since there is still disagreement among specialists as to the correct calibration curve, and this curve itself only extends as far back as about 5000 BC. But readers who want a rough guide to 'true' prehistoric dates may find it helpful to bear in mind that a radiocarbon date of 1000 BC is in all probability 1200 BC in calendar years, radiocarbon 2000 BC is about 2500 BC, while radiocarbon 3000 BC would be approximately 3700 BC.

Radiocarbon dating has no real bearing on the chronology of the Classic Maya period (*c.* AD 250–900), which depends on the accuracy of the correlation between the Long Count calendar and the European-Christian calendar. My colleague Dr Lounsbury has provided incontrovertible proof that the calendar correlation first advanced by Eric Thompson (the 584285 constant, for specialists) is correct, thus enabling scholars confidently to associate ancient astronomical events important to the Maya with historical dates.

And, finally, I would like to reiterate my continuing gratitude to Dr Glyn Daniel and to the late Dr Geoffrey Bushnell, without whose encouragement and support this book would never have existed in the first place, and to the editorial staff of Thames and Hudson.

Chronological table

DATES[*]	PERIODS	SOUTHERN AREA		CENTRAL AREA	NORTHERN AREA
		Pacific Coast	Highlands		
1530	Late Post-Classic		Mixco Viejo	Tayasal ↑	Independent States Mayapan
1200	Early Post-Classic	Tohil Plumbate	Ayampuc	(abandonment)	Toltec-Maya
900	Late Classic		Amatle-Pamplona	Tepeu	Puuc, Chenes ↑
600	Early Classic	Cotzumal-huapa ↑	Esperanza	Tzakol	Regional Styles Acanceh
250				Matzanel	
BC / AD	Late Preclassic	El Baúl Crucero	Aurora Santa Clara Miraflores	Chicanel	Late Preclassic
300	Middle Preclassic	Conchas	Las Charcas	Mamom	Middle Preclassic
				Xe	Maní Cenot
800	Early Preclassic	Cuadros	Arévalo		
		Ocós			Swasey
2000	(Archaic)				

*Dates for the pre-Christian era are given in uncalibrated radiocarbon years.

1
Introduction

The Maya are hardly a vanished people, for they number an estimated two million souls, the largest single block of American Indians north of Peru. Most of them have resisted with remarkable tenacity the encroachments of Spanish American civilization, although in the past decade these have taken an increasingly violent and repressive form. Besides their numbers and cultural integrity, the Maya are remarkable for an extraordinary cohesion. Unlike other more scattered indigenous peoples within Mexico and Central America, the Maya are confined with one exception (the Huastec) to a single, unbroken area that includes all of the Yucatán Peninsula, Guatemala, Belize, parts of the Mexican states of Tabasco and Chiapas, and the western portion of Honduras and El Salvador. Such homogeneity in the midst of such a miscellany of tongues and peoples testifies to their relative security from invasions by other native groups – the Aztec, for instance, never extended their empire to include any part of Maya territory, although they had important trading relationships with them.

There are few parts of the world where there is such a good 'fit' between language and culture: a line drawn around the Maya-speaking peoples would contain all those remains, and hieroglyphic texts, assigned to the ancient Maya civilization. It would be an error, though, to think of these peoples as existing in some kind of vacuum. An earlier generation of archaeologists, which included the late Sylvanus G. Morley of the Carnegie Institution of Washington, thought of the Maya as *the* great innovators and culture-givers to the rest of the peoples of Mexico and Central America. A later generation, which included myself, came to view this fundamentally 'Mayacentric' outlook as wrong: the ancient Maya had received much more from the non-Maya Mexican civilizations than they had given. I must now admit that Morley may have been more right than wrong, for reasons that will be made clear in this book.

In pre-Spanish times the Maya belonged to the larger grouping christened 'Mesoamerica' by Professor Kirchhoff. The northern frontier coincided approximately with the limits of aboriginal farming in Mexico, the desiccated plateau beyond holding out only the possibility of humble collecting and hunting. To the southeast, the Mesoamerican border ran from the Caribbean to the Pacific across what is now Honduras and El Salvador, although in late pre-Conquest times it is apparent that northwesternmost Costa Rica was thoroughly Mesoamerican in culture; the southeastern frontier generally divided the civilized Maya from simpler peoples of foreign tongue.

1   Major topographical features and cultural areas.

All the Mesoamerican Indians shared a number of traits which were more or less peculiar to them and absent or rare elsewhere in the New World: hieroglyphic writing, books of fig-bark paper or deerskin which were folded like screens, a complex permutation calendar, knowledge of the movements of the planets (especially Venus) against the background of the stars, a game played with a rubber ball in a special court, highly specialized markets, human sacrifice by head or heart removal, an emphasis upon self-sacrifice by blood drawn from the ears, tongue, or penis, and a highly complex, pantheistic religion which included nature divinities as well as deities emblematic of royal descent. Also in all Mesoamerican religions was the idea of a multi-tiered Heaven and Underworld, and of a universe oriented to the four directions with specific colors and gods assigned to the cardinal points and to the center.

131

While there are profound differences between the subsistence base of the lowlands and that of the highlands, the ancient triad of maize, beans, and squash formed then, as it still does, the basis of the Mesoamerican diet, but of course these foods were widely spread elsewhere – from the southwestern United States to Peru and Argentina in pre-Conquest times – wherever native cultures had advanced beyond a level of semi-nomadic simplicity. In Mesoamerica, none the less, the preparation of maize is highly distinctive: the hard, ripe kernels are soaked or boiled in a mixture of water and white lime, producing a kind of hominy which is then ground into unleavened dough on a quern (*metate*) with a handstone (*mano*, from the Spanish *mano de piedra*), later to be fashioned into steamed *tamales* or into the flat cakes called by the Spanish term *tortillas*. The latter, probably introduced into the Maya area in late pre-Conquest times from Mexico, are characteristically toasted on a clay griddle which rests upon a three-stone hearth.

124

From such profound similarities one can only conclude that all the Mesoamerican peoples must have shared a common origin, so far back in time that it may never be brought to light by archaeology. Yet there is some consensus among archaeologists that the Olmec of southern Mexico had elaborated many of these traits beginning about 3,000 years ago, and that much of complex culture in Mesoamerica has an Olmec origin. It is also reasonable to assume that there must have been an active interchange of ideas and things among the Mesoamerican élite over many centuries, a state of affairs which can be documented in the terminal Classic epoch thanks to recent research; this in itself would tend to bring about cultural homogeneity – for example, it might explain why both the Classic Maya and the very late Aztec held a snake-footed god to be the supernatural ruling their respective royal houses. It was out of such a matrix of cultural evolution and diffusion that Maya civilization was born.

The setting

There can be few parts of the globe as geographically diverse as Mesoamerica, which includes almost every ecological extreme from the snow-swept wastes of the high volcanoes to parched deserts and to rain-drenched jungle. The Maya area is situated in the southeastern corner of this topsy-turvy land, but actually is somewhat less varied than the larger unit of which it is a part. For instance, high-altitude tundra is not found, and deserts are confined to narrow stretches along the upper Río Negro and middle Río Motagua. It is also true that tropical forest is more extensive here than in Mexico outside the Maya area.

There are really two natural settings in the land of the Maya: highlands and lowlands. In geology, in animal and plant life, and in the form that human cultures took, these are well set off from each other. The Maya highlands by definition lie above 1,000 ft (305 m) and are dominated by a great backbone of volcanoes both extinct and active, some over 13,000 ft (3,960 m) in altitude, which curves down from southeastern Chiapas toward lower Central America. This mighty cordillera has been formed principally by massive explosions of pumice and ash of Tertiary and Pleistocene age which have built up a mantle many hundreds of feet thick, overlain by a thin cover of rich soil. Millennia of rain and erosion have produced a highly dissected landscape, with deep ravines between hog-back ridges, but there are a few relatively broader valleys, such as those of Guatemala City, Quetzaltenango, and Comitán, which have long been important centers of Maya life. Not all of the highlands are so recent in origin, however, for to the north of the volcanic cordillera is a band of more ancient igneous and metamorphic rocks, and beyond this a zone of Tertiary and Cretaceous limestones which in the more humid country bordering the lowlands take the fantastically eroded appearance of a Chinese

2   Lake Atitlán in the Maya highlands, Guatemala. This view, taken in the 1880s, shows native traders carrying loads of pottery to market.

landscape. Isolated to the northeast are the Maya Mountains, a formation of similar antiquity.

Highland rainfall is dependent, as in the rest of the New World tropics to the north of the Equator, upon a well-defined rainy season which lasts from May through early November. In effect, this follows a double-peaked distribution in both highlands and lowlands, with heaviest falls in June and in October. For the highlands, the highest figures are registered along the Pacific slopes of Chiapas and Guatemala, a zone noted in pre-Conquest days for its cacao production, but in general total precipitation for the Maya highlands is no greater than for the temperate countries of northern Europe.

The highland flora is closely related to soils and topography; on the tops of slopes and ridges, pines and grasses dominate, while further down in ravines where there is moisture, oaks flourish. Compared with that of the lowlands, the wild fauna is not especially abundant, but this may be due to a far denser human occupation.

Native farming practices in the highlands are quite different from those of the lowlands, although inhabitants of both regions depend upon the burning of unwanted vegetation and upon rest periods for farm plots. The moderate fallowing practiced in the highlands depends upon the position of the field on the slope, with only about 10 years of continuous cultivation possible in higher fields, after which the plot must be abandoned for as much as 15 years, while further down up to 15 years continuous use with only a 5-year rest is practicable. In populated areas of highland Guatemala, almost all the available land may be cleared or in second-growth. Several kinds of maize are planted over the year; tilling is by furrowing and, after the sprouts have appeared, by making hillocks. In these maize fields, or *milpas*, secondary crops like beans and squashes, or sweet manioc, are interplanted, as well as chili peppers of many sizes, colors, and degrees of 'hotness'. In summary, while it utilizes the same kinds of plants as in the lowlands, the highland system of agriculture seems to be well-adapted to an area of high population with good, deep soils where the competition posed by heavy forests and weeds is not a major problem.

But it is the lowlands lying to the north which are of most concern to the story of Maya civilization. A greater contrast with the highland environment can hardly be imagined, as every tourist flying to the ruins of Tikal from Guatemala City must have realized. The Petén-Yucatán peninsula is a single, great limestone shelf jutting up into the blue waters of the Gulf of Mexico which borders it on the west and north; its reef-girt eastern shores face the Caribbean. These limestones have risen from the sea over an immense period of time. In the older Petén and Belize region of the south, the uplift has been greatest, and the topography is more rugged with broken karst hills rising above the plain. As one moves north to Yucatán itself, the country becomes flatter – it looks like a featureless, green carpet from the air – but this is deceptive for on foot the pitting of the porous limestone is all too apparent. In the northern reaches of our peninsula, about the only topographical variation of any note is the Puuc range, a chain of low hills no more than a few hundred feet high strung out like an inverted 'V' across northern Campeche and southwestern Yucatán.

3

3 The Lacandón rain
forest, Chiapas, Mexico,
from a photograph by Dr T.
C. Schneirla.

Unlike the sierra to the south, there are few permanently flowing
rivers in the lowlands, except in the west and in the southeast, where
extensive alluvial bottom-lands have been formed. The great
Usumacinta with its tributaries is the most important system, draining
the northern highlands of Guatemala and the Lacandón country of
Chiapas, twisting to the northwest past many a ruined Maya 'city'
before depositing its yellow silts in the Gulf of Mexico. Sizeable rivers
flowing into the Caribbean are the Motagua, which on its path to the sea
cuts successively through pine and oak-clad hills, cactus-strewn desert,
and tropical forest; the Belize River; the New River; and the Río Hondo
which separates Belize from Mexico.

Lakes are also rare in the lowlands, especially in the Yucatán
Peninsula. The absence of ground water in many regions makes thirst a
serious problem. In the Petén of northern Guatemala, there are broad,
swampy depressions or *bajos* which fill during the summer but are often
dry in the rainless winter season. Smaller and similarly seasonal water-
holes called *aguadas* are found in some places in Yucatán, but there the
major source of drinking (and bathing) water for the inhabitants is the
cenote, a word corrupted by the Spaniards from the Maya *dzonot*.
These are circular sink holes, some of great size, formed by the collapse

of underground caves. Because they are perennially filled with water percolating through the limestone, they necessarily have served as the focal points for native settlement since the first occupation of the land.

The lowland climate is hot, uncomfortably so toward the close of the dry season. In May come the rains, which last through October, but compared with other tropical regions of the world these are not especially abundant. In much of the Petén, for instance, only about 70–90 inches (178–229 cm) fall each year, and as one moves north to Yucatán there is a steady decrease from even this level. Nor is there total reliability in these rains, for in bad years there may be severe droughts. Really heavy precipitation is found in the far south of the Petén and Belize; in the Lacandón country of Chiapas; and in the Tabasco plains which are covered with great sheets of water during much of the summer and for that reason were largely shunned by the pre-Conquest Maya.

A high monsoon forest covers the southern lowlands, dominated by mahogany trees towering up to 150 ft (45 m) above the jungle floor, by sapodillas, which gave wood to the ancients and chewing-gum to ourselves, and by the breadnut tree. In the middle and lower layers of this formation grow many fruit trees important to the Maya, such as the avocado. The forest is only partly evergreen, however, for in the dry season many species drop their leaves; but in a few places favored by higher rainfall, there is real, non-deciduous rain forest.

Interspersed in the monsoon forest, particularly in the Petén and southern Campeche, are open savannahs covered with coarse grasses and dotted with stunted, flat-topped trees. There is no real agreement on the origin of the savannahs, but modern opinion is against the idea that they were created by the ancient Maya through over-cultivation of the land. On the other hand, they are certainly maintained by the hand of man, for while they are avoided by farmers they are periodically burned off by hunters so as to attract game to new grasses which sprout in the ashes. When Cortés and his army crossed these grasslands on their way to the Itzá capital of Tayasal, they came upon a herd of sacred deer that had no fear of man, and thus allowed themselves to be easily slaughtered by the *conquistadores*.

To the north and west, where there is a profound drop in the annual rainfall, the forest turns into a low, thorny jungle, finally reaching the state of xerophytic scrub along the northern shore of the Yucatán Peninsula.

There is a rich fauna in the lowlands. Deer and peccary abound, especially in Yucatán, which the Maya called 'The Land of the Turkey and Deer'. Spider monkeys and the diminutive but noisy howler monkeys are easy to hunt and well-favored in the native cuisine. Among the larger birds are the ocellated turkey, with its beautiful golden-green plumage, the currasow, and the guan. More dangerous beasts are the jaguar, largest of the world's spotted cats, which was pursued for its resplendent pelt, and the water-loving tapir, killed both for its meat and for an incredibly tough hide employed in making shields and armor for Maya warriors.

Of more importance to the development of Maya civilization is the agricultural potential of the lowlands, which is by no means uniform.

4 Burning a lowland *milpa* or maize field at Uaxactún, Petén, Guatemala.

While some of the soils of the Petén, for instance, are relatively deep and fertile, those of Yucatán are the reverse. The sixteenth-century Franciscan bishop, Diego de Landa, our great authority on all aspects of Maya life, tells us that 'Yucatán is the country with least earth that I have seen, since all of it is one living rock and has wonderfully little earth.' It is little wonder that the early Colonial chronicles speak much of famines in Yucatán before the arrival of the Spaniards, and it might be that the province relied less upon plant husbandry than upon its famed production of honey, salt, and slaves.

It is now almost universally recognized, albeit unwillingly, that many tropical soils which are permanently deprived of their forest cover quickly decline in fertility and become quite unworkable as a layer of brick-like laterite develops on the surface. Tropical rainfall and a fierce sun do their destructive work in a surprisingly brief span, and agricultural disaster results. On such soils about the only kind of farming possible is that practiced by the present-day lowland Maya – a shifting, slash-and-burn system under which the forest is permitted to regenerate at intervals. While seemingly simple, it requires great experience on the farmer's part. A patch of forest on well-drained land is chosen, and cut down in late autumn or early winter. The felled wood

4 and brush are fired at the end of the dry season, and all over the Maya lowlands the sun becomes obscured by the smoke and haze which cover the sky at that time. The maize seed is planted in holes poked through

the ash with a dibble stick. Then the farmer must pray to the gods to bring the rain.

A *milpa* usually has a life of only 2 years, by which time decreasing yields no longer make it worthwhile to plant a third year. The Maya farmer must then shift to a new section of forest and begin again, leaving his old *milpa* fallow for periods which may be from 4 to 7 years in the Petén, and from 15 to 20 years in Yucatán. In inhabited regions, the forest seen from the air looks like some great patchwork quilt of varying shades of green, a veritable mosaic of regenerating plots and new clearings.

The long-held notion that shifting cultivation was the *only* system of food production practiced by the ancient Maya has now been discarded. In 1972, the geographer Alfred Siemens and the late Dennis Puleston reported their discovery from the air of extensive areas of raised fields in southern Campeche; these are narrow, rectangular plots elevated above the low-lying, seasonally inundated land bordering rivers on in *bajos*, and are remarkably similar to the *chinampas* on which Aztec agriculture was based in central Mexico. Ancient raised fields 5 have since been found over a wide area in northern Belize and in adjacent Quintana Roo.

Recent research suggests that at least some of the raised field systems of the southern lowlands may have been initiated in swampy areas as far back as the Late Preclassic (prior to AD 250), thus providing the

5 Prehistoric Maya raised fields in the Río Hondo area, northern Belize. Rectangular plots can be seen extending out from the *terra firma* side of the floodplain.

subsistence base for the remarkably precocious increase in population which we know for that period. In addition, space age technology has made it possible for Richard E. W. Adams to detect and map some of the large-scale features associated with these systems. Flights by aircraft of the National Aeronautic and Space Administration (NASA) over northern Guatemala and Belize have utilized Side-Looking Airborne Radar (SLAR) to reveal an impressive network of feeder canals beneath the usually impenetrable jungle canopy.

Stone-walled terraces which probably acted as silt traps are common in various localities in the lowlands, especially in western Belize and the Río Bec region of southern Campeche. Both these and the raised fields show that in favorable areas, perhaps in response to population pressure, the Maya turned to intensive, highly productive, fixed-field systems. At the same time, it should be remembered that the artificial aquatic environment created by raised field agriculture would have harbored abundant edible fish and crocodilians.

And yet the claims that the Classic Maya were almost totally dependent upon the techniques of intensive maize agriculture are probably exaggerated through the understandable enthusiasm created by new finds. Much of the Maya lowland area is and was unsuitable for raised fields or for terracing, and it remains a certainty that most of the maize eaten by the pre-Conquest lowland Maya was grown in *milpa* plots by the still-used methods of shifting cultivation.

Puleston, tragically struck down in 1978 by a bolt of lightning on the Castillo of Chichén Itzá, was a provocative champion not only of the raised-field theory, but also of the idea that the lowland Classic Maya may well have relied as much upon the cultivation of the breadnut or *ramón* tree (*Brosimum alicastrum*) as upon maize, since the breadnut fruit stores well and the tree itself is remarkably common around old Maya ruins. Stimulating though the idea was, recent research suggests that the breadnut was never much more than a famine food for the Maya, and that the frequency of its distribution near Maya sites is largely due to edaphic, or soil, factors and has little to do with human intervention.

Nevertheless, plants other than maize, particularly root crops, may have played an important role in the Maya diet, as was first suggested by Bennett Bronson. Sweet manioc, for instance, does very well in the lowlands, is easy to propagate, and requires very little attention.

What all this means is that the lowlands could have been far more densely occupied by the Classic Maya than we would have estimated under the old *milpa* hypothesis. This conclusion is reinforced by a recent aerial survey and mapping of ancient ruins in northern Yucatán, which revealed virtually continuous occupation from one end of the survey area to the other, implying a pre-Conquest population far higher than today's. Perhaps we should be talking of eight to ten million people in the lowlands at about AD 800. These new facts and hypotheses also bear upon the question of what proportion of this population would have been released from their agricultural pursuits to engage as full-time participants in the making and maintaining of Maya civilization; they may also bear upon the question of why it collapsed.

Areas

The Maya occupied three separate areas, which is hardly surprising   1
considering the great environmental contrasts within the Maya realm:
Southern, Central, and Northern, the latter two entirely within the
lowlands.

The Southern Area includes the highlands of Guatemala and
adjacent Chiapas, together with the torrid coastal plain along the
Pacific and the western half of El Salvador. In general, the Southern
Area is somewhat aberrant (many books on the Maya ignore it
altogether), almost surely because of the Mexican influence which has
been powerful here over a very long time. Some of the most characteristically 'Maya' traits are missing: the corbel vault in architecture and,
except in Late Preclassic times, the Maya Long Count and the stela-
altar complex. We must admit that in many ways the Southern Area
hardly seems Maya at all from a purely archaeological standpoint, while
some of it, such as the central and eastern Chiapas highlands, was only
occupied by Maya-speakers at a relatively late date.

In the Central Area, on the other hand, Maya civilization soared to
its greatest heights. Focused upon what is now the Department of
Petén in northern Guatemala, it reaches from Tabasco and southern
Campeche across the densely forested southern lowlands to include
Belize, the Río Motagua of Guatemala, and a narrow portion of
westernmost Honduras. All the most typically 'Maya' traits are present
– architectural features such as the corbel vault and roof comb, the fully
developed Long Count with all its complexities, hieroglyphic writing,
the stela-altar complex, and many others. These triumphs, however,
were registered during the Classic period. Since the opening decades of
the tenth century AD, most of the area has been a green wilderness.

As one would expect, the Northern and Central Areas have much in
common, since there are virtually no natural barriers to cultural
exchange or to movements of peoples between the two. There is, none
the less, a good deal of individuality to the Northern Area. In part this
may be due to the fact that agricultural potentialities in Yucatán are
poorer, and that places where people may live in large concentrations
(cities and towns) are pretty much dictated by the distribution of
cenotes; but it may also partly be the result of Mexican influences which
are almost as strong here as in the Southern Area. In contrast with the
situation in the southern lowlands, there was no mass abandonment of
the Northern Area (although many of the cities were depopulated), and
overall native population figures remain high.

Periods

The discovery of the ancient Maya civilization was a piecemeal process.
Following the imposition of Spanish power in the Yucatán Peninsula,
various persons such as the great Bishop Landa, or Fray Antonio de
Ciudad Real who visited the famous site of Uxmal in 1588, wondered at
the age of the mighty ruins which lay scattered across the land, but they
could discover little from the natives. Real interest in Maya remains
only began after the publication, in a London edition of 1822, of the

brutal 'explorations' which Captain Del Río had inflicted upon the site of Palenque in the late eighteenth century. Modern Maya archaeology, however, stems from the epic journeys undertaken between 1839 and 1842 by the American diplomat and lawyer, John Lloyd Stephens, and his companion, the English topographical artist Frederick Catherwood, which revealed the full splendor of a vanished tropical civilization to the world.

Stephens and Catherwood were the first since Bishop Landa to assign the ruined 'cities' which they encountered to the actual inhabitants of the country – to the Maya Indians rather than to the peripatetic Israelites, Welshmen, Tartars, and so forth favored by other 'authorities' – but they had no way of even roughly guessing at their age. It was not until the Maya calendrical script had been studied by Ernst Förstemann, the State Librarian of Saxony, and others, and the Maya inscriptions magnificently published by the Englishman Alfred P. Maudslay at the turn of the nineteenth century, that a real breakthrough was achieved in Maya chronology. In addition, large-scale excavations in Maya sites were begun at this time by the Peabody Museum of Harvard, to be followed by the Carnegie Institution of Washington, Tulane University, the University of Pennsylvania, and the Institute of Anthropology and History in Mexico.

The dating of the ancient Maya civilization now rests on four lines of evidence: 'dirt' archaeology itself, particularly the stratification of cultural materials like pottery; radiocarbon dating, in use since 1950; native historical traditions passed on to us by post-Conquest writers but bearing on the late pre-Conquest period; and the correct correlation of the Maya and Christian calendars.

The correlation problem is an unbelievably complex and still controversial topic which demands a few words of explanation. The Maya Long Count, which will be explained in greater detail in Chapters 3 and 8, is an absolute, day-to-day calendar which has run like some great clock from a point in the mythical past. Long Count dates began to be inscribed in 36 BC on present evidence and subsequently, during the Classic period, all over the ancient cities of the Central and Northern Areas. By the time of the Conquest, however, they were expressed in a very abbreviated and somewhat equivocal form. Now, it is explicitly stated in the native chronicles (the so-called Books of Chilam Balam) that the Spanish foundation of Mérida, capital city of Yucatán, which in our calendar took place in January 1542, also fell shortly after the close of a specified period of the truncated Long Count. Bishop Landa, an impeccable source, tells us that a certain date in a more primitive Maya system, the 52-year Calendar Round, fell on 16 July 1553 in the Julian calendar. All attempts to fit the Maya calendar to the Christian must take these two statements into account.

It so happens that there are only two correlations which meet these requirements as well as those of 'dirt' archaeology. These are the 11.16 or Thompson correlation, and the 12.9 or Spinden correlation, which would make all Maya dates 260 years earlier than does the former. Which of these is correct? The ancient Maya spanned the doorways of their temples with sapodilla wood beams, and these have not only survived but can be dated by the radiocarbon process. A very long

64

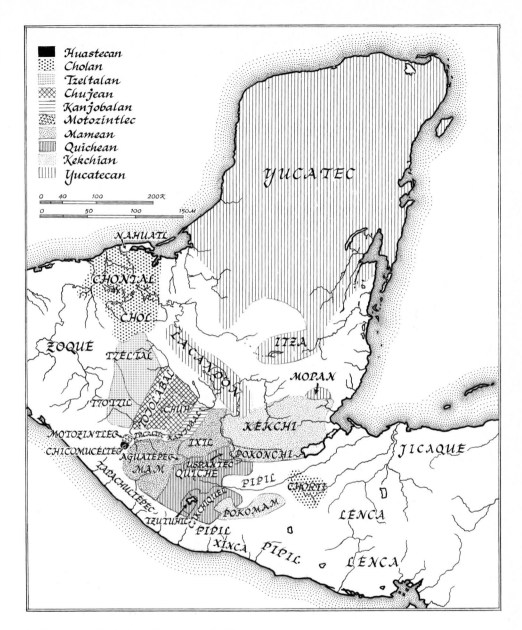

6   Present-day distribution of languages in the Maya area.

series of such samples has been run by the University of Pennsylvania, giving overwhelming support to the Thompson correlation. Most Mayanists have given sighs of relief, for any other chronology would play havoc with what we now think we know about the development of Maya culture over two millennia. Even further, any displacement in the dating of the Maya Classic period would disrupt the entire field of Mesoamerican research, for ultimately all archaeological chronologies in this part of the world are cross-tied with the Maya Long Count. Further details on the Maya-Christian correlation will be given in Chapter 8, for it bears directly on what we now know about ancient Maya astronomy.

As it now stands, the cultural sequence in the Maya area runs something like this. The earliest occupation of both highlands and lowlands was during the Early Hunters period, beginning by at least 13,000 years ago, and ending with the close of the Pleistocene, or Ice Age, about 7500 BC. Before 2000 BC there were simple horticulturalists, hunters, and farmers following a way of life called 'Archaic', far better known for the upland peoples of Mexico. During the Preclassic (or Formative) period, between 2000 BC and AD 250, village-farming became firmly established in all three areas, marking the first really intensive settlement of the Maya land. More advanced cultural traits like pyramid-building, the construction of cities, and the inscribing of stone monuments are found by the terminal centuries of the Preclassic, and some have even wondered why this early florescence should not be included in the Classic which it presages. The spectacular Classic period, lasting from AD 250 to 900, is defined as that interval during which the lowland Maya were erecting stone monuments dated in the Long Count. A great and as yet unexplained cataclysm shook the lowlands during the ninth century, by the end of which the Classic cities had been largely abandoned, while the Northern and Southern Areas seem to have received the impact of invasions either by Mexicans, or more likely, by Mexicanized Maya. Thus was inaugurated the Post-Classic, which endured until the arrival of the bearded adventurers from across the seas.

Peoples and languages

While the cohesion of the Maya-speaking peoples is quite extraordinary for any time or place, the linguistic family called 'Mayan' contains a number of closely related but mutually unintelligible languages, the result of a long period of internal divergence. A Maya from Yucatán would have the same trouble understanding an Indian from highland Chiapas as an Englishman would a Dutchman. There have been several attempts to correlate the various Mayan tongues in larger groups; the most recent one by the linguists Terence Kaufman and Lyle Campbell is the one we adopt here. An ingenious method of vocabulary comparison developed by the late Maurice Swadesh has enabled linguists to suggest approximate dates for the splitting-off of these from the ancestral Mayan language and from each other. It should be stressed, however, that there are many uncertainties built into this methodology, above all the assumption that the rate of change or divergence in 'basic' vocabularies is constant throughout time and space. Nevertheless, even if these dates prove to be wrong in absolute terms, they would still be valid for the relative sequence of events.

Prior to 2000 BC, near the end of the Archaic period, there was a single Mayan language, Proto-Mayan, perhaps located in the western Guatemalan highlands. About this time, according to the linguistic scenario, Huastecan and Yucatecan split off from the parent body, with Huastec migrating up the Gulf Coast to northern Veracruz and Tamaulipas in Mexico, and Yucatecan occupying the Yucatán Peninsula. Of the Yucatecan languages, Yucatec today is the dominant tongue, spoken by townspeople and rural farmers alike, while Lacandón is represented by only a few hundred remaining natives – primitive Maya who wear their hair long and still make bows and arrows (now entirely directed at the tourist trade) – inhabiting the Chiapas rain forest, or what is left of it, southwest of the Usumacinta. The Lacandón are pathetic survivors of a larger group which began diverging from Yucatec after the Classic Maya collapse, but which was probably always marginal to the more major tribes.

The parent body then split into two groups, a Western and an Eastern Division. In the Western group, the ancestral Cholan-Tzeltalan moved down into the Central Area, where they split into Cholan and Tzeltalan about 100 BC. The subsequent history of the Tzeltalans is fairly well known from linguistics and archaeology, for they seem to have left the Central Area by AD 400 and returned to the highlands, pioneering the settlement of the mountain valleys around San Cristóbal de las Casas, Chiapas. There many thousands of their descendants, the Tzotzil and Tzeltal, maintain unchanged the old Maya patterns of life. Of the Cholans, who played a major role in the Maya story, we will see more later. Other Western language groups include the little known Kanjobal, Tojolabal, Motozintlec, and Chuj, which stayed close to the parental homeland and which seem to have had little to do with the main developmental line of Preclassic and Classic Maya civilization.

The Eastern Division includes the Mamean group of languages; Mam itself is a rather archaic tongue which has spilled down to the Pacific coastal plain in relatively late times. Another Mamean language is spoken by the Ixil, a very conservative Maya group centered on the ancient town of Nebaj; they have been the principal target of a particularly bloody repression within the past decade. Much of the late pre-Conquest history of the Southern Area concerns the powerful Quiché and Cakchiquel of the Eastern Division. They and their relatives, the Tzutuhil, who live in villages along the shores of the volcano-girt Lake Atitlán, speak languages which only 1,000 years ago were one, Quichean. Since the Spanish Conquest, a more dominant role has been taken by the Kekchi, who have expanded from a center in the Alta Verapaz of Guatemala to colonize southern Belize and the once Cholan-speaking lowlands around Lake Izabal, Guatemala.

What, then, was the language recorded by the ancient Maya inscriptions and books? A glance at the linguistic map will show that the Yucatán Peninsula is occupied by Yucatec to the exclusion of all others, and there can be no quibbling that this was the speech of the Maya scribes of the Northern Area, including those who produced the four surviving codices. Yucatecan was probably spoken over much of Belize during the Classic, for Mopán in the southern part of the country belongs to this group, and phonetic writing on the walls of Naj Tunich cave, not far from the Belize border in Guatemala, is a sure indication of Yucatecan in use there during the Late Classic.

But much of the Central Area appears as a blank on the map, with the exception of those lands occupied by the Lacandón, by the surely recent Kekchi, and by the Yucatecan Itzá who are known to have moved into the Petén from the north no earlier than the thirteenth century AD and probably a good deal later. The idea that the language of most of the inscriptions of the Central Area was Yucatecan has little to recommend it.

Some years ago the late Sir Eric Thompson proposed that the Central Area was inhabited by Cholan-speakers during the Classic period. From its present distribution alone – with Chontal and Chol in the low hills and plains in the northwest, and Chorti in the southeast – it seems certain that Cholan once predominated across a great arc extending right through the Central Area, at least to the Belize border, and we have some Spanish documents which confirm this point. It can hardly be coincidental that Chol is still spoken around the great Classic site of Palenque, and Chorti in the vicinity of Copán; phonetic readings of the Classic texts support this fact.

It seems inescapable, therefore, that much of the great civilization of the Central Area was the creation of the Cholan Maya, although during the Early Classic some Tzeltalans may have played a part, and the Yucatecans may well have dominated the land to the east of northern Petén. At any rate, hieroglyphic writing appears on present evidence to have been in use only among Cholan and Yucatecan speakers.

Languages other than Mayan are found in isolated pockets, indicating either intrusions of peoples from foreign lands or remnant populations engulfed by the expansion of the Mayan tongues. The somewhat shadowy Pipil, whose speech is very close to Nahuatl, the official language of the Aztec Empire, are concentrated in western El Salvador, but there are other Pipil communities on the Pacific coast and in the Motagua valley of Guatemala. Some authorities think that they invaded the Maya country from Mexico during the Toltec disruptions of the Early Post-Classic, an idea which is not out of line with the lexicostatistic evidence on them, but they could have come earlier. Tiny populations of Zoquean speakers near the Pacific coast in the Chiapas-Guatemala border region are probably vestiges of a once more-widespread distribution of this language family. Xincan, with no known affiliations, seems to have extended over all of the eastern part of the Pacific coastal plain before the arrival of Mayan and Pipil, but the Xincan territory is an archaeological and ethnological blank. Nahuatl itself, as a great trading *lingua franca*, was spoken at the time of the Conquest at the port of Xicallanco on the Laguna de los Términos in southern Campeche.

Loan words from other languages do appear in Mayan, testifying to early contacts and cultural contributions. Those from the Mixe-Zoquean family of the Isthmus of Tehuantepec (locus of the very early

Olmec civilization) include high-culture words such as *may*, 'to count or divine', and *pom*, 'copal incense', and it has been suggested that Mixe-Zoquean was the tongue of the Olmec, of whom we shall speak more in the next chapter. The Zapotec of Oaxaca, who probably invented the essentials of the Mesoamerican calendar and who were surely the first to use hieroglyphic writing, contributed several names for the days in the 260-day count so fundamental to Maya thought. And in late times, during the Post-Classic epoch, many words, names, and titles were introduced into the Maya area from Nahua speech by Mexican or Mexicanized warlords.

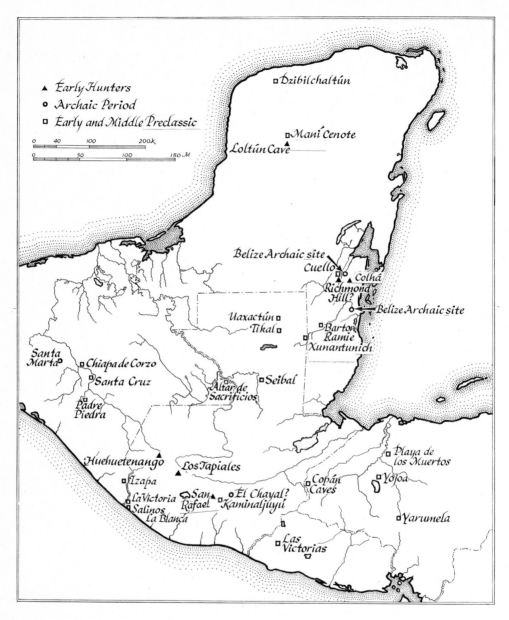

▲ Early Hunters
○ Archaic Period
□ Early and Middle Preclassic

□ Dzibilchaltún

□ Maní Cenote
Loltún Cave ▲

Belize Archaic site
Cuello □ ▲
□ Colhá
Richmond ○
Hill?
├─ Belize Archaic site

Uaxactún □
Tikal □
□ Barton
Ramie
Xunantunich

Santa
Marta ○
□ Chiapa de Corzo
□ Santa Cruz
Altar de
Sacrificios □
□ Seibal

□ Padre
Piedra

Huehuetenango ▲
▲ Los Tapiales
□ Playa de
los Muertos

□ Izapa
La Victoria □ ▲ San ▲ □ El Chayal?
Salinos Rafael Kaminaljuyú
La Blanca
□ Copán
Caves
○ Yojoa

□ Yarumela

□ Las
Victorias

7   Sites of the Early Hunters, Archaic, and Early and Middle Preclassic periods.

The earliest Maya

The Popol Vuh, the great epic of the Quiché Maya, recounts that the forefather gods, Tepeu and Gucumatz, brought forth the earth from a watery void, and endowed it with animals and plants. Anxious for praise and veneration after the creation, the divine progenitors fashioned man-like creatures from mud, but to mud they returned. Next a race of wooden figures appeared, but the mindless manikins were destroyed by the gods, to be replaced by men made from flesh. These, however, turned to wickedness and were annihilated as black rains fell and a great flood swept the earth. Finally true men, the ancestors of the Quiché, were created from maize dough.

Neither tradition nor archaeology have thrown much light on Maya origins. Tribal memories are weak, and a combination of luxuriant vegetation and unfavorable geological conditions has made the search for really early remains difficult. There are few caves and rock-shelters suitable for habitation by primitive hunters and gatherers, and open sites are virtually impossible to detect, especially in the monsoon forests.

7

Early hunters

In spite of more than a half century of research, there is little agreement among archaeologists as to when the first settlement of the New World took place. The initial colonization of this hemisphere must have been made by Asiatic peoples crossing over the Bering Strait land bridge during the latter part of the Pleistocene, when sea level was far lower than it is today. Radiocarbon dates from human occupations in Pennsylvania, the Valley of Mexico, the Andean highlands of Peru, and most recently Brazil, suggest to some scholars that American Indians had colonized both North and South America by at least 20,000 years ago, but many authorities do not accept these dates as valid, preferring a post-14,000 year arrival. By the ninth millennium BC, the first Indians were already camped on the wind-swept Straits of Magellan, at the southern tip of South America, and so we may assume that primitive hunters had by then occupied all that part of the Americas that was worth inhabiting. Large areas of both continents were grassland over which roamed great herds of herbivores – mammoths, horses, camels, and giant bison.

In the western United States, Canada, and Alaska, where a number of camps belonging to this ancient epoch have been located, the earliest

8 A fluted point of obsidian of the Early Hunters period from San Rafael. L. 2¼ in. (5.7 cm).

culture which has stood up to archaeological scrutiny is called Clovis, well dated to about 12,000 to 10,000 years ago. If we can rely upon the remains in several slaughtering sites in the American Southwest, the Clovis people lived mainly off mammoth-hunting, although in lean times they must have been content with more humble foods. These great elephants were killed with darts hurled from spear-throwers, fitted with finely chipped and 'fluted' points from the bases of which long channel flakes had been removed on one or both faces. Clovis points are widely distributed, from Alaska to Nova Scotia, down through Mexico and into Central America. They have even been found in Costa Rica and Panama.

One of the earliest known artifacts from Maya country is a small projectile point of obsidian, found by a picnicking schoolboy at San Rafael, in the pine-clad hills just west of Guatemala City. Even a neophyte would recognize this as a Clovis: fluting has been carried out on one side, the edges are ground down where the object was to be lashed to a dart or spear shaft. It is remarkably similar in outline to several such points which have been collected in Mexico, and to the smaller Clovis points of the United States.

In 1969 the archaeologists Ruth Gruhn and Alan Bryan discovered the highland Guatemalan site of Los Tapiales, which they excavated in 1973; it lies in an open meadow on the Continental Divide, in a cold, rainy, foggy environment, and probably represents a small, temporary camp of hunters located on an important pass. The stone tool industry is mainly basalt, and includes the base of a Clovis fluted point, bifaces, burins (for slotting bone), gravers, scrapers, and blades. Unfortunately no bone material has survived, but the site did produce radiocarbon dates extending back to 8760 BC, within the Clovis span.

The kind of game that these ancient people may have hunted may be revealed by a butchering site on the outskirts of the highland town of Huehuetenango, first investigated in 1977 by Herbert Alexander. This

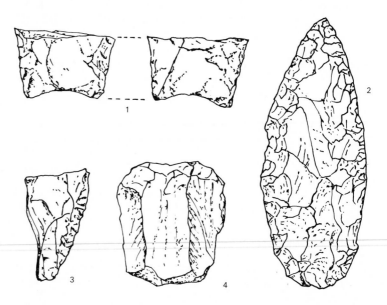

9 Early Hunters period stone tools from Los Tapiales, Totonicapan, Guatemala. 1, base of fluted point; 2, obsidian uniface; 3, burin; 4, scraper.

was located on or near the edge of a large, Pleistocene lake. Limited excavations have turned up the bones of at least three mastodons and one or more horses. Butchering marks are frequent on the bones, and four stone tools used in the process were found *in situ*, comprising a granite chopper and three unifacially worked tools.

The difficulties of prospecting for stone tools of the Early Hunters period in the Maya lowlands have already been mentioned. One of the few areas favorable for this kind of search is northern Belize, where there are extensive inland areas of low, eroded, sandy ridges with widely scattered pine cover. There, the Belize Archaic Archaeological Project directed by Dr Richard S. MacNeish found four different sites of what he calls the Lowe-Ha Phase, perhaps to be dated on typological grounds to 9000–7500 BC. These were the campsites of nomadic microbands; although little bone has survived in this acid environment, projectile points similar to fluted examples from Panama and Ecuador show that they hunted, and snub-nosed scrapers and sidescrapers testify to skin-working. Bifacial stone choppers found at Lowe-Ha sites may have been used both in butchering and general food preparation.

Further north, in Yucatán, a Mexican project has discovered an Early Hunters period occupation with bones from extinct animals including wild horses in a corner of Loltún Cave, an enormous cavern complex utilized by the Maya for millennia.

There would thus be general agreement that the Maya area was peopled by at least 11,000 years ago. But is there anything older? The answer may (or may not) come from the site of Richmond Hill in northern Belize, discovered in 1972 and excavated by Dennis Puleston in 1973–4. There, many thousand apparent tools made of chert are found on the eroded surface of low knolls. There are nodules from which flakes have been removed, a few primary flakes, and some secondary ones. The industry, if it is such, is as crude as anything found in the famed Olduvai Gorge of East Africa, and some have doubted whether they are man-made at all; however, microscopic wear patterns suggest that they are indeed artifacts. The closest parallels to Richmond Hill in the New World would be crude stone tools from the earliest levels in the caves near Ayacucho, Peru, with dates going back to 20,000 years ago. While there are no radiocarbon determinations available for Richmond Hill, it may yet turn out to be an important piece of evidence for the oldest American Indians.

Archaic collectors and cultivators

By about 7000 BC, the ice sheets which had covered much of North America in the higher latitudes were in full retreat, and during the next 5,500 years the climate of the world was everywhere warmer than it is today. In Europe, this interval has been called the 'Climatic Optimum', but in many parts of the New World conditions were by no means so favorable, least of all for hunters. A fatal combination of hot, dry weather, which turned grasslands into desert, and over-hunting by man had finished off the big game. In upland Mexico, the Indians were diverted to another way of life, based on an intensified collection of the seeds and roots of wild plants, and upon the killing of smaller, more solitary animals. In their economy, in their semi-nomadic pattern of settlement, and even in the details of their tool-kits, the Mexican Indians of the Archaic period were only part of the 'Desert Culture', extending at that time all the way from southern Oregon, through the Great Basin of the United States (where it survived into the nineteenth century), and down into southeastern Mexico.

It was in Mexico, however, and in this 'Desert Culture' context, that all the important plant foods of Mesoamerica – maize, beans, squashes, chili peppers, and many others – were first domesticated. It seems likely that the practice of plant cultivation must have reached the Maya area at some time during the Archaic period.

An earlier generation of scholars, particularly Sylvanus G. Morley, firmly believed that the Maya themselves had been the first to domesticate Indian corn (*Zea mays*). This idea was rooted on the often-revived premise that the wild progenitor of maize was *teosinte*, a common weed in cornfields of the western Guatemalan highlands. Whether this premise is correct is still a subject of acrimonious dispute among botanists. One school of thought, led by Paul C. Mangelsdorf, contends that *teosinte* is not the ancestor of maize but is its offspring through hybridization with another grass, *Tripsacum*, and that the real progenitor was a tiny-cobbed wild species of corn with small, hard kernels that could be popped. Cobs of this sort have been found by MacNeish and his colleagues in dry caves in the Tehuacán Valley of Puebla, Mexico, in levels dating to about 5000 BC. According to Mangelsdorf, they represent ancestral maize; according to his opponents, they are probably *teosinte*. This complex problem has not yet been resolved.

Even if *teosinte*, which admittedly is extremely close botanically to maize, should prove to be the antecedent of domestic maize, this does not necessarily mean the domestication process took place in Guatemala, for it is widespread in southern and western Mexico as well. Nevertheless, Guatemala (which is no larger than the state of Ohio) has more distinct varieties of maize than can be found in all the United States put together, which suggests that this must have been a very old center for the evolution of this plant under the tutelage of man. Quite probably all the uplands, from southern Mexico through Chiapas and highland Guatemala, were involved in the processes leading to the modern races of this most productive of all food plants.

It will be recalled that, according to a linguistic method of dating called lexicostatistics, the Proto-Mayan language was already present in the highlands of western Guatemala, and probably Chiapas too, before 2000 BC, well within the Archaic span and before the most ancient pottery-using cultures, and it may have been they who brought maize and other cultigens to our area. Beyond the western border of the Maya area, the rock-shelter of Santa Marta in Chiapas may record traces of this *ur*-Maya group. Unfortunately, somewhat wetter conditions than those in the Tehuacán Valley have destroyed any perishables which may have been left by the ancient inhabitants of the shelter, but nut-cracking stones with pecked depressions, and pebble *manos* and *metates* tell us that seeds and other plant foods were well exploited. Other artifacts of the Santa Marta Complex, including

7

10 Milling stones from
Archaic sites in northern
Belize.

chipped projectile points, choppers, and scrapers, strongly resemble
those of the Tehuacán and Tamaulipas caves, and the whole
assemblage, which is estimated to last from 7000 to 3500 BC, obviously
belongs with the Mexican Archaic and more generally with the 'Desert
Culture'.

Evidence for the Archaic period is generally poor in the highlands,
but it is improving in the Maya lowlands. We have some idea of what
the Petén looked like then, based on analysis of windblown pollen
recovered from a long core drilled into the bottom of Lake Petenxil, in
the heart of the Central Area. It used to be thought that the savannahs
which punctuate the tropical forest had resulted from an over-use of
their fields by the Classic Maya, with a consequent invasion of
unwanted grasses. This notion has now been turned upside-down. At
2000 BC, the Petén was like a parkland, with broad savannahs
surrounded by copses of oak, the tropical forest being considerably
more restricted than at present. The strong dominance of forest over
grasslands has been shown to have begun only during the Classic
period (AD 250–900), reaching peak intensity after the Maya had fairly
deserted the Petén.

The same pollen core has also provided an unexpected bit of
information, namely that by 2000 BC a little maize was being grown
near the margins of the lake, a good 1,000 years before the first pottery-
using farmers are known for the region. Who were these people? If we
accept the word of the linguists, they could have been the Yucatec on
their trek north to Yucatán from the Maya homeland, but since their

33

sites have not been located this is mere speculation. While some African peoples raise their crops in tropical grasslands, it is unlikely that the pioneer Maya, lacking metal tools, could have tilled the savannahs. More plausibly, they would have colonized patches of tropical forest which offered good soils and the possibility of clearing by the slash-and-burn method, avoiding the open country as assiduously as did the early Neolithic farmers of Europe.

In 1980, Richard S. MacNeish of the R. S. Peabody Foundation began a three-year investigation of the Archaic or Preceramic occupation of Belize. With his long experience in uncovering the early, incipient agricultural prehistory of highland and northeast Mexico, MacNeish was in a good position to recognize similar sequences in the Maya lowlands, unlike the usual Maya archaeologist more familiar with Classic pyramids than with humble, chipped-stone artifacts. The result has been the establishment of a tentative Archaic sequence running from about 7500 BC until after 2000 BC, with a slowly increasing number of grinding tools related to the processing of seeds and other vegetal materials, and gradually expanding and perhaps seasonal dependence upon marine resources. Unfortunately, preservation of plant materials and faunal remains is poor in his Belize sites, so that the data on the introduction and use of domesticated plants are virtually non-existent. Nevertheless, the question of whether native populations, ancestral Maya or not, had occupied the lowlands prior to the beginning of the Preclassic has now been answered in the affirmative.

Early Preclassic villages

Really effective farming, in the sense that densely inhabited villages were now to be found throughout the Maya area, was an innovation of the Preclassic period, which lasted from 2000 BC to about AD 150. What brought it about? Some scholars favor the theory that it was a major improvement in the productivity of the maize plant, perhaps through back-crossing with its offspring (or ancestor), *teosinte*. At any rate, villages made up of thatched-roof houses, in no way different from those in use among the modern Maya peasantry, now dotted the land.

Still, we must not assume that the advance to Preclassic life took place everywhere at the same time. Rather, it is in those environments which abounded on the one hand in easily obtained wild animal and plant foods, and on the other in fertile and workable soils, that a precocious development of permanently occupied villages is to be expected.

One such ecological zone is the Pacific littoral of Guatemala, near the Chiapas frontier. This region may not have been Maya-speaking in ancient times, but its early cultures must bear a likeness to the sort of evolution toward fully settled life that some day will be found elsewhere in the Maya area. In that hot fertile land one of the oldest village
11   cultures is Ocós, which may begin by 1500 BC, followed by Cuadros (fixed by radiocarbon dates to 1000–850 BC), both of which are Early Preclassic. In those days, settlements were little more than tiny hamlets of some three to twenty families each, placed just above the muddy banks of mangrove-lined estuaries and lagoons.

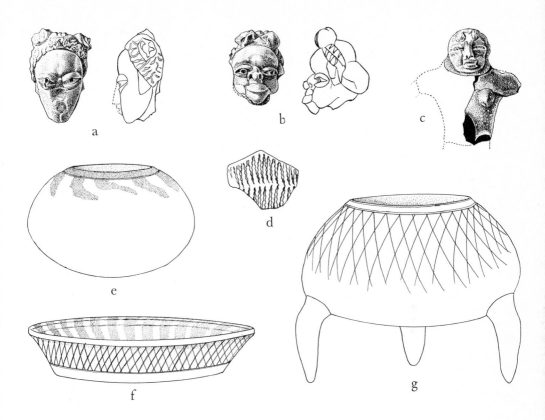

The Early Preclassic villagers efficiently exploited the rich, brackish-water environment, gathering mangrove oysters and marsh clams in great numbers, and taking turtles and crabs, while iguanas (a harmless lizard of fearsome appearance) were caught for their tasty flesh and eggs. In the lagoons and nearby rivers they fished for gar, snook, porgy, and catfish. In slightly higher lands adjacent to their settlements, they cleared the tropical forest for their cornfields; cobs miraculously preserved in the debris of a Cuadros village show that the maize grown was of the well-known race Nal-Tel, still favored by many lowland Maya farmers.

The scarcity or in some cases complete absence in Ocós and Cuadros sites of bones from animals which would have required an effort to secure, such as deer and peccary, testify to the sit-at-home propensities of these people. The arts of settled life were allowed to flourish, particularly pottery which makes its first appearance in the Maya area at this time. But fired clay vessels are known even earlier than this in Mexico, especially in the Purrón phase at Tehuacán, where an extremely crude, gravel-tempered ware was manufactured by about 2000 BC. The interesting thing about Purrón pottery is that there are only two shapes: the *tecomate*, or globular, neckless jar, and the flat-bottomed dish with outslanting sides. It is just those forms which are found in the ground-stone containers of the preceding culture, Abejas, and it is reasonable to assume that regardless of where the *idea* of firing

11 Figurines and reconstructed vessels of the Ocós culture (Early Preclassic period). *a–c*, fragments of pottery figurines; *d*, fragment of neckless pottery jar, with rocker-stamping; *e*, neckless jar with red paint on rim and body; *f*, bowl with striping in iridescent paint on interior; *g*, tripod neckless jar with iridescent paint on interior; $2\frac{1}{2}$ in. (6.4 cm) high; *b*, *c*, to scale; *d*, $2\frac{1}{2}$ in. (6.4 cm) wide; *e*, 9 in. (22.9 cm) wide; *f*, *g*, to scale.

the clay originated, the first Mesoamerican ceramics were evolved in part from prototypes in stone.

It is no surprise, then, to find *tecomates* and flat-bottomed bowls the predominant shapes of Ocós and Cuadros, as they are of other Early Preclassic cultures elsewhere in Mesoamerica, such as the related Chiapa I or Cotorra phase of central Chiapas. Quite unexpected, however, is the surprising sophistication of Ocós ceramics: the most unusual plastic techniques are used to embellish surfaces, the roughened zones usually contrasting with the smooth, and on many vessels a deep red, sparkling slip made from specular hematite was applied. Rocker-stamping was often carried out with the crinkly edge of a shell, by 'walking' the edge of the shell in zigzags across the wet clay. But two kinds of decoration deserve special mention. Many Ocós potsherds were found to have been impressed with cord or twine (sometimes so fine, it must have been a cotton thread) which had been wrapped around a paddle. Cord-marking is known on Neolithic ceramics in much of the Old World, and is characteristic of the first pottery in northern North America; its appearance in Ocós, thus far unique for Mesoamerica, cannot yet be explained. Another oddity is the use of a special glossy clay slip, giving a coppery-metallic sheen when seen at the right angle, known elsewhere only on the coast of Ecuador during the Preclassic period.

11f,g

Less spectacular artifacts – stone *manos* and *metates* for grinding maize kernels into dough, notched potsherds utilized as weights for fish-nets, and so forth – belong to the mundane life of the period. There is another element already present in Ocós culture which is worthy of mention, ceremonialism. In Ocós debris at La Victoria were found a number of solid, hand-made, female figurines of pottery. Such objects were made by the thousands in many later Preclassic villages of both Mexico and the Maya area, and while nobody is exactly sure of their meaning, it is generally thought that they had something to do with the fertility of crops, in much the same way as did the Mother Goddess figurines of Neolithic and Bronze Age Europe. For the New World, the earliest appear by 3000 BC in Ecuador and it may be that those of Mesoamerica were ultimately derived from that direction.

Every Ocós house, its pole walls daubed with mud and whitewashed, was raised above the ground on a low, earthen platform so as to avoid the inundations of the summer rainy period. In an Ocós site not very far from La Victoria is a much larger mound, reaching a height of about 25 ft (7.6 m), so lofty that it surely was a temple platform. All temples in pre-Spanish Mesoamerica, even the towering pyramids of the Maya lowlands, are essentially nothing more than a magnification of the humble peasant dwelling – the simple, rectangular house on its own flat mound. Far back in time, near the very beginnings of Preclassic life, the adoption of completely sedentary ways had given rise not only to full- or part-time specialists in the arts of pottery, weaving, and the like, but also to religious practitioners. Perhaps at first only the houses of leading persons in the community were used for their rites; eventually, a more grandiose structure was built for the purpose, raised up higher and higher to the sky by enlarging the supporting mound, finally resulting in a temple to which several of the surrounding villages could have been

drawn. As ordinary men were buried beneath the floors of their own houses, so the great men of the élite class began to be interred inside the platforms of these temples. The evidence at hand suggests that this could have taken place already by Ocós times.

12 Excavated portion of plastered platform of the Swasey phase at Cuello, northern Belize (Early Preclassic period?).

Away from the Pacific coast, we know little about the Early Preclassic. It is possible that a deep layer of broken water jars, bearing a surprising resemblance to Roman amphorae, which was uncovered by the late George Brainerd on the edge of a *cenote* at Maní, in Yucatán, belongs to this early horizon, since it underlies pottery typical of the Middle Preclassic period. In the highlands, the *tecomate*-using Arévalo people, known from a modest excavation at Kaminaljuyú on the outskirts of Guatemala City, can best be placed late in the Early Preclassic (*c.* 850 BC).

In the northern part of Belize, that land of archaeological surprises, the recently excavated site of Cuello has produced what may be an Early Preclassic phase, called Swasey, which according to Professor Norman Hammond is radiocarbon-dated between 2000 and 1000 BC. In Swasey deposits there have been preserved tiny cobs of pop corn, and root crops such as native yam (*Dioscorea*), cocoyam (*Xanthosoma*), and possibly manioc. There is also some evidence of architectural beginnings, with plastered platforms which once supported perishable superstructures. Swasey ceramics are admittedly a puzzle, since they bear no resemblance to Early Preclassic ceramics elsewhere in Mesoamerica; in fact, to some specialists they look Middle or even Late Preclassic. A more recent series of radiocarbon dates suggest that these doubts are well-founded, and that we are not dealing with an Early Preclassic manifestation after all.

12

The Middle Preclassic expansion

If conditions before 800 BC were perhaps not optimum for the spread of effective village farming except for a few favored regions, in the following centuries the reverse must have been true. Heavy populations, all with pottery, began to establish themselves in both highlands and lowlands during the Middle Preclassic period, which lasted until about 300 BC. In no instance do we have remains suggesting that these were anything more than simple peasants: there was no writing, little that could be called architecture, and hardly any development of art. In fact, nothing but a rapidly mounting population would make us think that the Maya in this period were much different from their immediate ancestors.

There was, however, something very different that had been taking place in Mexico, in the hot coastal plain of southern Veracruz and adjacent Tabasco. This was the developing Olmec civilization, which began in the Early Preclassic, reached its peak toward the end of the Middle Preclassic, and then collapsed as suddenly as did the Maya at a much later time. So far, the oldest known Olmec site is San Lorenzo, lying near a branch of the Coatzacoalcos River in Veracruz. Excavated by a Yale expedition between 1966 and 1969, fully developed Olmec culture, represented typically by gigantic basalt sculptures fashioned in a distinctive style, proved to date back to 1200 BC. By 900 BC, San Lorenzo had been destroyed by an unknown hand, but during the three centuries of its *floruit*, Olmec influence emanating from this area was to be found throughout Mesoamerica, with the curious exception of the Maya domain – perhaps because there were few Maya populations at that time sufficiently large to have interested the expanding Olmec.

During the Middle Preclassic, following the demise of San Lorenzo, the great Olmec center was La Venta, situated on an island in the midst of the swampy wastes of the lower Tonalá River, and dominated by a 100-ft-high (30 m) mound of clay. Elaborate tombs and spectacular offerings of jade and serpentine figurines were concealed by various constructions, both there and at other Olmec sites. The Olmec art style was centered upon the representations of creatures which combined the features of a snarling jaguar with those of a weeping human infant; among these were-jaguars almost surely was a rain god, one of the first recognizable deities of the Mesoamerican pantheon. From the unity of the art style, from the size and beauty of the sculptured monuments, and from the massive scale of the public architecture, there can be no doubt that there was a powerful Olmec state on the Gulf Coast which even at this early time was able to command enormous resources both in manpower and in materials.

More important to the study of the Maya, there are also good reasons to believe that it was the Olmec who devised the elaborate Long Count calendar, and the Olmec – or, more likely, the Zapotec of Oaxaca – who invented writing. Whether or not one thinks of the Olmec as the 'mother culture' of Mesoamerica, the fact is that many other civilizations, including the Maya, were ultimately dependent on the Olmec achievement. This is especially true during the Middle

13

13 (*opposite*) Monument 52 at San Lorenzo, Veracruz, an Olmec were-jaguar deity of the San Lorenzo phase (1200–900 BC). Early Preclassic period.

38

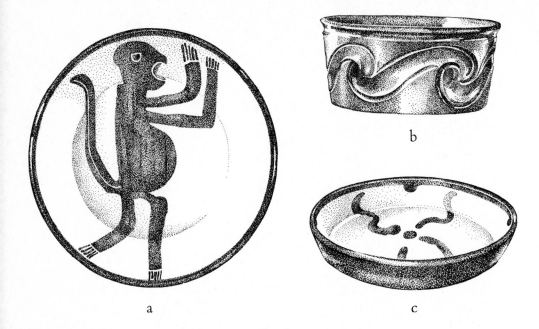

a

b

c

14 Pottery vessels of the Las Charcas culture (Middle Preclassic period). *a, c,* interiors of red-on-white bowls; *b,* grey-brown bowl with modeled decoration. *a,* 12 in. (30.5 cm) diam.; *b, c,* to scale.

15 (*opposite*) A Middle Preclassic pottery figurine of a seated woman, from the Las Charcas culture site of Copolchí. Ht *c.* 4 in. (10 cm).

Preclassic, when lesser peasant cultures away from the Gulf Coast were acquiring traits which had filtered to them from their more advanced neighbors, just as in ancient Europe barbarian peoples in the west and north eventually had the benefits of the achievements of the contemporaneous Bronze Age civilizations of the Near East.

One of the greatest of all archaeological sites in the New World is Kaminaljuyú, on the western margins of Guatemala City in a broad, fertile valley lying athwart the Continental Divide. Although it consisted of several hundred great temple mounds in Maudslay's day, all but a handful have been swallowed up by the rapidly expanding slums and real estate developments of the capital. Rescue operations by the Carnegie Institution of Washington and Pennsylvania State University have shown that whereas part of the site was constructed during the Early Classic, the great majority of the mounds were definitely Preclassic. The loss to science through the depredations of brickyards and bulldozers has been incalculable.

22

It has been no easy task, under these circumstances, to work out an archaeological succession for Kaminaljuyú, but the oldest culture is probably Arévalo, for which we have little more than some sherds from *tecomates* and red-slipped bowls. This is followed by Las Charcas, which marks a major occupation of the Valley of Guatemala, for Las Charcas remains are scattered widely. Its stratigraphic position underneath deposits of the Late Preclassic, backed up by a number of slightly contradictory radiocarbon dates, suggests that this village culture falls toward the end of the Middle Preclassic, around the fifth or fourth century BC.

The best-preserved Las Charcas remains come from a series of bottle-shaped pits which had been cut in ancient times down through

the topsoil into the underlying volcanic ash. No one has a firm idea of the purpose of these excavations. Perhaps some may have been cooking pits, and it is entirely possible that as among the historic Hidatsa Indians of the Great Plains others may have been for the storage of maize and beans, but surely their final use was as refuse containers. In them have been found carbonized avocado seeds, maize cobs, and remnants of textiles, basketry and probably mats, and rope fragments.

14 The magnificent Las Charcas white ware, manufactured from a kaolin-like clay, is extremely sophisticated, with designs in red showing spider monkeys with upraised arms, grotesque dragon masks, and other more 15 abstract motifs. Las Charcas figurines are predominantly female, but with a liveliness of concept seldom found elsewhere. Again, as with coeval cultures in other parts of Mesoamerica, there is good evidence for the construction of clay temple mounds of considerable size, perhaps already arranged around plazas.

In the Maya lowlands, both in the Central and in the Northern Areas, we now have for the first time substantial evidence for a Maya population. The oldest occupation, the little-known Xe culture, appears in deep levels at the site of Altar de Sacrificios and at Seibal in the western part of the Petén, and may represent some kind of intrusion from the highlands via the Lacantún drainage system. But it is in the northern Petén where the Middle Preclassic has been best defined. Considerable excavations at the great Maya centers of Uaxactún and Tikal have shown that Mamóm is the dominant culture of this time, and have thus far failed to turn up anything substantially earlier. It should be kept in mind that the Petén may have been no promised land for more ancient peoples intruding into it, particularly if annual rainfall was at one time somewhat below its present amount.

Mamóm, which has a radiocarbon date within the fifth century BC, looks like a simple village culture since, with the exception of one small structure at Altun Ha, in Belize, no examples of public architecture have yet been revealed by the archaeologist's spade. The special conditions of excavations in the Petén, however, must be considered. The lowland Maya almost always built their temples over older ones, so that in the course of centuries the earliest constructions would eventually come to be deeply buried within the towering accretions of rubble and plaster. Consequently, to prospect for Mamóm temples in one of the larger sites would be extremely costly in time and labor, and the question of their existence should be kept open.

Mamóm pottery is quite simple when compared with Las Charcas to which it is related. The commonest wares are red and orange-red monochromes, with polychrome decoration absent. Usually the only embellishment is simple incising on the inside of bowls, or daubing of necked jars with red blobs. The figurine cult, if such it may be called, is present in Mamóm, with a wide range of stylistic treatment carried out by punching and with applied strips of clay. At Tikal, a cache of Mamóm ceramics was discovered in a sealed *chultun*. This is a bottle-shaped chamber below the plaza floor, quite comparable in shape and perhaps in use to those of Las Charcas. *Chultuns* are ubiquitous in sites of the Central and Northern Areas, cut down into the limestone marl from the surface. We know that by the Late Classic, they were used for burials and reached some degree of elaboration; they also may have functioned as sweat baths. Initially, however, they could have been utilized as sources of the fine *sascab* lime employed in construction by Maya architects, but their use as storage pits (perhaps for the fruit of the breadnut tree, as suggested by Puleston) should not be overlooked. However, they are often so damp that stored food may have rotted. Whatever the answer to the '*chultun* mystery', they are as old as the Mamóm phase.

Something like Mamóm has been found throughout the Maya lowlands wherever serious excavations have been undertaken – even at the site of Dzibilchaltún in northern Yucatán.   7

The Middle Preclassic sees the establishment of Maya-speaking peasants everywhere; the flowering of Maya culture could only have taken place on this base. But there is absolutely nothing to suggest that Maya civilization as we understand it – the vaulted masonry architecture, the naturalistic painting and relief style, Long Count calendar and hieroglyphic writing – had even begun to germinate during this epoch.

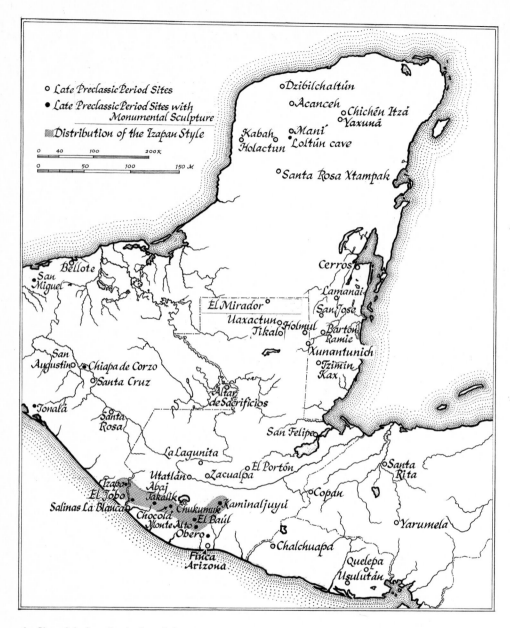

○ Late Preclassic Period Sites
● Late Preclassic Period Sites with
      Monumental Sculpture
▨ Distribution of the Izapan Style

0   40   100   200K
0   50   100   150 M

Dzibilchaltún
○Acanceh
      ○Chichén Itzá
Kabah ○Maní Yaxuná
Holactun ○Loltún cave
○Santa Rosa Xtampak

Bellote
San
Miguel

Cerros
Lamanai
El Mirador ○ San José
Uaxactun○ Holmul
Tikal○   Barton
            Ramie
San   ○Xunantunich
Augustin○ ○Chiapa de Corzo ○Tzimin
○Santa Cruz   Kax
Tonalá
Santa   Altar
Rosa   de Sacrificios
                San Felipe
La Lagunita
Utatlán○ ○Zacualpa ○El Portón ○Santa
Izapa Abaj   Rita
El Jobo ○Tak'alik ○Chukumuk ○Kaminaljuyú ○Copan
Salinas La Blanca Chocola○El Baúl
            Monte Alto ○Yarumela
            Obero○
            Finca   ○Chalchuapa
            Arizona Quelepa
                     Usulután

16 Sites of the Late Preclassic period.

3
The rise of Maya civilization

It is a long step from the village cultures that we have thus far been considering to the awe-inspiring achievements of the Classic Maya, but by no means an impossible one. The all-important questions are, what happened during the intervening time covered by the Late Preclassic period, and how did those traits considered as typical of the Classic Maya actually develop?

16

There have been a number of contradictory theories to account for the rise of Maya civilization. One of the most persistent holds that the previously undistinguished Maya came under the influence of travelers from shores as distant as the China coast; as a matter of interest to the lay public, it should be categorically emphasized that *no* objects manufactured in any part of the Old World have been identified in any Maya site, and that ever since the days of Stephens and Catherwood few theories involving trans-Pacific or trans-Atlantic contact have survived scientific scrutiny.

The possibility of some trans-Pacific influence on Mesoamerican cultures cannot, however, be so easily dismissed. Its most consistent proponent has been Professor David Kelley of the University of Calgary, who has long pointed out that within the twenty named days of the 260-day calendar so fundamental to Mesoamericans (see below) is a sequence of animals that can be matched in similar sequence within the lunar zodiacs of many East and Southeast-Asian civilizations. To Kelley, this resemblance is far too close to be merely coincidental. Furthermore, Asian and Mesoamerican cosmological systems, which emphasize a quadripartite universe of four cardinal points associated with specific colors, plants, animals, and even gods, are amazingly similar. Both Asian and Mesoamerican religions see a rabbit on the face of the full moon (whereas we see a 'Man in the Moon'), and they also associate this luminary with a woman weaving at a loom.

Even more extraordinary, as the historian of science Dr Joseph Needham reminds us, Chinese astronomers of the Han Dynasty as well as the ancient Maya used exactly the same complex calculations to give warning about the likelihood of lunar and solar eclipses. These data would suggest that there was direct contact across the Pacific. As oriental seafaring was always on a far higher technological plane than anything ever known in the prehispanic New World, it is possible that Asian intellectuals may have established some sort of contact with their Mesoamerican counterparts by the end of the Preclassic.

Lest this be thought to be idle speculation along the lines of the lunatic fringe books so common in this field, let me point out one further piece of evidence. Dr Paul Tolstoy of the University of Montreal has made a meticulous study of the occurrence of the techniques and tools utilized in the manufacture of bark paper around the Pacific basin. It is his well-founded conclusion that this technology, known in ancient China, Southeast Asia and Indonesia, as well as in Mesoamerica, was diffused from eastern Indonesia to Mesoamerica at a very early date. The main use of such paper in Mesoamerica was in the production of screenfold books to record ritual, calendrical, and astronomical information. It is not unreasonable to suppose that it was through the medium of such books, which are still in use by Indonesian people like the Batak, that an intellectual exchange took place.

This by no means implies that the Maya – or any other Mesoamerican civilization – were merely derivative from Old World prototypes. What it does suggest is that at a few times in their early history, the Maya may have been receptive to some important ideas originating in the Eastern Hemisphere.

Another school of thought holds that, because of the supposedly low agricultural potential of the Petén and Yucatán, civilization was introduced to the lowlands from an outside area with a more favorable ecology. There are others who claim that this potential has been gravely underrated, and that Maya culture as it is known for the Classic period is completely *sui generis*, with no trace of outside influence. Needless to say, both of these points of view are overstated, and both are at least partly wrong. The fact is that the Maya of both highlands and lowlands have never been isolated from the rest of Mesoamerica, and that Mexican influences have sporadically guided the course of Maya cultural history since very early times, as we shall see in this and subsequent chapters. It is also increasingly apparent that the reverse was also the case: strong Maya influence can be detected in central Mexico and the Gulf Coast of Veracruz, particularly during the last phase of the Classic.

How are we to define the word 'civilization'? How do the civilized differ from the barbaric? Archaeologists have usually dodged this question by offering lists of traits which they think to be important. Cities are one criterion. The late V. G. Childe thought that writing should be another, but the obviously advanced Inca of Peru were completely illiterate. Civilization, in fact, is different in degree rather than in kind from what precedes it, but has certainly been achieved by the time that state institutions, large-scale public works, temple buildings, and widespread, unified art styles have appeared. With few exceptions, the complex state apparatus demands some form of records, and writing has usually been the answer; so has the invention of a more-or-less accurate means of keeping time.

Yet all civilizations are in themselves unique. The Classic Maya of the lowlands had a very elaborate calendar; writing; temple-pyramids and palaces of limestone masonry with vaulted rooms; architectural layouts emphasizing buildings arranged around plazas with rows of stone stelae lined up before some; polychrome pottery; and a very

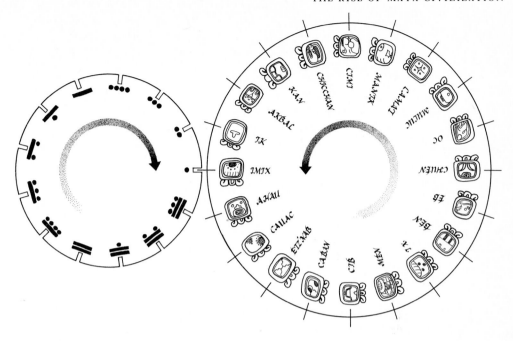

17 Schematic representation of the 260-day count.

sophisticated art style expressed in bas-reliefs and in wall paintings. These traits are now known to have been developed in the Late Preclassic (300 BC–AD 250) period.

The birth of the calendar

Some system of recording time is essential to all higher cultures – to fix critical events in the lives of the persons ruling the state, to guide the agricultural and ceremonial year, and to record celestial motions. The Calendar Round of 52 years was present among all the Mesoamericans, including the Maya, and is presumably of very great age. It consists of two permutating cycles. One is of 260 days, representing the intermeshing of a sequence of the numbers 1 through 13 with twenty named days. Among the Maya, the 260-day count (sometimes called by the *ersatz* term *tzolkin*) began with 1 Imix, followed 2 Ik, 3 Akbal, 4 Kan, until 13 Ben had been reached; the day following was Ix, with the coefficient 1 again, leading to 2 Men, and so on. The last day of the 260-day cycle would be 13 Ahau, and it would repeat once again commencing with 1 Imix. How such a period of time ever came into being remains an enigma, but the use to which it was put is clear. Every single day had its own omens and associations, and the inexorable march of the twenty days acted as a kind of perpetual fortune-telling machine guiding the destinies of the Maya and of all the peoples of Mexico. It still survives in unchanged form among some isolated folk in southern Mexico and the Maya highlands, under the care of calendar priests.

Meshing with the 260-day count is a 'Vague Year' of 365 days, so called because the *actual* length of the solar year is about a quarter-day more, a circumstance that leads us to intercalate one day every four

17

18

POP	UO	ZIP	ZOTZ	TZEC
XUL	YAXKIN	MOL	CHEN	YAX
ZAC	CEH	MAC	KANKIN	MUAN
PAX	KAYAB	CUMKU		UAYEB

18 Signs for the months in the 365-day count.

years to keep our calendar in march with the sun, but which was ignored by the Maya. Within it, there were eighteen named 'months' of twenty days each, with a much-dreaded interval of five unlucky days added at the end. The Maya New Year started with 1 Pop, the next day being 2 Pop, etc. The final day of the month, however, carried not the coefficient 20, but a sign indicating the 'seating' of the month to follow, in line with the Maya philosophy that the influence of any particular span of time is felt *before* it actually begins and persists somewhat beyond its apparent termination.

From this it follows that a particular day in the 260-day count, such as 1 Kan, also had a position in the Vague Year, for instance 2 Pop. A day designated as 1 Kan 2 Pop could not return until 52 Vague Years

(18,980 days) had passed. This is the Calendar Round, and it is the only annual time count possessed by the highland peoples of Mexico, one that obviously has its disadvantages where events taking place over a span of more than 52 years are concerned.

Although it is usually assumed to be 'Maya', the Long Count was widely distributed in Classic and earlier times in the lowland country of Mesoamerica; but it was carried to its highest degree of refinement by the Maya of the Central Area. This is really another kind of permutation count, except that the cycles used are so large that, unlike the Calendar Round, any event within the span of historical time could be fixed without fear of ambiguity. Instead of taking the Vague Year as the basis for the Long Count, the Maya and other peoples employed the *tun*, a period of 360 days. The Long Count cycles are:

20 kins	1 uinal or 20 days	138
18 uinals	1 tun or 360 days	
20 tuns	1 katun or 7,200 days	
20 katuns	1 baktun or 144,000 days.	

Long Count dates inscribed by the Maya on their monuments consist of the above cycles listed from top to bottom in descending order of magnitude, each with its numerical coefficient, and all to be added up

19 Schematic representation of part of the 52-year Calendar Round.

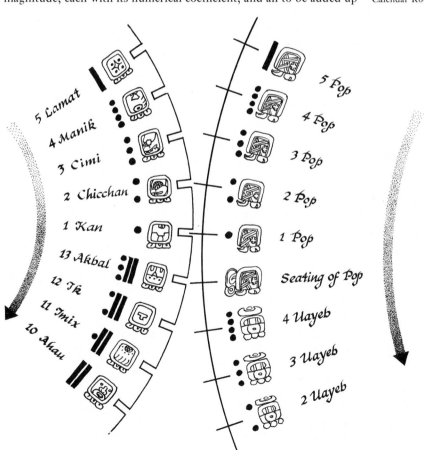

5 Lamat
4 Manik
3 Cimi
2 Chicchan
1 Kan
13 Akbal
12 Ik
11 Imix
10 Ahau

5 Pop
4 Pop
3 Pop
2 Pop
1 Pop
Seating of Pop
4 Uayeb
3 Uayeb
2 Uayeb

so as to express the number of days elapsed since the end of the last Great Cycle, a period of 13 baktuns whose ending fell on the date 4 Ahau 8 Cumku. The starting point of the present Great Cycle corresponds, in the Thompson correlation, to 13 August 3114 BC (Gregorian calendar). Thus, a Long Count date conventionally written as 9.10.19.5.11 10 Chuen 4 Cumku would be calculated as follows:

9 baktuns	1,296,000 days
10 katuns	72,000 days
19 tuns	6,840 days
5 uinals	100 days
11 kins	11 days

or 1,374,951 days since the close of the last Great Cycle, reaching the Calendar Round position 10 Chuen 4 Cumku.

cf.137   Something should also be said about the coefficients themselves. The Maya, along with a few other groups of the lowlands and the Mixtec of Oaxaca, had a number system of great simplicity, employing only three symbols: a dot with the value of 'one', a horizontal bar for 'five', and a stylized shell for 'nought' or 'completion'. Numerals up to four were expressed by dots only, six was a bar with a dot above, and ten two bars. Nineteen, the highest coefficient in calendrical use, took the form of four dots above three bars. The treatment of higher numbers, for which the 'nought' symbol was essential, will be discussed in Chapter 8.

It is generally agreed that the Long Count must have been set in motion long after the inception of the Calendar Round, but by just how many centuries or millennia is uncertain. Be that as it may, the oldest recorded Long Count dates fall within Baktun 7, and appear on 16 monuments which lie *outside* the Maya area. At present, the most ancient seems to be Stela 2 at Chiapa de Corzo, a major ceremonial center which had been in existence since Early Preclassic times in the dry Grijalva Valley of central Chiapas: in a vertical column are carved the numerical coefficients [7.16.]3.2.13, followed by the day 6 Ben, the 'month' of the Vague Year being suppressed as in all these early inscriptions. This would correspond to 7 December 36 BC (Gregorian calendar). Five years later, the famous Stela C at the Olmec site of Tres Zapotes in Veracruz was inscribed with 7.16.6.16.18 6 Eznab. On the Chiapa de Corzo monument, the initial coefficients are missing but reconstructable.

Now, the 16th katun of Baktun 7 would fall within the Late Preclassic, and we can be sure that unless these dates are to be counted forward from some base *other* than 13.0.0.0.0 4 Ahau 8 Cumku (as the end of the last Great Cycle is sometimes recorded), which seems improbable, then the 'Maya' calendar had reached what was pretty much its final form by the first century BC among peoples who were under powerful Olmec influence and who may not even have been Maya. From them, writing and the calendar were spread along the Pacific coast of Guatemala and into the Maya highlands, eventually reaching the developing states of the Petén forests.

Izapa and the Pacific Coast

Crucial to the problem of how higher culture came about among the Maya is the Izapan civilization, for it occupies a middle ground in time   16 and in space between the Middle Preclassic Olmec and the Early Classic Maya. Its hallmark is an elaborate art style, found on monuments scattered over a wide zone from Tres Zapotes on the Veracruz coast, to the Pacific plain of Chiapas and Guatemala, and up into the Guatemala City area.

Izapa itself is a very large site made up of over eighty temple mounds of earthen construction faced with river cobbles, just east of Tapachula, Chiapas, in the moist, slightly hilly country about 20 miles inland from the Pacific shore. Whether it belongs with Mexico, culturally speaking, or with the Maya area is debatable, but the tongue anciently spoken here was not Maya but Tapachulteco, a vestigial member of the once   6 more widespread Mixe-Zoquean group. While Izapa was founded as a ceremonial center as far back as Early Preclassic times and continued in use until the Early Classic, the bulk of the constructions and probably all of the many carved monuments belong to the Late Preclassic era. The Izapan art style consists in the main of large, ambitiously conceived but somewhat cluttered scenes carried out in bas-relief. Many of the activities shown are profane, such as a richly attired person decapitating a vanquished foe, but there are deities as well. One of these is a 'Long-lipped God', part human and part fish (most likely shark),   27 who apparently is the prototype of God GI of Palenque and thus the ancestral form of Chac, the ubiquitous Maya patron of lightning and rain. Another supernatural being present at Izapa has one leg ending in a serpent's body and head, and is thus the earliest known representation of God K, in Classic times the presiding deity of Maya ruling houses. But by far the leading figure in the crystallizing Maya pantheon as seen in Izapan monumental art, extending to the giant stucco masks of Late Preclassic temples in the Petén and Belize, is the monstrous form of Vucub Caquix, an anthropomorphic vulture who shows up in the Popol Vuh as the arrogant 'sun' of the creation preceding this one.

Certain recurrent elements must represent well-understood iconographic motifs, such as a U-shaped form between diagonal bars above the principal scene, perhaps an early occurrence of the sky-band so ubiquitous in Classic Maya art; the 'U' itself is most likely the prototype of the Maya glyph for the moon, and is found repeated many   139d times on the same relief.

Izapa, then, is a major center with some of the features which we consider more typical of the lowland Maya already in full flower – the stela-altar complex, the Long-lipped God who becomes transformed into the Maya rain god Chac, and a highly painterly, two-dimensional art style which emphasizes historical and mythic scenography with great attention to plumage and other costume details. Writing and the calendar are absent, but as one moves along the Pacific slopes east into Guatemala, one finds sites with inscriptions and Baktun 7 dates.

One of these Guatemalan stations is Abaj Takalik, situated in a lush, well-watered piedmont zone that in the days of the Conquest was a great producer of chocolate, and is now devoted to coffee. Like Izapa, it is made up of earthen mounds scattered about the site with little attention to formal arrangement. That the Olmec had once intruded here is apparent from a large boulder located less than a mile from the main group of mounds, carved in relief with a bearded were-jaguar in the purest Olmec style. Stela 1 from the site is purely Izapan but dateless. On the other hand, Stela 2, now somewhat damaged, bore on its carved face two richly attired Izapan figures with tall, plumed headdresses, facing each other across a vertical row of glyphs, below a cloud-like mass of volutes from which peers the face of a sky god. The topmost sign in the column is beyond doubt a very early form of the Introductory Glyph which in later Classic inscriptions stands at the head of a Long Count date. Just beneath is the baktun coefficient, which is pretty clearly the number 7. In the last few years, a University of California expedition has found a number of significant new monuments at Abaj Takalik, including a stela with two Baktun 8 dates, so that this site may have equaled Izapa in importance.

A more complete Baktun 7 inscription appears on Stela 1, the 'Herrera Stela', from El Baúl, a coffee plantation considerably to the southeast of Abaj Takalik in a region studded with Early Classic centers of the Cotzumalhuapa culture. This object has attracted fairly hot debate ever since it was found in 1923, some refusing to believe it even as old as the Classic period, and its very discoverer claiming it as Aztec! On the right, a profile figure is stiffly posed with spear in hand below a cloud-scroll; over the lower part of his face is some sort of covering,

20   Stela 1 from El Baúl, the earliest dated monument (AD 36) in the Maya area proper. On the right a figure in profile stands stiffly posed beneath a cloud-scroll.

21 Monument 1 at Monte Alto, a site of the Late Preclassic period. Ht 4 ft 8 in. (1.42 m).

while to his headdress is attached a chin strap, a feature known to be extremely early in the Maya lowlands. In front of him are two vertical columns of glyphs, the right-hand of which consists of little more than empty cartouches which were probably meant to be painted. Let us, however, consider the row on the extreme left, for this is almost surely the earliest dated monument in the Maya area proper. At the top is the coefficient 12 above a fleshless jaw, a Mexican form of the day sign Eb. Then there are four indecipherable signs, followed by a series of Long Count numbers which can be reconstructed as 7.19.15.7.12, reaching the Calendar Round position 12 Eb; in terms of our own calendar, this would be in the year AD 36, some 256 years prior to the first such date in the Maya lowlands, but significantly later than the precocious inscriptions of Chiapas and the Veracruz coast.

We cannot leave the Pacific coastal zone without mentioning a second sculptural tradition which reaches some degree of popularity both there and at Kaminaljuyú. This is expressed in large, crude, pot-bellied statues with puffy faces and lower jaws so inflated that they have been compared with the late Il Duce of Italy. At Monte Alto, not far

21 from El Baúl, a group of these monstrous forms is placed in a row along with a colossal head carried out in the same style, and some believe that the entire pot-bellied complex is connected with the Olmec culture and precedes the Izapan. However, since Monte Alto is strewn with Late Preclassic pottery sherds, it is most likely that this was a subsidiary cult that coexisted with the Izapan Rain God, just as Egyptian and Graeco-Roman religious art flourished side-by-side in ancient Alexandria. But a cult to what deity? A fairly good case can be made out for this being none other than the Fat God, without known functions but ubiquitous among the peoples of Mexico and the Northern Maya Area in Classic times.

Kaminaljuyú and the Maya highlands

A Late Preclassic rival to Izapa in size and number of temple mounds and in the splendor of its carved monuments was Kaminaljuyú during the Miraflores phase. This, it will be recalled, was once a major ceremonial site on the western outskirts of Guatemala City. The majority of the approximately 200 mounds once to be found there were probably constructed by the Miraflores people, whose rulers must have possessed a formidable economic and political power over much of the Maya highlands at this time.

22 View of Kaminaljuyú, looking west, from a photograph taken by A. P. Maudslay. Most of the earthen mounds are temple substructures of the Miraflores culture.

The excavation of two Miraflores tombs has thrown much light on the luxury to which these rulers were accustomed. Mound E-III-3 at Kaminaljuyú consists of several superimposed temple platforms, each a

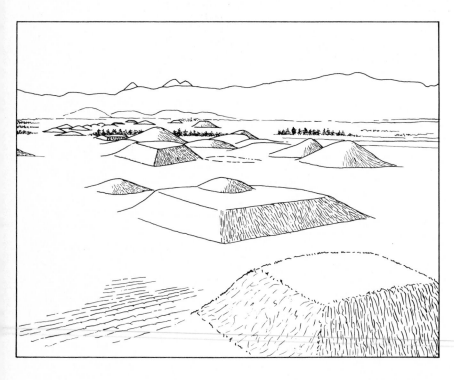

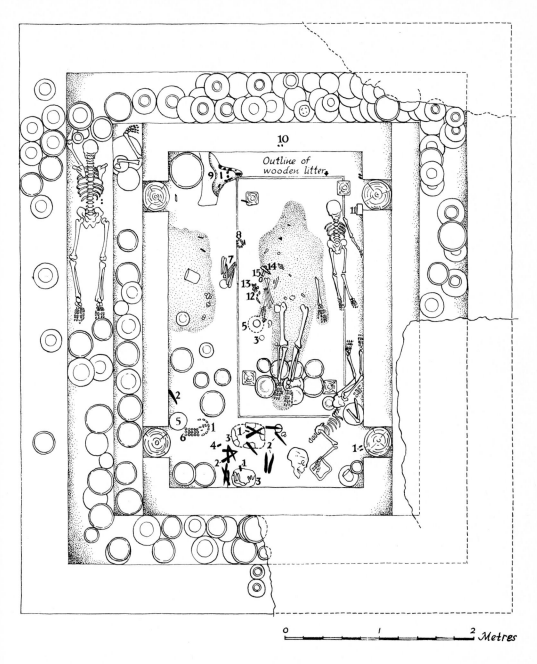

23 Plan of Tomb II, mound E-III-3, a burial of the Miraflores culture at Kaminaljuyú. *1*, jade beads; *2*, obsidian flake-blades; *3*, mica sheets; *4*, jade mosaic element; *5*, stuccoed gourds; *6*, pebbles; *7*, basalt implements; *8*, human teeth; *9*, jade mosaic mask or headdress; *10*, obsidian stones; *11*, pyrite-incrusted sherd; *12*, soapstone implement; *13*, bone objects, fish teeth, and quartz crystals; *14*, sting-ray spines; *15*, spatulate bone object. All other circular objects are pottery vessels.

flat-topped, stepped pyramid fronted by a broad stairway; in its final form it reaches a height of more than 60 ft (18 m). In lieu of easily worked building stone, which was unavailable in the vicinity, these platforms were built from ordinary clay and basketloads of earth and household rubbish. Almost certainly the temples themselves were thatched-roof affairs supported by upright timbers. Apparently each successive building operation took place to house the remains of an

23 exalted person, whose tomb was cut down from the top in a series of stepped rectangles of decreasing size into the earlier temple platform, and then covered over with a new floor of clay. The function of Maya pyramids as funerary monuments thus harks back to Preclassic times.

The corpse was wrapped in finery and covered from head to toe with cinnabar pigment, then laid on a wooden litter and lowered into the tomb. Both sacrificed adults and children accompanied the illustrious dead, together with offerings of an astonishing richness and profusion. In one tomb, over 300 objects of the most beautiful workmanship were placed with the body or above the timber roof, but ancient grave-robbers, probably acting after noticing the slump in the temple floor caused by the collapse of the underlying tomb, had filched from the corpse the jades which once covered the chest and head. Among the finery recovered were the remains of a mask or headdress of jade plaques perhaps once fixed to a background of wood, jade flares which once adorned the ear lobes of the honored dead, bowls carved from

24 chlorite-schist engraved with Miraflores scroll designs, and little
25 carved bottles of soapstone and fuchsite.

26 Miraflores pottery vessels from E-III-3 and elsewhere belong to a ceramic tradition prevalent throughout southeastern Mesoamerica during the Late Preclassic horizon, from Izapa to El Salvador, and up into the Central and Northern Maya area, but are set off from this in their refinement and sophistication. Shapes have now become exuberant, with re-curved outlines, elaborate flanges on rims and bodies, and the appearance of vessel feet. Some of the most amusing examples of the potter's art are effigy vessels, a few of which show smiling old men. Painted stucco is often used to achieve effects in colors such as pink and green, unobtainable in fired slips. Most bowls and jars are embellished with engraved and carved scroll designs. A more peculiar kind of decoration which is virtually a marker for the Late Preclassic period in the Maya area is Usulután, believed to originate in El Salvador where it attains great popularity. On this widely traded ware, a resistant substance such as wax or thin clay was applied to bowls with a multiple-brush applicator; after smudging or darkening in a reducing fire, the material was removed to leave a design of wavy, parallel, yellowish lines on a darker orange or brown background.

As for stone carving on a large scale, it was once believed that the Miraflores people made only 'mushroom stones'. These peculiar objects, one of which was found in an E-III-3 tomb, are of unknown use. Some see vaguely phallic associations. Others, such as Dr Borhegyi, connect them with the cult of the hallucinogenic mushrooms still to this day prevalent in the Mexican highlands, and it is claimed that the mortars and pestles with which the stones are so often associated were used in the preparatory rites.

24 A Late Preclassic effigy of grey-green chlorite schist from Tomb I, Mound E-III-3 (Miraflores culture) at Kaminaljuyú. Overall length 8¼ in. (21 cm).

25 A grey soapstone jar from Tomb I, Mound E-III-3 at Kaminaljuyú. Ht 3½ in. (9.2 cm).

26 A fine-line incised bowl from Tomb I, Mound E-III-3 at Kaminaljuyú. W. 12 in. (30.5 cm).

27 A man wearing masks of long-lipped gods is carved on this granite stela from Kaminaljuyú. Ht 6 ft (1.8 m).

28 Broken Miraflores stela from Kaminaljuyú depicting Izapan gods (right) and a human figure with down-pointing trident eyes.

But we have much more to go by than that, thanks to the devastation of Kaminaljuyú by modern real-estate entrepreneurs. It now appears that there were Miraflores artists capable of creating sculpture on a large scale, in an Izapan style that can only be called the forerunner of the Classic Maya. Moreover, the élite of this valley were fully literate at a time when other Maya were perhaps just learning that writing existed. Two of these monuments were encountered by accident in a drainage ditch. One is a tall, granite stela embellished with a striding 27 figure wearing a series of grotesque masks of Izapan gods (the one over his face is the head of the bird-monster Vucub Caquix), and carrying a chipped flint of eccentric form in one hand. On either side of him are spiked clay incense burners exactly like those found in Miraflores excavations. The other is even more extraordinary. It must have been of gigantic proportions before its deliberate breakage; the surviving 28 fragments show that there were several Izapan gods, one bearded, surrounding a human figure with downpointing tridents in place of eyes, probably a precursor of a god who later appears at Tikal; he too, wields an eccentric flint. The glyphs associated with these figures may be their calendric names, for in ancient Mesoamerica, both gods and men were identified by the days on which they were born. A much longer text in several columns is incised below in a script which is otherwise unknown but which, in the opinion of Miss Proskouriakoff and others, may foreshadow Classic Maya writing, since there are strong similarities in form if not in specific characters. It cannot, however, yet be read.

Not only were stelae of major size carved by the Miraflores artisans, but also tenoned figures called 'silhouette sculptures', which were perhaps originally meant to be stuck upright into temple and plaza floors; frog- or toad-effigy figures of all sizes; and many other forms. Once more, the pot-bellied figures are ubiquitous: did they represent a cult of the people, separate from the more aristocratic religion of the rulers? Or do they, as some believe, belong to an earlier horizon? Archaeology has unfortunately arrived on the scene too late to answer this.

The astonishing wealth of the Miraflores people, their artistic and architectural capabilities, their obvious relation to the Classic Maya in matters of style, iconography, and script – all these things lead one to believe that the Izapan culture of the highlands must have had a good deal to do with the adoption of civilized life in the Central and Northern Areas. While the pre-eminence of Kaminaljuyú during the Late Preclassic period is plain to see, its star began to sink by the second and third centuries AD, and most of it was left in ruin at the close of the Late Preclassic. It was not until the Mexican invasions of the Early Classic that this great center regained its former splendor.

Elsewhere in the Guatemalan highlands, the French archaeologist Alain Ichon has excavated the mound site of La Lagunita, located in the Chixoy drainage some 40 km northeast of the Quiché center of Chichicastenango. There he encountered a number of relief sculptures in a terminal Late Preclassic style related to the Izapan culture, but somewhat aberrant, including one representation of Vucub Caquix. There were four stone sarcophagi, one containing two superimposed human skeletons with a wealth of offerings, including jade, variously colored obsidian, and white flint, along with a pottery effigy of a terrifying deity with long nose and gaping mouth revealing a lolling tongue and huge fangs.

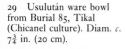

29   Usulután ware bowl from Burial 85, Tikal (Chicanel culture). Diam. *c.* $7\frac{3}{4}$ in. (20 cm).

The Petén and the Maya lowlands

While the Maya highlands and Pacific Coast were experiencing an extraordinary cultural efflorescence in the Late Preclassic, the Central and Northern Areas were hardly slumbering. Within the boundless forests, the agricultural economy and society had advanced to such a degree that massive temple centers were already rising in jungle clearings. But it is clear that from the very beginning the people of the lowlands were taking a somewhat different course from that of their kinsmen to the south, and it is their unique qualities which so distinguish them in the Classic period which was soon to be inaugurated.

Although there are minor differences from region to region, a single widespread culture, Chicanel, dominated the Central and Northern Areas at this time. Usulután ware and vessels with widely everted lips, elaborate rim flanges, or complex outline are, as in the Southern Area, hallmarks for the period. Most pottery is legless, and confined to a simple black or red monochrome, with thick glossy slips that feel waxy to the touch. It is strange that in most known Chicanel sites, figurines are not found, from which it may be supposed that there was a change in popular cults.

The most unusual feature of Chicanel culture, however, is the high elaboration of architecture, above all in the latter part of the Late Preclassic, from 100 BC to AD 250. It must be remembered that the Petén-Yucatán shelf is blessed with an inexhaustible supply of easily

30 The north side of Pyramid E-VII-sub, Uaxactún, a Late Preclassic site belonging to the Chicanel culture. On top of this stucco-faced pyramid had once been a pole-and-thatch temple. Ht 26 ft 4 in. (8 m).

29

cut limestone, and with abundant flint for tools with which to work it. Moreover, the Maya of the lowlands had discovered as far back as Mamóm times that if limestone fragments were burnt, and the resulting powder mixed with water, a white plaster of great durability was obtained. And finally, they quickly realized the structural value of a concrete-like fill made from limestone rubble and marl.

With these resources at hand, the Maya temple architect was able to create some elaborate constructions at a very early date. At the great Petén sites of Uaxactún, Tikal, and El Mirador, deep excavations have shown that major pyramids, platforms, and courts were already taking shape by late Chicanel times. There is general agreement, for instance, that the E-VII-sub pyramid at Uaxactún was built late in the Chicanel phase; beautifully preserved by the overlay of later structures, this truncated temple platform is faced by brilliantly white plaster and rises in several tiers each having the apron moldings which are so distinctive a feature of Maya architecture in the lowlands. On all four sides are centrally placed, inset stairways flanked by great monster masks which apparently represent the Jaguar God of the Underworld (the night sun), as well as sky-serpents. Postholes sunk into the floor show that the superstructure was a building of pole and thatch.

Even more advanced temples have been uncovered at Tikal, which lies only a half-day's walk south of Uaxactún. Two late Chicanel structures, for instance, had superstructures with masonry walls, and it is possible, though certainly not proved, that the rooms were spanned by the corbel vault, or so-called 'false arch'. Some quite extraordinary paintings embellished the outer walls of one of these temples, showing human figures standing in a background of cloud-like scrolls, carried out by a sure hand in black, yellow, red, and pink. Another set of murals, this time in black on a red background, was found inside a late Chicanel burial chamber at Tikal. The subject matter comprises six richly attired figures, probably both human and divine. The two sets, which are thought to date from the last half of the first century BC, are pretty clearly in the Izapan style characteristic of Kaminaljuyú.

Some of the Late Preclassic tombs at Tikal prove that the Chicanel élite did not lag behind the nobles of Miraflores in wealth and honor. Burial 85, for instance, like all the others enclosed by platform substructures and covered by a primitive corbel vault, contained a single skeleton. Surprisingly, this individual lacked head and thigh bones, but from the richness of the goods placed with him it may be guessed that he must have perished in battle and been despoiled by his enemies, his mutilated body being later recovered by his subjects. The remains were carefully wrapped-up in textiles, and the bundle placed in an upright position. A small, greenstone mask with shell-inlaid eyes and teeth seems to have been sewn to the bundle to represent the head. A sting-ray spine, the symbol of self-sacrifice among the Maya, and a spondylus shell were added to the gruesome contents. Packed around the burial chamber were no less than twenty-six vessels of the late Chicanel period, one of which contained pine-wood charcoal dated by the radiocarbon process to AD 16 ± 131.

The towering achievements of the Classic Maya in building and maintaining their enormous centers have blinded us to the equally

30

31

31 A greenstone mask, with shell-inlaid teeth and eyes, from Burial 85, Tikal. Ht 5 in. (12.7 cm).

remarkable florescence of Late Preclassic Maya culture. Two sites in Belize have provided exciting new data shedding light on this phenomenon. The first is Cerros, a relatively compact site located on a small, narrow peninsula near the mouth of the New River, on the southern edge of Chetumal Bay. Excavations and mapping carried out by David A. Freidel of Southern Methodist University have shown that this Late Preclassic center, with four primary pyramidal structures along with a host of other buildings, was surrounded by a moat-like canal which may have been connected with raised agricultural fields. One such pyramid was a two-tiered temple platform; its central stairway was flanked by four elaborate plaster-sculpture masks. Freidel interprets this as an elaborate cosmological diagram involving four important gods, and its relationship to the huge platform masks found on E-VII-sub pyramid at Uaxactún and on early buildings at Tikal is obvious.

Far up the New River, a considerable distance to the southwest of Cerros, is the important site of Lamanai (known as 'Indian Church' on older maps of Belize), which has been excavated by David M. Pendergast of the Royal Ontario Museum during a series of field seasons beginning in 1974. Lamanai lies on a long lake formed by the river, and its 718 mapped structures are stretched out in strip form along its shore. There is even an ancient harbor in the northern part of the site, testifying to its entrepreneurial importance in the regulation of ancient Maya trade. While it was occupied from earliest times right into the post-Conquest period, much of its importance lies in the large, imposing, Late Preclassic temple-pyramids which usually underlie 32 Early Classic constructions, including one with a plaster-work mask closely resembling those from Cerros.

32 Structure N10-43 at
Lamanai, Belize, as it
appeared *c.* 100 BC. Ht 33 m.
Typical of large Late
Preclassic temple-pyramids,
the lower stairs are flanked
by gigantic god-masks of
stucco.

But the full scope of this Late Preclassic achievement in the southern
Maya lowlands has only come to light at El Mirador, located in the
northernmost Petén only a few miles from the Mexican border. This
has turned out to be the oldest Maya capital city, far in advance of
Tikal, which it dwarfs by its size and lessens by its antiquity. The
investigations and mapping carried out by Professors Bruce Dahlin and
Ray Matheny have shown that El Mirador is almost entirely of Late
Preclassic (Chicanel) date; it was abandoned throughout the Early
Classic, but there is a shoddy, Late Classic reoccupation which had
little importance. There are two groups of monumental construction,
connected by a causeway, and in fact a whole network of causeways
radiates out from El Mirador across the surrounding swampy
landscape.

The East Group is dominated by the Danta pyramid and its
associated platforms, which cover an area of 18 hectares; the pyramid
and the structure upon which it sits reach a height of 230 ft (70 m), and
thus must comprise an overall bulk which may be the largest in
Mesoamerica, if not the New World. The Tigre pyramid in the west
group is no less than 141 ft (43 m) high. As at Cerros, Lamanai, Tikal,
and Uaxactún, gigantic stucco masks of deities flanked stairways, on
the testimony of one excavated structure.

All of this suggests that there was a flowering of culture in the
southern lowlands just prior to the beginning of the Christian era,
several centuries before the so-called Classic, and that this might well
have been connected with a kind of population explosion as remarkable
as that which we associate with the Late Classic. Certainly further
intensive excavations are called for at the key site of El Mirador.

Such Late Preclassic splendor is found throughout the lowlands
wherever the spade has gone deep enough. Even in the seemingly less-
favorable Northern Area, there are enormous constructions datable to

this era, such as the great high mound at Yaxuná, a temple substructure having a ground plan of 197 by 427 ft (60 by 130 m).

By the terminal Late Preclassic of the second and third centuries AD we are on the threshold of Classic Maya civilization. Temples arranged around plazas, construction with limestone and plaster, apron moldings and frontal stairways on pyramids, tomb building, and frescoes with naturalistic subjects – all had already taken shape by the end of the Late Preclassic. This brief epoch sees the intrusion of new ceramic traits which seem to have been first elaborated in El Salvador and later in Belize, the most important of these being the addition of hollow, breast-shaped supports to bowls, hour-glass-shaped pot-stands, and polychrome. Maya polychrome is distinguished by a brilliant range of colors applied over a glossy, translucent orange underslip, but wherever it was first invented it certainly was not native of the Petén region. Corbeling of rooms must have evolved from methods employed in the construction of tombs, and by AD 250 began to be in universal use at Petén sites. The principle is simple: above the springline of the walls, successive courses of stones were set in   cf.75
overlapping rows up to the vault summit, which was capped by flat   55
stones. However, there is an inherent structural weakness, and the great thrust from above is taken up in Maya buildings by massive walls and by the strength of the rubble-cement fill. Nevertheless, once adopted it became the badge of Maya architecture in the lowlands, as opposed to the thatched or flat-beam roofs of Mexico.

The list is impressive, and one would think on the face of it that Maya civilization had emerged independently here in the lowlands, several centuries before the opening of the Classic era. But two items are missing or exceedingly rare: monuments with Long Count dates, and writing. These we know were present among the coeval Izapan centers of the highlands and Pacific Coast, and it is probable that they were derived from the even older Olmec civilization of the Gulf Coast. The Izapan style was spread from outside into the Central and Northern areas – a broken carving from a terminal Late Preclassic level of the Tikal acropolis, the early Tikal frescoes, and a human figure in relief on the walls of Loltún cave in Yucatán all testify to this – but literacy and a concern with recording dates did not become prevalent in the lowlands until the eve of the Classic period.

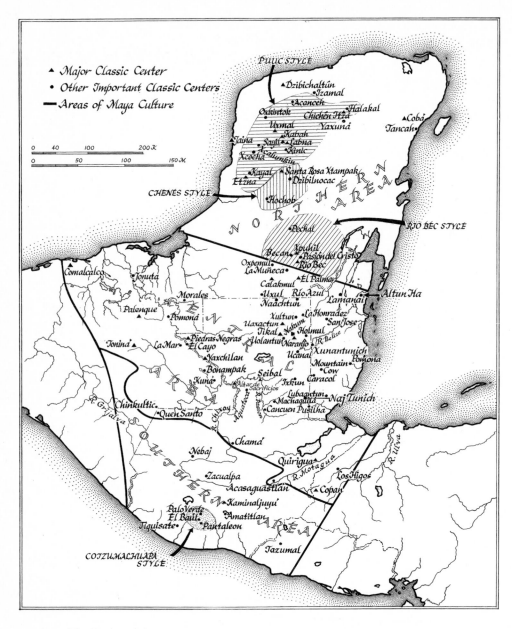

▲ Major Classic Center
• Other Important Classic Centers
— Areas of Maya Culture

PUUC STYLE

▲ Dzibichaltún
• Izamal
• Acanceh
Oxkintok • • Halakal
Chichén Itzá
Uxmal ▲ Yaxuná
• Kabah
Jaina ▲ • Sayil • Labna
• Xcocha • Kinic
• Hunkin
• Kayal • Santa Rosa Xtampak
Etzna ▲ • Dzibilnocac
Hochob •
Pechal •

CHENES STYLE

NORTHERN AREA

RIO BEC STYLE

Comalcalco ▲ • Jonuta
Xpuhil
Becan • • Pasión del Cristo
Oxpemul • Río Bec
La Muñeca • • El Palmar
Calakmul •
Morales • Uxul Río Azul
Náachtún Lamanai •
Palenque ▲ • Pomoná Xultun • • La Honradez Altun Ha
Uaxactun • • Nakum • San José
Tonina ▲ Tikal ▲ • Holmul
La Mar • • El Cayo • Uolantun Naranjo • R. Belize
Piedras Negras • Ucanal Xunantunich
Yaxchilan • Pomona
Mountain
Bonampak • Seibal Cow
Kuna • • Ixkun Caracol
Altar de • Sacrificios
Chinkultic • Lubaantún
Quen Santo • Machaquilá • Naj Tunich
Cancuen Pusilha •
Chamá •
Nebaj •
Quirigua •
Zacualpa • Los Higos •
Acasaguastlan • • Copán
Kaminaljuyú •
Palo Verde • Amatitlan
El Baúl • Pantaleon
Tiquisate • Pantaleon

SOUTHERN AREA

CENTRAL AREA

COTZUMALHUAPA
STYLE

Tazumal •

33 Sites of the Classic period.

4
Classic splendor: the Early period

During a span of six centuries, from about AD 250 to 900, the Maya, particularly those of the Central Area, reached intellectual and artistic heights which no others in the New World, and few in the Old, could match at that time. The Classic period was a kind of Golden Age, not only for them but for the rest of the Mesoamerican peoples. Large populations, a flourishing economy, and widespread trade were typical of the Classic, but although it was once thought to have been a period of relative peace and tranquillity in comparison with what followed, that notion has in the main been disproved. It is an equally unfounded assumption that the Classic peoples were ruled by priests. On the contrary, we shall see that the ancient Maya were just as warlike and had as thoroughly secular a government as the supposedly more bloodthirsty states of the Post-Classic. 33

The Classic in fact can only be defined accurately as that span during which the lowland Maya were using the Long Count calendar on their monuments. In 1864, workmen engaged in digging a canal near Puerto Barrios, on the steamy Caribbean coast of Guatemala, came across a jade plaque which subsequently found its way to Leiden, Holland. The Leiden Plate, generally agreed to have been made at Tikal, has engraved on one face a richly bedecked Maya lord at his accession, trampling underfoot a sorry-looking captive, a theme repeated on so many Maya stelae of later times. On the other side is inscribed the Long Count date 8.14.3.1.12, corresponding to a day in the year AD 320. The style of the glyphs and the costume and pose of the person depicted call to mind the Late Preclassic monuments of the highlands and Pacific Coast, but in this case the date is preceded by the typical Maya Introductory Glyph, and the bar-and-dot numbers are followed by the signs for baktun and lesser periods. Until recently the Leiden Plate was considered the most ancient object dated in Maya fashion, but now we have Stela 29 from Tikal, erected in 8.12.14.8.15 (AD 292). 34

The possibility that even earlier objects dated in the Maya system will some day be found in the Maya lowlands should be kept open, especially in the light of the Hauberg Stela, a miniature monument in a Seattle, Washington, private collection. This depicts a masked Maya lord in the act of a mystic blood-letting rite, and its very aberrant date (probably because of its antiquity) has been interpreted by the art historian Dr Linda Schele and the linguist John Justeson as a day in the year AD 199. This important relief would thus be intermediate in time between dated inscriptions of the Izapan culture and the dawn of Classic Maya civilization.

Thus, the lowland Maya had definitely received the Long Count by the close of the third century AD. From this event until the Classic downfall, we have a very closely dated archaeological sequence governed by the carving of stelae and other monuments, which themselves have been tied at Uaxactún and other sites with the construction of floors, building stages, and tombs. The Classic very conveniently divides itself into an Early and a Late period at about AD 600; however, this division is not merely an invention of the archaeologist, for not only did a profound upheaval take place in the Central Area at that time, but there are considerable cultural differences between the two halves.

Two things set off the Early from the Late Classic: firstly, the strong Izapan element still discernible in Maya culture, and secondly, the appearance in the latter part of the Early Classic of powerful waves of influence from the site of Teotihuacan in central Mexico. This city was founded at about the time of Christ in a small but fertile valley opening onto the northeast side of the Valley of Mexico itself. On the eve of its destruction at the hands of unknown peoples, at the end of the sixth century AD, it covered an area of over 8 square miles. Teotihuacan is

34   The Leiden Plate, a jade plaque found in 1864, shows a Maya lord trampling a captive underfoot and, on the reverse side, carries the Long Count date 8.14.3.1.12, corresponding to a day in the year AD 320. Ht 8½ in. (21.6 cm).

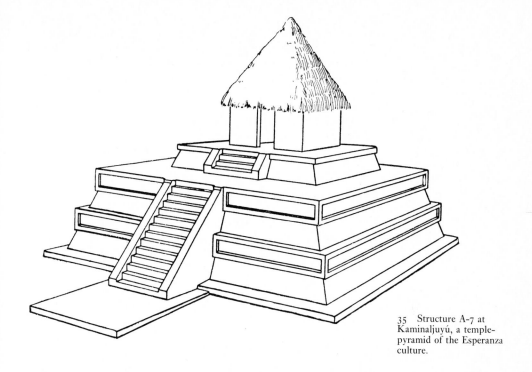

35 Structure A-7 at Kaminaljuyú, a temple-pyramid of the Esperanza culture.

noted for the regularity of its great avenues, for its Pyramids of the Sun and Moon, and for the delicacy and sophistication of the wall paintings which graced the walls of its luxurious palaces. So mighty was the city that it held dominion over most of Mexico in the Early Classic, as the center of an empire which may well have been greater than that of the much later Aztec. From what economic base such political and cultural power derived is unclear, but it may have been linked to adoption of the unique and incredibly productive system of *chinampa* cultivation carried out by draining and cultivating the swampy margins of the Great Lake which then filled the Valley of Mexico. This was the city which interfered in such a significant way with the course of Maya history.

The Esperanza culture

The disintegration of Maya culture in the highlands began with the close of the Miraflores period, when building activity slackened at major sites. In fact, by the end of the Preclassic, the great ceremonial center of Kaminaljuyú, focal point of Maya cultural and political affairs in the Southern Area, appears to have been a virtual ruin.

Shortly after AD 400, the highlands fell under Teotihuacan domination. An intrusive group of central Mexicans from that city seized Kaminaljuyú and built for themselves a miniature version of their capital. An élite class ruling over a captive population of Maya descent, they were swayed by native cultural tastes and traditions and became 'Mayanized' to the extent that they imported from the Central

Area pottery and other wares with which to stock their tombs. The Esperanza culture which arose at Kaminaljuyú during the Early Classic, then, is a kind of hybrid.

There are several complexes of Esperanza architecture at Kaminaljuyú, all built on a plan which is not in the least bit Maya. Essentially these are stepped temple platforms with the typical Teotihuacan *talud-tablero* motif, in which a rectangular panel with inset (*tablero*) is placed over a sloping batter (*talud*). The good building stone which is so abundant in the Mexican highlands is missing at Kaminaljuyú, so that the architect, almost certainly a Teotihuacano himself, had to be content with clay faced with red-painted stucco. A single stairway fronted each stage of the platform, while on top a temple sanctuary was roofed either with thatch or with the more usual flat-beam-and-mortar construction of Teotihuacan.

The foreign lords of the Esperanza phase chose the temple platforms themselves as their final resting-places. As with the earlier Miraflores people, each platform was actually built to enclose the ruler's tomb, a log-roofed chamber usually placed beneath the frontal staircase, successive burials and their platforms being placed over older ones. The honored deceased was buried in a seated posture upon a wooden bier and was accompanied to the other world not only by rich offerings of pottery and other artifacts, but also by one to three persons sacrificed for the occasion, generally children or adolescents. Surrounding him were rich funerary vessels, undoubtedly containing food and drink for his own use, as well as implements such as *metates* and *manos* needed to prepare them.

Jade ornaments, some in the process of manufacture, were recovered in quantity from the Esperanza tombs: beads, complex ear ornaments in the form of flared spools, pendants, and spangles are ubiquitous. Underneath one staircase was found a 200-lb (90-kg) boulder of jade from which V-shaped slices had been sawn, indicating that the Esperanza élite had access to a major source of this substance so precious to all the peoples of Mesoamerica.

Few of the pottery vessels from the Esperanza tombs are represented in the rubbish strewn around Kaminaljuyú, from which it is clear that they were intended for the use of the invading class alone. Some of these were actually imported from Teotihuacan itself, probably carried laboriously over the intervening 800 or 900 miles on back racks such as those still used by Indian traders in the Maya highlands. The ceramic hallmarks of the Teotihuacan civilization are the cylindrical vessel with three slab feet and cover; a little jug with open spout and handle; the '*florero*', so called from its resemblance to a small flower-vase; and Thin Orange ware, made to Teotihuacan taste in northern Puebla. All are present in Esperanza, but so are polychrome bowls from the Petén, with their peculiar 'basal flanges'.

Certain of the tripod vessels have been stuccoed and painted in brilliant colors with feather-bedecked Teotihuacan lords, or seated Maya personages and both Maya and Teotihuacan deities, including the Butterfly Goddess so popular in Mexico. One Petén Maya polychrome bowl had even been overpainted with processional figures in Teotihuacan style, speech scrolls curling from their mouths.

35

36

37

38

36 A long jade bead carved with a human figure, from Tomb A-VI, Kaminaljuyú, (Esperanza culture). L. 6 in. (15.6 cm).

37 Restored Thin Orange ware vessel in the form of a seated man, from Tomb X, Kaminaljuyú (Esperanza culture). This ware was manufactured to Teotihuacan taste in northern Puebla, and appears wherever the Teotihuacan people had penetrated. Ht of vessel *c*. 11¾ in. (30 cm).

38 An Esperanza culture tripod vessel with cover, from Tomb B-II, Kaminaljuyú. The exterior had been stuccoed and painted in buff, red and light green. The figures on the vessel are Maya, while the glyphs on the lid are Teotihuacanoid. Ht $12\frac{1}{2}$ in. (32 cm).

All sorts of other valuables were placed with the dead. That Esperanza pomp, perhaps the funeral itself, was accompanied by music is shown by shell trumpets and by large turtle carapaces used with deer-antler beaters as percussive instruments. On a large effigy incense burner from one grave, a seated person strikes a two-toned slit drum. Besides jade, the corpse was ornamented with pearls, cut-out pieces of mica, and rich textiles which have long since rotted away. Included in several tombs were pairs of jaguar paws, symbols of royal power among the highland Maya. The highest technical achievement is seen in the mirrors made up of pyrite plates cut into polygonal shapes and fitted to each other over a circular disk of slate. These are in all likelihood another import from Teotihuacan, but the back of one proved to have remarkable carving in an elaborate scrollwork style that is associated with the Classic Veracruz civilization then developing on the Gulf

Coast of Mexico. The ability of the Esperanza rulers to amass luxurious objects from the most distant parts must have been considerable.

The Esperanza culture may have its spectacular side, but almost as striking are omissions. The Long Count calendar had disappeared from the Southern Maya area for good, which is strange considering its ancient roots here. The figurine cult had utterly disappeared. Nor is there any sure indication of stone sculpture on any scale in Esperanza Kaminaljuyú. The evolution of Maya culture in the Southern Area, especially in the highlands, had come to a very abrupt end with the establishment of Teotihuacan hegemony, and apart from the imports of Petén products, Maya ways of doing things were replaced with Mexican from the Early Classic on. Were these intruders warriors or traders? They may well have been both. By Aztec times in central Mexico there was a special caste of armed merchants called *pochteca*, who journeyed into distant countries in search of rare manufactures and raw materials not available in the homeland, all of which were destined for the king. From representations of the *pochteca* god at Teotihuacan, we know that the institution is at least as old as the Early Classic. Thus, Kaminaljuyú may have been a southeasterly outpost of long-distance traders from that great city, established for the purpose of exporting Maya riches for the Teotihuacan throne. As will be seen, the presence of this foreign group was felt through the Petén and as far north as Yucatán itself.

39 Pottery incense burner with heads of the Death God and Xipe Totec, Mexican god of the springtime, from the Zarzal underwater site, Lake Amatitlán, Guatemala. Ht $9\frac{1}{2}$ in. (24 cm).

40 Pottery of the Tzakol phase at Uaxactún (Early Classic period). *a, b,* polychrome basal-flange bowls; *c,* spouted jug; *d, e,* tripod cylindrical vessels. *a,* 9⅜ in. (23.8 cm) wide; *b–e,* to scale.

As for the vanquished Maya of the Guatemalan highlands, they must have continued on as before, rendering tribute to Mexican rather than native overlords, tillers of the land and laborers on public construction projects. The great public ceremonials of Kaminaljuyú may even have been forbidden to them. But one cult in which they were certainly allowed to participate was centered upon Lake Amatitlán, not far south of the Esperanza capital, where hot springs and fumaroles along the southern shore must have attracted annual processions rendering homage to the gods of water and fire. Skin-divers have brought up many hundreds of blackened vessels from the hot mud of the lake bottom, ranging from extraordinary incense burners to the pots and pans of the peasant household, all cast by devotees into the steaming waters.

In 1969 farm tractors plowing the fields in the Tiquisate region of the Pacific coastal plain of Guatemala, an area located south-southwest of Lake Atitlán that is covered with ancient (and untested) mounds, unearthed rich tombs and caches which contained a total of over 1,000 ceramic objects. These have been examined by Nicholas Hellmuth of the Foundation for Latin American Archaeological Research, and proved to consist of two-piece censers, slab-legged tripod cylinders, hollow moldmade figures, and other objects, all in the Teotihuacan style. Numerous finds of fired clay molds suggest that these were mass-produced from Teotihuacan prototypes by military-merchant groups intrusive from central Mexico during the last half of the Early Classic.

39

Tzakol culture in the Central Area

Early Classic remains in the Central Area are burdened with towering constructions of Late Classic date, and it has only been quite recently that the elaboration of Maya civilization during this period has been fully realized. The Tzakol culture, as the civilization of the Petén and surrounding regions is called, endures until about 9.8.0.0.0, or to round it off in Christian years, until AD 600.

Already Maya civilization is in full flower, with enormous ceremonial centers crowded with masonry temples and 'palaces' facing onto spacious plazas covered with white stucco. Stelae and altars are carved with dates and embellished with the figures of men and perhaps gods. Polychrome pottery, the finest examples of which were sealed up in the tombs of honored personages, emphasizes stylized polychrome designs of cranes, flying parrots, or men, often on bowls with a kind of apron or basal flange encircling the lower part. Along with these purely Maya ceramics are vessels which show the imprint of distant Teotihuacan: again, the cylindrical vase supported by three slab legs, the small, spouted jug, and the *florero*.

The wonderful Maya mural art has its roots in the Chicanel wall paintings of Tikal, but by Tzakol times it had reached a very high degree of elaboration. Now mutilated by local vandals, the lovely Early Classic wall paintings of Temple B-XIII at Uaxactún were executed in

40

cf.49

41   The tomb chamber of Burial 48, Tikal (Tzakol culture). On its walls is painted the Long Count date 9.1.1.10.10 4 Oc (19 March AD 457), together with other glyphs of probably stellar significance.

42 Polychrome two-part ceramic effigy from Burial 10, Tikal (Tzakol culture). This may represent an old god receiving a severed head as an offering. Ht 14 in. (36 cm).

43 (*opposite*) Side view of Stela 31 at Tikal, with a warrior shown in relief in Teotihuacan costume. In one hand he carries an *atlatl* or spear-thrower, and in the other a shield with the face of Tlaloc, the Mexican Rain God.

muted tones of red, brown, tan, and black. The scene is one from real life: before a palace building sheltering three Maya ladies, two male figures, one painted a warlike black, are in conversation (which is undoubtedly recorded in several columns of indecipherable glyphs). At one side are two horizontal rows of figures, probably meant to be standing on two levels of a stepped platform, painted with a strong feeling for individual caricature; a few are chattering in excited discourse. Some are singers shaking rattles, while a small boy beats time on a skin-covered drum.

Burials of great richness have been uncovered beneath Tzakol temples in several Petén sites. Among the most striking is the 'Painted Tomb' chamber, 9 ft (2.7 m) long by 5 ft (1.5 m) wide, cut from the soft bedrock underlying an Early Classic temple facing the Great Plaza at

41

Tikal. There were three interments here, two of them adolescent victims sacrificed to accompany the principal personage, a headless and handless corpse presumably recovered by his followers from the scene of a military disaster. The white, stuccoed walls had been covered with glyphs applied in black paint by a sure hand, including the Long Count date 9.1.1.10.10 (19 March AD 457 in the Gregorian calendar), in all likelihood the day of the man's death or of his funeral. *A metate* and *mano*, and vessels once filled with food (one had contained some pigeon-sized birds), show that the soul was to be nourished in the afterlife. Marine shells and sting-ray spines, imported from distant shores, were placed with the dead. Besides pottery vessels, the tomb contained a travertine pedestal bowl encircled by a row of incised glyphs, the lines of which were filled with red cinnabar.

During the 1960s and early 1970s, a period which saw the apogee (or nadir) of Maya tomb robbery in the southern lowlands, the modestly sized site of Río Azul in the northeasternmost Petén was heavily looted, and produced for the international market an extraordinary variety of élite objects of the utmost beauty, mainly but not entirely of Early Classic date. Three of these emptied tombs had Tzakol culture murals painted in red and black on the bare walls, including glyphic texts of dynastic nature, and a scene depicting the undulating surface of the Underwater world, a theme linked by Dr Hellmuth with Xibalbá, the Maya realm of the dead. In the last several years, a project led by Dr R. E. W. Adams has uncovered an intact tomb with further murals and Early Classic offerings, although not on the scale or magnificence of those already stripped of their finery.

Although influence from Teotihuacan, or from its Kaminaljuyú outpost, had for some time been suspected for the Central Area during the Early Classic, the full extent of this has only begun to become clear through modern excavations at Tikal, in the very heart of the Petén. It is also apparent that the foreign impact is strongest at about AD 500, in the last century of the Early Classic.

43   Stela 31 from Tikal, erected in AD 445, hints at the nature of this influence. This elaborate relief sculpture is, according to the hieroglyphic specialist Peter Mathews, largely concerned with the historical annals of Tikal, leading from a time anterior to the accession recorded on the Leiden Plate, up to the day when the ruler 'Stormy Sky' (a nickname bestowed by modern epigraphers) celebrates the end of his first katun in power at the great city. 'Stormy Sky' himself is loaded down with jade ornaments almost to the point of obscuring him; he carries in the crook of his left arm the head of a god wearing in its headdress the Tikal 'Emblem Glyph' (see Chapter 8). On either side is a standing warrior whose dress and armament (rectangular shield and *atlatl*, or spear-thrower) brand him as a foreigner from Teotihuacan. One of the shields shows the face of the great Teotihuacan Rain God, Tlaloc. Was Tikal, like Kaminaljuyú, a suzerainty of Teotihuacan? Or were those foreign mercenaries in the employ of a native king? The city-dwellers of Teotihuacan were a mercantile people, and it would have been greatly in the interest of an armed *pochteca* group to have seized the Petén so as to control the commerce originating in the Maya jungles. Perhaps also it was the resplendent, gold-green tail feathers of

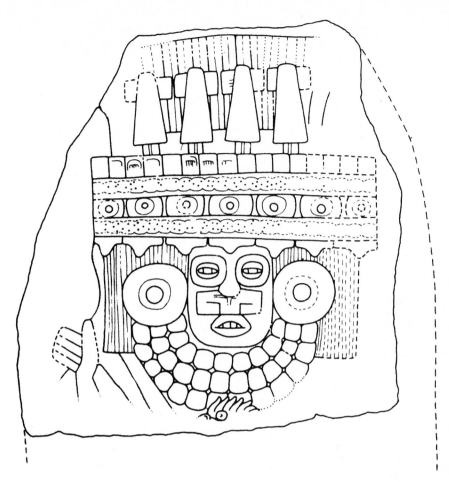

the shy quetzal, located in the cloud forests south of the Petén, that they were seeking, to adorn the headdresses of Teotihuacan nobles.

They might also have tried to impose the worship of Teotihuacan gods upon the Petén Maya, substituting their own rain god for the native Chac. To this the upper part of a shattered stela from Tikal, showing a large Tlaloc face exactly like that upon the shield of Stela 31, is testimony. On finely stuccoed and painted vessels from the Tikal tombs is the blue-faced Tlaloc again, together with the Mexican god of spring, Xipe Totec, recognized by the open mouth and the pairs of vertical lines which pass through the eyes across the cheeks. Some of these vessels are Thin Orange ware manufactured in the Mexican highlands, another comes from the Tiquisate region on the Pacific Coast of Guatemala, while others represent hybrids in shape and decoration between Maya and Teotihuacan traditions.

There almost certainly was a heavy trade between the Petén and the Valley of Mexico. Tzakol sherds from basal flange bowls have been found at Teotihuacan, and green obsidian blades from central Mexico were placed with the Tikal dead. However, of all the perishable products which must have traveled the same routes – textiles, quetzal

44 Fragmentary stela in Teotihuacan style from Tikal showing a large Tlaloc face exactly like that upon the shield in Stela 31 (ill. 43).

45

45 Lid of a stuccoed bowl from Burial 10, Tikal (Tzakol culture). The head and hands painted here in Teotihuacan style belong to Xipe Totec, the Mexican god of the springtime.

feathers, jaguar pelts, wooden objects, and so forth – nothing at all remains.

Not only in the northern Petén, but at many other places in the Central Area, major Maya centers were well established by the sixth century AD and even earlier. At these, Teotihuacan domination is less easy, or even impossible, to demonstrate, and one can suppose that this was restricted to the Tikal-Uaxactún area alone. None the less, Yaxhá, a small Maya city located southeast of Tikal, has a stela in pure Teotihuacan style apparently depicting a warrior-goddess with Tlaloc mask, and a city plan which combines the amorphous Maya pattern with formal 'streets' laid out in the central Mexican fashion. Whatever

cf.46–48 might be the nature of Teotihuacan influence on the affairs, both political and cultural, of the Petén Maya, in the last half of the sixth century a serious crisis shook the Central Area. No more stelae were erected, and there are signs of widespread and purposeful mutilation of public monuments. It is not clear what all this means, but although none of the Petén sites actually seems to have been abandoned near the

46   Early Classic jade plaque of the bird-monster god
Vucub Caquix, from Copán, Honduras. Ht 4¼ in.
(10.7 cm).

47   A jade object shaped like an ear flare from
Pomona, Belize (early Tzakol culture). The four
glyphs refer to gods. Diam. 7 in. (17.8 cm).

49 A double-chambered
vessel of the Tzakol culture,
possibly from Campeche,
Mexico. On the two lids one
of the Hero Twin gods faces
Vucub Caquix. Ht 11⅞ in.
(30.3 cm).

close of the Early Classic, there might have been fierce internecine
warfare or perhaps even a popular revolt.

When the smoke clears, in the first decades of the seventh century,
Classic Maya life is seen to have been reconstituted much as before,
possibly with new rulers and new dynasties. But Teotihuacan is no
longer a factor in Maya civilization. In some great event of which we
have no written record, that city was destroyed, and the empire of
which it was the capital came to an end. This took place by AD 600, and
probably was the decisive factor resulting in the Maya disturbances in
the closing decades of the Early Classic. However, the release from a
foreign yoke which was economic and probably also political enabled
the lowland Maya of the Central Area to reach unparalleled heights in
the Late Classic period.

The Northern Area

A good deal less is known about the Early Classic in the stony land of
Yucatán and Campeche than in the south. In both ceramics and
architecture, these Maya closely adhered to Petén standards. One of the
earliest centers is Oxkintok in the scrubby plain of western Yucatán,
with a stone lintel carved in the fifth century AD, and some
contemporary but aesthetically inferior reliefs.

49

48 (*opposite*) The finest Maya
wood carving known, this
seated figure from Tabasco,
Mexico, represents a
moustachioed lord with
folded arms; traces of
hematite pigment remain on
the piece. Ht 14 in. (35.5
cm). Cf. frontispiece
illustration.

83

A more interesting site is Acanceh, southeast of Mérida, the present-day capital of Yucatán. On the one hand, there is a stepped pyramid-platform with inset stairway of apron moldings of straightforward Petén Maya type. On the other, there is an extraordinary platform with a *talud-tablero* façade, stuccoed with relief figures in Teotihuacan style: anthropomorphic bats, birds of prey, a squirrel, and a representation of the central deity of Teotihuacan, known as the Feathered Serpent or Quetzalcoatl. There is nothing Maya about this building. On the contrary, it is evidence that the dynamic people of Teotihuacan had established outposts not only in the Southern and Central Areas, but also here in the Northern Area, foreshadowing the great Mexican invasions that were to take place in Yucatán five centuries later.

The Cotzumalhuapa problem

The Pipil have always been an enigmatic people. Their language is Nahuat, a close relative of Nahuatl, the official tongue of the Aztec, differing mainly from the latter by a substitution of *t* in place of *tl*. Having intruded into the Maya area at some unknown time from an equally unknown region in Mexico, by the Spanish Conquest the Pipil had established a major settlement in a small zone within the well-watered piedmont zone just above the Pacific plain of Guatemala. From traditions recorded in Colonial times, however, it is known that

50 The stuccoed figure of a jaguar or puma, a speech scroll issuing from its mouth, is shown in Teotihuacan style on the upper façade of an Early Classic building at Acanceh, Mexico.

their domain had once extended somewhat to the west into lands later claimed by the Cakchiquel Maya.

This once-Pipil territory is the locus of a vanished civilization which was indisputably Mexican, centering upon the town of Santa Lucía Cotzumalhuapa, in a region which once was famed for its production of cacao, the chocolate beans used not only for drink but as currency. There are only about a half-dozen Cotzumalhuapan sites known, or perhaps just one large one, for all lie within a tiny area of only 20 square miles. Each is a compact ceremonial center consisting of temple substructures arranged on a single large platform measuring only a few hundred yards on its long axis; structures have earthen cores faced with river cobbles, but stairways and some courts were occasionally covered with dressed stone.

From the evidence of art style and pottery, the Cotzumalhuapan culture must have arisen in the latter part of the Early Classic, and endured into the Late. A more hard, cruel, and unsympathetic sculptural style can hardly be imagined, or one less Maya in its general aspect. As the late Sir Eric Thompson noted, the Cotzumalhuapan sculptors showed 'a haunting preoccupation with death'. Reliefs of skulls and manikin figures of skeletons are not uncommon. Their second obsession was the rubber ball game. Secure evidence for the

51 A stone relief of the Crab God from El Baúl (Cotzumalhuapa culture). On either side are the Mexican dates 2 Monkey and 6 Monkey. Ht 3 ft 3 in. (1 m).

51

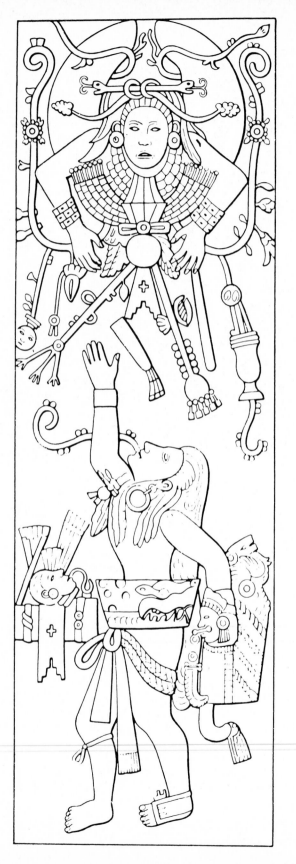

52 A ball-player salutes the Moon Goddess. Monument 4 from Santa Lucía Cotzumalhuapa (Cotzumalhuapa culture, end of the Early Classic or beginning of the Late Classic).

53 A thin stone head (*hacha*) from El Baúl (Cotzumalhuapa culture). Objects of this sort were probably ball-court markers. Ht *c.* 1 ft (30.5 cm).

game comes from certain stone objects which are frequent in the Cotzumalhuapan zone and in fact over much of the Pacific coast down to El Salvador. Of these, most typical are the U-shaped stone 'yokes' which represented the heavy protective belts of wood and leather worn by the contestants; and thin heads or *hachas* with human faces, grotesque carnivores, macaws, and turkeys, generally thought to be markers for the zones of the court, but worn on the yoke during post-game ceremonies. Both are sure signs of a close affiliation to the Classic cultures of the Mexican Gulf Coast, where such ball-game paraphernalia undoubtedly originated.

53

Among the relief and in-the-round sculptures of the Cotzumalhuapan sites are representations of some purely Mexican gods: Xipe Totec; the Wind God Ehecatl, shown as a horrifically snouted monster with one extruded eyeball; Tlaloc; Tlalchitonatiuh, god of the rising sun; the Old Fire God, Huehueteotl; and Quetzalcoatl as Feathered Serpent. On some magnificent stelae, ball players wearing 'yokes' and protective gloves reach up to celestial deities, usually the Sun or Moon. From the bodies of gods and men may sprout the fronds and pods of cacao, the apparent source of Cotzumalhuapan wealth.

52

Not only their religion, but their very calendar was Mexican. The majority of the glyphs on the monuments are recognizable as the kind of day-names prevalent among the peoples of southern Mexico, while the numbers and coefficients are expressed in the Mexican fashion by dots or circles only, without the use of the bar for 'five' so characteristic of the Maya. Again, as in Mexico, individuals (and perhaps gods, too) were identified by the day of their birth.

The creators of the Cotzumalhuapan civilization, then, were not Mayan but Mexican, most likely the Pipil themselves. Yet, while some of their art and a few of their pottery vessels can be related to Teotihuacan, they could not have come from that city. There are surer connections with the Gulf Coast plain, where there is a similar concentration upon the ball game, death, human sacrifice, and the cultivation of cacao. If these were the Pipil, then there might have been an ancient center of Nahuat speakers in southern Veracruz who, as another *pochteca* group, could have invaded the southern Maya area across the Isthmus of Tehuantepec. It will be recalled that there is a further enclave of Pipil on the other side of the highlands in the Motagua Valley of Guatemala, and it is probably no accident that isolated sculptures in Cotzumalhuapan style have been found there at Quiriguá and at near-by Copán, both otherwise purely Classic Maya centers. But the Cotzumalhuapa problem is very far from solved.

5
Classic splendor: the Late period

The great culture of the Maya lowlands during the Late Classic period is one of the 'lost' civilizations of the world, its hundreds of cities and towns often buried under an almost unbroken canopy of tropical forest. At one time it could be said that we did not know who lived in these now-decayed centers, and how the Maya realm was then governed. It was even thought that the major sites which are often called 'cities' were nothing of the sort.

Large masonry buildings are easy to map, but, curiously enough, so are the simple huts of the common people, for the ancient Maya conveniently raised their houses on low, rectangular mounds of earth and stone to avoid the summer floods. Topographic surveys of large Maya sites like Tikal and Seibal in the Petén, or Dzibilchaltún in northern Yucatán, reveal a very amorphous pattern of structures ranging from great temple-pyramids and so-called 'palaces' down to individual house mounds arranged around tiny plazas (these were probably family compounds). This pattern is a far cry from the neat gridiron layout of Teotihuacan in central Mexico, which conforms far more to our idea of what a city should be. An earlier generation of archaeologists considered the great sites to be nothing more than relatively empty ceremonial centers, staffed only by the priest-rulers and their retinues, and bustling with populace only during great rituals and times of corvée labor.

The intellectual tide has changed in the light of new data and new concepts. While it is true that, with the exception of the Teotihuacan-influenced Yaxhá in the Petén, there are no streets to be discerned in lowland sites during the Classic, these nevertheless functioned as cities, since they were the administrative and ritual centers for city-states and had populations as large as many post-Roman cities of the Old World. In early, pre-industrial cities and towns of the Western Hemisphere, we are used to seeing city walls, but these are not found at Classic Maya sites. Because of the seemingly unplanned nature of the settlement pattern, the boundaries of Maya cities are difficult to determine. Becán in the Río Bec region is surrounded by a moat, and Uaxactún and Tikal are separated by a defensive earthwork, but these are exceptions to the rule.

The late Sylvanus G. Morley once classified all known Maya centers, both Classic and Post-Classic, according to their supposed degrees of relative importance, ranging from Class 1 giants like Tikal and Copán down to Class 4 centers such as Bonampak and Acanceh. In 1946 he

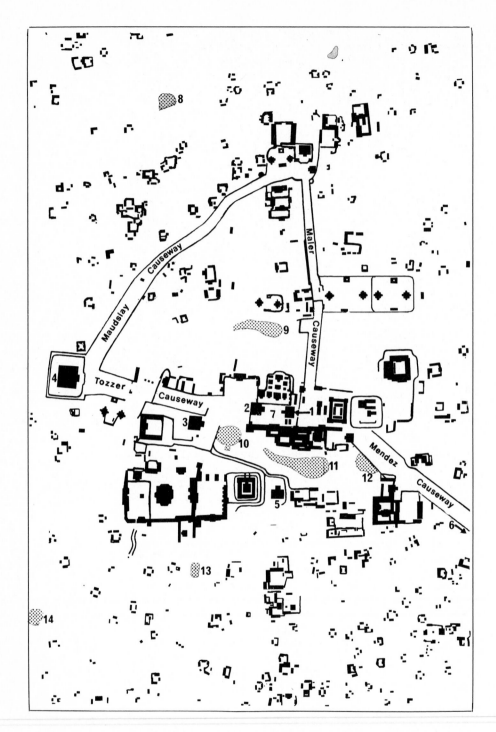

54 Plan of the central part of Tikal (the area covered is slightly over 1 sq. mile). *1–5* Temples I–V; *6* Temple of Inscriptions; *7* Great Plaza; *8–14* Reservoirs: *8* Bejucal, *9* Causeway, *10* Temple, *11* Palace, *12* Hidden, *13* Madeira, *14* Perdido.

55 A room in the Five-Story Palace at Tikal, from a photograph taken by Teobert Maler. The use to which these 'palaces' were put remains uncertain. As seen here, there are usually one or more plastered benches along the back wall of the rooms.

listed a total of 116 sites in the Northern and Central Areas, but explorations since then suggest that the figure could probably be doubled.

How large were the great cities in terms of size and population? Tikal is the largest of all Maya sites and has been completely mapped down to the last house mound, although in view of the difficulty of drawing boundaries around any settlement of the lowlands it is hard to say exactly where it ends. Within a little over 6 square miles, there are about 3,000 structures, ranging from lofty temple-pyramids and massive palaces to tiny household units of thatch-roofed huts. Estimates of the total Tikal population in Late Classic times vary all the way from 10,000 to 40,000 persons. If one accepted the latter figure, which many Mayanists think is the most likely, this would mean a density higher than that of an average city in modern Europe or America. A glance at the Tikal layout will show that this is a concentration of a basically dispersed population, with a slight increase in frequency and size of house as one moves closer to the heart of the site itself, where the dwellings of aristocrats and bureaucrats alike would have been more splendid.

The same somewhat 'colloidal' appearance is typical of all other known Classic centers, which in the northeast Petén were always placed on low ridges so that they could be easily seen for several miles, if the trees around them were cut. They look, in fact, rather like artificial

56 A restoration drawing of the site of Copán, Honduras, by Tatiana Proskouriakoff. To the right is the Acropolis, to the left the Great Plaza. The bulk of the construction shown here is of the Late Classic period.

57 The Ball Court at Copán from the south (Late Classic period).

mountains. The same can be said for the sites of much of the Northern Area, although in the northern part of the Yucatán Peninsula, where ground water is scarce, the presence of large *cenotes* often determines the position of major ceremonial centers. But water was also scarce in the Petén, and at huge centers like Tikal there are several artificial reservoirs of some size, surrounded by embankments, which provided sufficient water to the inhabitants over the winter dry season.

Classic sites in the Central Area

A Classic Maya center typically consists of a series of stepped platforms topped by masonry superstructures, arranged around broad plazas or courtyards. In the really large sites such as Tikal there may be a number of building complexes interconnected by causeways. Towering above all are the mighty temple-pyramids built from limestone blocks over a rubble core. Although the temples themselves contain one or more corbeled and plaster-covered rooms, these are so narrow that they could only have been used on the occasion of ceremonies meant to be kept from plebeian eyes. Tall they are, but the Maya architects were not content and almost always added a further extension to the upper temple, a so-called roof comb, which along with the temple façade was highly embellished with painted stucco reliefs.

55   The bulk of the construction at a Maya site, however, is taken up by the palaces, single-storied structures built on similar principles to the temple-pyramids but on much lower platforms and containing more plastered rooms, sometimes up to several dozen in the same building. Occasionally, there may be one or two interior courtyards within the palaces. There is little agreement on just what a 'palace' was used for. Did the rulers and other members of the élite live in these? They seem singularly uncomfortable (and bat-infested) to those archaeologists forced by circumstances to camp in them, and it seems more likely that the royal household was sheltered in perishable buildings which have not survived the lowland climate. It has also been suggested on the evidence of their cell-like rooms that they might have been monasteries or quarters for the priesthood, but it is entirely uncertain whether there were ecclesiastical or monastic orders in Classic times.

In any Classic center in the Central Area with a claim to importance, standing stelae were placed in the stucco floors of the plazas, usually fronting certain important temples but sometimes palaces as well. At times the stelae appear on platforms supporting temple-pyramids, but the rule seems to have been that certain stelae were always associated with specific structures, for reasons which until recently were something of a mystery. Generally a stela will have a low, round, flat-topped 'altar' standing before it. The subject-matter of the relief carvings on one or both stela faces seems always the same: a richly attired Maya ruler, generally a male, carrying peculiar emblems such as 58   the so-called ceremonial bar or manikin scepter, or else a similarly garbed person with spear and shield, trampling a captive underfoot. We shall examine these reliefs and the Long Count dates and glyphs which are inscribed on them in Chapter 8, for the story that they tell is now unfolding.

58   Stela 4, Machaquilá, Guatemala (Late Classic period). The figure holds a 'Manikin Scepter' (God K), the symbol of rulership.

57 Ball courts seem to be present at many sites in the Central Area, but they are more frequent and better made in the southeast, at sites like Copán. These courts are of stucco-faced masonry, and have sloping playing surfaces. At Copán, three stone markers were placed on each side, and three set into the floor of the court, but the exact method of scoring in the game is obscure. Toward the western part of the Central Area, in centers along the Usumacinta River, sweat baths are known, possibly adopted from Mexico where such structures can still be found in many highland towns.

Awe-inspiring though the great Maya 'cities' are, there is little overt indication of any overall planning in their arrangement. Rather, the typical center seems to have grown by accretion as temples, palaces, and entire complexes were rebuilt over and over again through the centuries. There was a gradual accumulation of architectural features that seem to have had social and political functions of a special (but still largely undetermined) nature. Nothing could be more foreign or inappropriate to the Maya center than the kind of grid plan seen in some of the great urban sites of Mexico, such as Teotihuacan.

56 Certainly one of the loveliest of all Classic Maya ruins is Copán, situated above a tributary of the Río Motagua in a section of western Honduras famed for its tobacco. Stephens, who explored the site in 1839 (and bought it for 50 dollars!) called it 'a valley of romance and wonder, where . . . the genii who attended on King Solomon seem to have been the artists.' The principal temple-pyramids rest on an artificial acropolis which has been partly carried away by the Copán River, but many of the structures remain intact. Among them is the Temple of the Hieroglyphic Stairway, completed in the eighth century AD, with a staircase every one of whose sixty-three steps is embellished on the risers with an immensely long text of about 2,500 glyphs. The ball court at Copán is the most perfect known for the Classic Maya, with tenon sculptures in the shape of macaw heads as its markers. But it 59, 60 is the wonderfully baroque qualities of its carving in the round which distinguish this site from all others, for the Copán artists worked in a greenish volcanic tuff superior to the limestone in use among the Petén centers. Not only were doorways, jambs, and façades of the major temples ornamented with stone figures of the Rain God, young Maize God, and other deities, but no fewer than twenty stelae were carved and 61 erected in Early and Late Classic times, together with fourteen 'altars'. It appears that the majority of the stelae were placed on the north end of the site, in a broad court bounded by narrow stepped platforms from which the populace could gaze upon the spectacles involved with the stela cult.

In recent years, Copán has been the focus of a large-scale international archaeological project that has thrown much light on the most important Maya site in the southeast lowlands. Apparently founded by Olmec who had come to this region to exploit the apple-green jade native to the nearby Motagua valley, this remained one of the great regional city-states until the Classic collapse. Dynastic records preserved on the stelae and Hieroglyphic Stairway indicate that Copán had its ups and downs. For instance, the eighth-century ruler of the site, 18 Rabbit, was captured and presumably eventually sacrificed

59 Stone head and torso of the Young Maize God, from Copán, one of the wonderfully baroque carvings at this site. Ht 28 in. (71 cm).

60 Head of a torchbearer on the Reviewing Stand, Copán, from a photograph by Dr Gordon Ekholm. This grotesque sculpture is very reminiscent of the Cotzumalhuapa style. Approximately life-size.

61 Stela D and its 'altar', north side of the Great Plaza at Copán, from a lithograph published by Frederick Catherwood in 1844. The 'altar' represents the Death God with fleshless jaws. On the stela is the *tun* ending date 9.15.5.0.0 (26 July AD 736 in the Gregorian calendar). Ht of stela 11 ft 9 in. (3.6 m).

by the lord of Quiriguá, a nearby site (see below) which had largely been under Copán's thumb. Perhaps the most exciting new discovery at Copán resulted from excavations in a palace complex austerely known as Structure 9N-82, which proved to be dedicated to the Monkey-man Scribes of the Classic Maya, and which may well have been inhabited by a high-ranking noble scribe and his family (see Chapter 8).

Quiriguá lies only 30 miles north of Copán; it is a far humbler Classic center which seems on the testimony of the inscriptions to have been one of the latter's suzerainties, at least at certain times of its history. Situated not far from the western bank of the Río Motagua, in its lush lower reaches, Quiriguá contains a few architectural groups of no great distinction. Its enormous sandstone stelae and carved zoomorphic stones, however, are quite another matter; indeed Stela E, erected late in the eighth century, might claim to be the greatest stone monument of the New World, its shaft measuring 35 ft (10.7 m) in height. On the front face it is carved with the figure of a bearded ruler holding a small hand shield and a 'manikin scepter' in either hand, while the sides are covered with texts containing several Long Count dates. The great skill of the Quiriguá sculptors can be seen in the grotesque full figures which take the place of cycle glyphs in the inscriptions of several other stelae,

62 (*opposite*) Stela D at Quiriguá, Guatemala, from a photograph taken by A. P. Maudslay in 1885. This monument was erected on 9.16.15.0.0, or 18 February AD 766. Ht 19 ft 6 in. (5.9 m).

62

63　Altar of Zoomorph O at Quiriguá. On the left of this enormous monument, which was dedicated on the *katun* ending 9.18.0.0.0 (11 October AD 790), is the figure of the rain god dancing in the coils of a serpent. L. 12 ft 4 in. (3.8 m).

63

in the stone 'zoomorphs' representing crouching earth monsters or sky deities with humans seated among their snake-like coils, and in the richly embellished boulders ('altars') associated with them.

It is more than likely that the ruins of Tikal, in the very heart of the Petén, were first encountered by the brave Father Avendaño and his companions in 1695. Lost and starving among the swampy *bajos* and thorny forests of northern Guatemala, they came across a 'variety of old buildings, excepting some in which I recognized apartments, and though they were very high and my strength was little, I climbed up them (though with trouble).' Tikal, now partly restored by the University of Pennsylvania, is a giant among Maya centers; it is the largest Classic site in the Maya area, and one of the greatest in the New World. Particularly impressive are its six temple-pyramids, veritable skyscrapers among buildings of their class. From the level of the plaza floor to the top of its roof comb, Temple IV, the mightiest of all, measures 229 ft (70 m) in height. The core of Tikal must be its great plaza, flanked on west and east by two of these temple-pyramids, and on the north by the acropolis already mentioned in connection with its Late Preclassic and Early Classic tombs. Some of the major

64 A carved wooden lintel from Temple IV at Tikal. Beneath the body of a double-headed serpent is seated a Maya king upon a throne, with spear in one hand and shield in the other. The terraced platform below is apparently a sort of palanquin. Probably dedicated in AD 747. L. in greatest dimension 6 ft 9 in. (2.1 m).

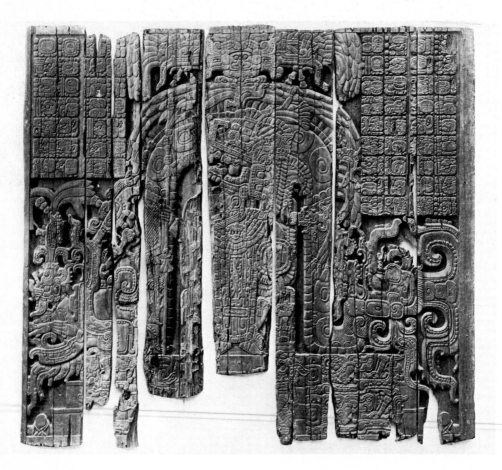

architectural groups are connected to the Great Plaza and with each
other by broad causeways, over which many splendid processions must
have passed in the days of Tikal's glory. The 'palaces' are also
impressive, their plastered rooms often still retaining in their vaults the
sapodilla-wood spanner beams which had only a decorative function.

65   Temple I at Tikal, the
largest site in the Maya area.
This is the funerary pyramid
of the ruler Ah Cacau ('Lord
Cacao').

Tikal is not particularly noteworthy for its stone sculptures. Among
the many limestone stelae lined up in the Great Plaza before the
acropolis, the best are of the Early Classic period. None the less, there
were great artists in the service of Tikal's rulers, for the fortunately
preserved wooden lintels above the doorways of the temple-pyramids
are covered with lovely reliefs of Maya rulers in various poses
accompanied by lengthy glyphic texts. Artistry of a different sort can be
seen in the remarkable offerings accompanying the splendid tomb
underneath Temple I, discovered in 1962 by Aubrey Trik of the
University of Pennsylvania. In it, a very great man, 'Lord Cacao', had
been laid to rest with his riches – his ornaments of jade and shell – and

64

65

99

66 Two incised bones from the Temple I tomb, Tikal. *Top*, three Chacs (Rain Gods) are catching fish. *Above*, seven Maya deities travel in a canoe into the Underworld. In the middle is the Maize God.

with food-filled pottery vessels. But what was really unusual was a large collection of bone tubes and strips which had been delicately incised with scenes of gods and men carried out with the most extreme sophistication. The fine drawing and calligraphy give us some idea of what a Classic Maya codex may have looked like, none of these bark-paper books having survived except in the most fragmentary form in tombs at sites like Altun Ha and Uaxactún.

There are ten reservoirs at Tikal from which the Maya obtained their drinking water, one of which was perforce refurbished by the modern archaeologists in lieu of any other potable source. These are often surrounded by artificial earthen levees, and contain sufficient water throughout the dry season. Some of them no doubt began as quarries, although the latter are known in many other places around the site, where outcrops and half-worked blocks of limestone still bear the marks of the crudely chipped tools with which they were hewn by the stone-masons of over one thousand years ago.

67 Incised bone of the Late Classic period from the tomb beneath Temple I, Tikal. A hand holding a brush pen appears from the jaws of Itzamná, inventor of writing, in his serpent form.

The many dozens of Classic Maya centers scattered over the Petén and Belize – such as Uaxactún, Nakum, Naranjo, Xunantunich, and Altun Ha – are witnesses to the importance of this region before its abandonment. Maya sites are as numerous along the banks of the Usumacinta and its tributaries, in the southwestern part of the Central Area. Yaxchilán is a major center strung out along a terrace of the Usumacinta, with some of its components perched on the hills above. While its temple-pyramids reach no great height, their upper façades and roof combs were beautifully ornamented with figures in stucco and stone. Yaxchilán is famous for its many stone lintels, carved in relief with scenes of conquest and ceremonial life, with which are associated dates and glyphic texts providing clues to the real meaning of the Classic Maya inscriptions. All this must wait, however, until Chapter 8. Further downstream is Piedras Negras, which has also produced similar data. This site is more extensive than Yaxchilán, and has a large number of particularly fine stelae set in place before its temples, as well as eight sweat baths, complete with stone-built hearths lined with

72

68

68 Stela 14, from Piedras
Negras, Guatemala. The
monument marks the
accession to the throne in AD
761 of the young lord seated
in the niche. At the foot of
the platform stands a
middle-aged woman, perhaps
the new king's mother. Ht 9
ft 3 in. (2.8 m).

69 (*right*) A detail of one of the remarkable wall paintings in Room 1 at Bonampak, dating to *c.* AD 790. Musicians sing and beat time, while to the left a group of mummers perform masked as water gods.

70 (*below*) A Maya lord is seated on a dais above three lesser figures on this engraved stone from Bonampak, Mexico. First half of seventh century AD. Ht $38\frac{1}{2}$ in. (98 cm).

71 (*above*) A wall painting in Room 2 at Bonampak, *c.* AD 790. On a terraced platform stands the ruler of Bonampak and his subordinates. Below, captives taken in a jungle skirmish are being tortured by having their finger-nails removed.

72 (*right*) A richly robed woman, Lady Xoc, kneels before the Yaxchilán ruler 'Shield Jaguar', and draws blood by passing a rope with thorns through her tongue. This relief from Yaxchilán, Guatemala, was dedicated AD 709, not long after 'Shield Jaguar' had captured his enemy 'Death'. Ht 3 ft 7 in (1.1 m).

potsherds, masonry benches for the bathers, and drains to carry off water used in the bath.

Few discoveries in the Maya area can rank with that of Bonampak, an otherwise insignificant Late Classic center clearly under the cultural and political thumb of Yaxchilán. Bonampak, which lies not far from the Río Lacanhá, a tributary of the Usumacinta system, was first stumbled across in February 1946 by two American adventurers who were taken there by Lacandón Indians among whom they had been living. Three months later, the photographer Giles Healey was led by a group of Lacandón to the same ruins, and he was the first non-Maya to gaze at the stupendous paintings which covered the walls of three rooms in one of the structures.

69, 71   The Bonampak murals, which can be dated to shortly before AD 800 on the basis of Long Count texts and stylistic considerations, obviously relate a single narrative, a story of a battle, its aftermath, and the victory celebrations. Against a background of stylized jungle foliage, a skirmish takes place among magnificently arrayed Maya warriors, while musicians blow long war trumpets of wood or bark. The scene shifts to a stepped platform in Bonampak itself; the miserable prisoners have

71   been stripped, and are having the nails torn from their fingers. An important captive sprawls on the steps, perhaps tortured to exhaustion, and a severed head lies nearby on a bed of leaves. A naked figure seated on the platform summit pleads for his life to the central figure, the great lord Chaan-muan, king of Bonampak, clad in jaguar-skin battle-jacket surrounded by his subordinates in gorgeous costume. Among the noble spectators is a lady in a white robe, holding a folding-screen fan in one hand. Chaan-muan's principal wife, she is identified by the glyphic text as coming from Yaxchilán. One of the final ceremonies includes a group of mummers fantastically disguised as water gods, accompanied by an

69   orchestra of rattles, drums, turtle carapaces (struck with antlers), and long trumpets. Perhaps the culminating scene is the great sacrificial dance performed to the sound of trumpets by lords wearing towering headdresses of quetzal plumes; in preparation for it, white-robed Maya ladies seated on a throne draw blood from their tongues, and a strange, pot-bellied dwarf-like figure standing on a palanquin is carried on-stage.

A more profound and subtle meaning than mere Maya saber-rattling has been ascribed to these murals by the art historian Mary Miller, who tells us that the three rooms 'record a splendid pageant of rulership'. At different times in its history, which goes back to the Early Classic, Bonampak was both an ally and enemy of Yaxchilán (a recently discovered causeway goes off in the direction of the latter). In 790, relations between the two powers were close: the real theme of the paintings is the presentation and consecration of a little male heir who may also have been heir to the Yaxchilán throne. His father Chaan-muan took his troops into battle to secure prisoners for the celebrations in honor of the heir apparent; the great occasion was eventually solemnized by the torture and decapitation of these captives, and by the ritual shedding of their own blood by great lords and ladies.

No verbal description could do justice to the beautiful colors and to the skill of the hand (or hands) which executed these paintings. Suffice it to say that Bonampak has thrown an entirely new light on the warlike interests of the Maya leaders, upon social organization and stratification in a Maya center, and upon the magnificence of Late Classic Maya culture in general, before time destroyed most of its creations. Bonampak was abandoned before the murals were finished, and the artists dispersed. The heir apparent probably never ascended this or any other throne, as Maya civilization went into eclipse.

The late Sylvanus Morley considered Palenque to be the most beautiful of all the Maya centers, albeit in comparison with a giant like Tikal it is of no great size. The setting is incomparable: Palenque lies at the foot of a chain of low hills covered with tall rain forest, just above the green flood plain of the Usumacinta. Parrots and macaws of brilliant plumage fly at tree-top level; on rainy days the strange roar of howler monkeys can be heard near the ruins. A small stream runs through the site and is carried underneath the principal complex, the Palace, by a corbel-vaulted aqueduct. A veritable labyrinth, the Palace is about 300 ft long and 240 ft wide (91 by 73 m), and consists of a series of vaulted galleries and rooms arranged about interior courtyards or patios, dominated by a unique four-story square tower with an interior

73 View from the southwest of the Late Classic Palace and Tower, Palenque. In the distance is the floodplain of the Río Usumacinta.

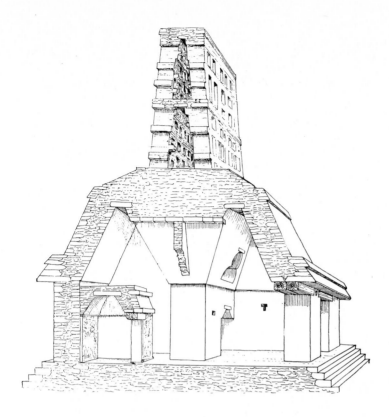

75 Cross-section of the Temple of the Cross at Palenque, showing construction of the roof comb, vaults, and inner sanctuary.

stairway. A Venus glyph painted on one of the landings suggests that the tower was used as an observatory, but it commands a wide view and could also have served as a watch-tower. Arranged along the sides of two of the patios are grotesque reliefs, almost caricatures, of prisoners showing submission by the usual means, one hand raised to the opposite shoulder, and it could have been in these courts that the captured enemies of Palenque were arraigned, tortured, and sacrificed.

The Palenque artists excelled in stucco work, and the exteriors of the   74
pilasters ranged along the galleries of the Palace are marvellously embellished in that medium with Maya lords in relief, carrying the symbols of their authority, while lesser individuals sit cross-legged at their side. All these stuccoes were once painted, and the noted Palenque authority Merle Greene Robertson has found a definite color code: for instance, the exposed skin of humans was painted red, while that of gods was covered with blue.

Of the temple-pyramids of Palenque, three were constructed on more or less the same plan, and must have served somewhat the same function. These are the Temples of the Sun, the Cross, and the   76
Foliated Cross, arranged about three sides of a plaza on the eastern side
75   of the site. Each temple rests on a stepped platform with frontal stairway, each has a mansard roof with comb, and each has an outer and an inner vaulted room. Against the back wall of the latter is a 'sanctuary', a miniature version of the larger temple; in its rear is set up a magnificent low relief tablet carved with long hieroglyphic texts and exhibiting the same motif, two Maya men, one taller than the other,

74 (*opposite*) Decorated pier on the Palace, Palenque, from a photograph by A. P. Maudslay. In this Late Classic stucco relief, both figures grasp a fantastic serpent.

facing each other on either side of a ceremonial object. In the case of the Temple of the Sun, the most perfect of all Maya buildings, this central object is the mask of the Jaguar God of the Underworld, the sun in its night aspect, before two crossed spears. The two other temples have in its place a branching world-tree (which bears an astonishing resemblance to the Christian cross) surmounted by a quetzal bird. The exterior pilasters of the sanctuaries also bear stone reliefs of standing figures, the one on the right side of the Cross sanctuary unusual in that it shows God L, one of the aged Lords of the Underworld, smoking a cigar.

Thanks to some remarkable recent advances in our understanding of the Palenque inscriptions, we now know why these three temples are so similar: the tablets in their sanctuaries all record the accession in AD 683 of the king known as Lord 'Chan-Bahlum' (or 'Snake-Jaguar'). He is the taller of the two figures on each tablet; the shorter is his great predecessor Lord Pacal, of whom more below.

From time to time over the past sixty years that excavations have been carried out at Palenque, finds have been made of fairly well-stocked tombs that were intruded into temple platforms and into the Palaces itself. But these are nothing compared with the remarkable discovery made in June 1952 by the Mexican archaeologist Alberto Ruz. The Temple of the Inscriptions rests on a 65-ft-high (19.8-m) stepped pyramid approached by a noble frontal stairway. On the walls of its portico and central chamber are three panels containing a total of 620 hieroglyphs with many dates, the latest of which corresponds to AD 692. The floor of the temple itself is covered by large stone slabs, but Ruz was particularly curious about one which had a double row of holes provided with removable stone stoppers; on removing this it was clear that he had hit upon a vaulted stairway leading down into the interior of the pyramid, but intentionally choked with rubble. In four field seasons he had completely cleared the stairs, which changed direction half-way down, finally reaching a chamber on about the same level as the base of the pyramid. It too had been filled, but on its floor were encountered the skeletons of five or six young adults, probably all sacrifices. At its far end, the passage was blocked by a huge triangular slab which filled the entire vault.

It was on removing this slab that Ruz first looked into the great Funerary Crypt, a discovery rivaling that of Bonampak in importance. 77 The chamber is 30 ft long and 23 ft high (9 by 7 m), and its floor lies underneath the frontal stairway but below the level of the plaza, some 80 ft (24 m) down from the floor of the upper temple. Around its walls stride stucco relief figures of men in very archaic costume, perhaps the Nine Lords of the Night of Maya theology, but it is equally possible that they were meant to be distant ancestors of the deceased. A huge rectangular stone slab, $12\frac{1}{2}$ ft (3.8 m) long and covered with relief carvings, was found to overlie a monolithic sarcophagus within which an ancient Maya ruler had been put to rest. A treasure-trove of jade accompanied the corpse: a life-sized mosaic mask of jade was placed 78 over the face, jade and mother-of-pearl disks served him as ear spools, several necklaces of tubular jade beads festooned the chest, and jade rings adorned his fingers. A large jade was held in each hand and

76 (*opposite*) View from the northeast of the Temple of the Sun, Palenque, dating from the late seventh century AD.

another was placed in the mouth, a practice documented for the late Yucatec Maya, for the Aztec, and for the Chinese. Two jade figures, one representing the Sun God, lay at his side. Finally, pottery vessels and two sensitively modeled heads in stucco were placed on the floor of the funerary chamber.

Epigraphic detective work has revealed that the man in the Funerary Crypt was the mightiest of all of Palenque's rulers, Lord Pacal (or 'Hand-shield'), who had ascended the throne when he was twelve years old and had died in AD 683 at the venerable age of eighty. It is immediately evident that this great man had the Crypt built to contain his own remains; further, that he might have had the entire temple-pyramid above it raised in his own lifetime. Thus it seems that the Temple of the Inscriptions was a funerary monument with exactly the same primary function as the Egyptian pyramids. And this, of course, leads one to look upon most Maya temple-pyramids as sepulchral monuments, dedicated to the worship of deceased kings.

77 Funerary Crypt in the Temple of the Inscriptions, Palenque, dated to AD 683. The sarcophagus of Lord Pacal lies below and supports the great stone slab. Around the walls of the corbeled chamber are nine stuccoed figures.

78 Life-sized jade mosaic mask of Lord Pacal, from the Funerary Crypt, Temple of the Inscriptions, Palenque, and dated to AD 683. The eyes are fashioned of shell and obsidian, and all the pieces were once affixed to a wooden backing, now rotted away.

Such a conclusion is backed up by many finds in the Central Area, and not just at the really large sites. Altun Ha, for example, is a relatively small center – perhaps qualifying only as a Maya town – in northern Belize, with an antiquity reaching back into Preclassic times. It has no stelae, and thus played no great role on the Classic political stage, but some fairly spectacular finds have been made there by David M. Pendergast of the Royal Ontario Museum. One of these was the famous 'Sun God's Tomb' constructed in a modestly sized funerary pyramid. Before the interment of the honored deceased (an adult male), virtually the entire crypt had been draped in cloth. The corpse had then been placed on a wooden platform, and accompanied by the skins of jaguars or pumas, by matting and cordage, and by necklaces and pendants of jade and *Spondylus* (thorny oyster) shell. The *pièce de résistance* was the largest carved jade ever found in Mesoamerica, a 14.9-cm-high effigy head of the monstrous bird-deity Vucub Caquix, according to the Popol Vuh epic the 'sun' of the era preceding our own.

Classic sites in the Northern Area:
Río Bec, Chenes, and Cobá

The deserted forests of southern Campeche and Quintana Roo form the wildest part of the Maya region, but scattered through them are many ruined centers which have as yet been untouched by pick or spade. Our knowledge of these sites, as Miss Proskouriakoff has pointed out, is owed 'to the gum-chewing habit of our sedentary city-dwellers', for it is the chicle hunters who have come across them while searching for the sapodilla trees from which the gum is extracted. Several share in an aberrant architectural style named after the large site of Río Bec. Here showiness rather than function is what was apparently sought, for characteristic of this style of the Late Classic is the decoration of perfectly ordinary small 'palaces' with high towers imitating the fronts of temple-pyramids; these towers are solid, however, the steps being impossibly narrow and steep, and the 'doorway' at the summit leading to nothing. It is as though the Río Bec architects wished to imitate the great Tikal temples without going to any trouble. In the Río Bec sites, such as Xpuhil and Hormiguero, we begin to see on façades and roof combs the elaborate ornamentation emphasizing masks of the sky-serpent, which becomes of increasing concern to Maya architects as one moves further north into the Yucatán

79 North façade of Structure V at Hormiguero, Mexico (Río Bec culture), from a photograph taken by Karl Ruppert in 1933. The figure stands before the doorway of the one-room temple, entered through the jaws of a monstrous mask. On the west side are the remains of a false tower.

Peninsula. To today's 'functionalists', the fakery of the Río Bec style is somewhat repellent, but no one could help but be awed at these mysterious sites crumbling in their jungle fastness.

Between the Río Bec area and the Puuc Hills of Yucatán is the Chenes, a well-populated zone of northern Campeche. Like those of Río Bec, with whom they must have been in close contact, the Chenes architects lavishly ornamented façades with sky-serpent masks and volutes, but the false towers of the former are missing. And, as at the Puuc sites to the north, the ornamentation consists of hundreds of small sculptural elements set into the buildings. One enters the front room through the fantastic jaws of the sky-serpent, and is faced with tiers of such masks, one over the other, on the corners.

While the two sub-areas that we have been discussing are clearly intermediate in space and style between the Petén and the terminal Late Classic Puuc styles, there are centers in the wild eastern half of the peninsula which are obviously direct extensions of central Petén ideas and perhaps peoples. One of these is Cobá, a name implying something like 'ruffled waters', a fitting epithet since it was built among a small group of shallow, reedy lakes in northern Quintano Roo; until recently the zone was frequented only by Maya hunters who occasionally burned incense before the stelae scattered among its ruins. Cobá is not a single site but a whole group linked to a central complex by long,

80   Palace at Xpuhil (Río Bec culture), from a reconstruction drawing by Tatiana Proskouriakoff. The three towers are completely solid and served no other function than decoration.

perfectly straight masonry causeways usually called by the Maya term *sacbe* ('white road'). There are more than sixteen of these, but what the idea was behind their construction we cannot even guess, for quite often a *sacbe* several miles in length will reach a ruin of very paltry dimensions. *Sacbe* No. 1 is the strangest of all, for it continues west from Cobá in a generally straight direction for no less than 62 miles, finally reaching the site of Yaxuná, some 12 miles southwest of Chichén Itzá. Some have claimed that the Maya *sacbe* were arteries of commerce, but a purely ceremonial function is far more plausible.

The buildings of Cobá are in a sorry state of preservation, but there appear to have been temple-pyramids and palaces like those of the Petén. It continued to be inhabited into Post-Classic times, for there are a few structures like those of Tulum (a very late town on the east coast of the peninsula), and there are references to Cobá in late Maya legends in which the center is associated with the Sun God.

Classic sites in the Northern Area: the Puuc

'If Yucatán were to gain a name and reputation', wrote Bishop Landa in 1566, 'from the multitude, the grandeur and the beauty of its buildings, as other regions of the Indies have obtained these by gold, silver and riches, its glory would spread like that of Peru and New Spain.' Landa was not exaggerating, for ruins there are by the hundreds. Sylvanus Morley saw this as evidence for what he called a 'New Empire' founded by refugees from the derelict civilization of the Central Area, his so-called 'Old Empire', and he claimed to find references in the late Maya chronicles to a double-pronged migration from the south. However, ceramics recovered from excavations, along with a better reading of the ethnohistoric sources, led Eric Thompson and George Brainerd to the view that many of the Yucatecan sites were coeval with the Petén centers which were claimed to pre-date them.

It will be remembered that a group of very low hills, the Puuc, is to be found in southwestern Yucatán. It is there that the dominant Classic architectural style of the peninsula takes form, probably toward the close of the Late Classic period. The problem of dating is acute, for some of these centers are mentioned in the chronicles by late upstart lineages who claimed to have founded them, but there are truncated Long Count dates painted on capstones in the late ninth and early tenth baktun; the very latest reads 10.3.17.12.1, or AD 905, but Thompson believed on excellent grounds that the Puuc style may have lasted until 10.8.0.0.0 (AD 987), when Toltec invaders usher in the Post-Classic.

Characteristic of Puuc buildings are facings of very thin squares of limestone veneer over the cement-and-rubble core; boot-shaped vault stones; decorated cornices; round columns in doorways; engaged or half-columns repeated in long rows; and the exuberant use of stone mosaics on upper façades, emphasizing the usual sky-serpent faces with long, hook-shaped noses, as well as frets and lattice-like designs of criss-crossed elements. In the perfection of architectural façades, the Puuc is far ahead of the more sloppy Petén style.

Uxmal is by far the largest Puuc site, and one of the triumphs of Maya civilization. Traditionally, this was the seat of the Xiu family, but

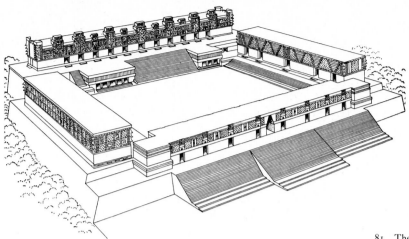

81   The Nunnery
Quadrangle at Uxmal.

this was a johnny-come-lately lineage of Mexican origin which could not possibly ever have built the site. Uxmal is dominated by two mighty temple-pyramids, the Great Pyramid and the House of the Magician, the upper temple of the latter entered through a monster-mask doorway like those of the Chenes. Next to the Magician is the imaginatively named Nunnery, actually a palace group made up of four separate rectangular buildings arranged around an interior court; although the group could be entered from the corners, the principal gateway with its corbel arch lies on the south side. The mosaic elements making up the masonry façades of the Nunnery Quadrangle are particularly interesting; they include miniature representations of the thatched-roof huts of the ordinary folk of the time. There are certainly hints in some of these elements of influences from Mexico, particularly from the Totonac site of Tajín in central Veracruz. One such element from the House of the Magician depicts a Tlaloc face surrounded by Mexican year-signs.

Below the Great Pyramid on its own artificial terrace, is the House of the Governor, the finest structure at Uxmal and the culmination of the Puuc style. The upper façade or frieze of the three long interconnected structures of this building is covered by a fantastically elaborate mosaic of thousands of separate masonry elements set into the rubble core, a symphony of step-and-fret, lattice-work, and sky-serpent-mask motifs combined into a single harmonious whole.

There are only a handful of carved stelae at Uxmal; not only are they sloppily executed, but they are in a sorry state of preservation. Nevertheless, Professor Jeff Kowalski has been able to work out a partial dynastic history dominated by the figure of Lord Chac, during whose reign the House of the Governor was built, probably as his administrative headquarters.

That the Puuc style reached east as well as north is evident at the great site of Chichén Itzá in eastern Yucatán, where a number of buildings at this otherwise Toltec center closely resemble those to the west, with the proviso that Puuc veneer masonry is seldom present. Among these are the three-storied Nunnery, the Akab Dzib ('dark   84

82 West wing of the Palace at Sayil, Mexico (Puuc culture). Seemingly three-storied, each row of rooms actually rests on a solid rubble core. The vaults have collapsed in the lower 'story'.

83 Arch at Labná, a Puuc culture site in Mexico, from a view published by Frederick Catherwood in 1844.

84 East wing of the Nunnery (Puuc culture) at Chichén Itzá, Mexico, from a lithograph by Frederick Catherwood. The masks repeated so many times on this kind of façade are believed to be of the sky-serpent.

85 The five-storied structure at Etzná, Campeche (Late Classic period).

writing', so called from the reliefs containing glyphic texts on one of the inner doorways), and the Temple of the Three Lintels; there may be more, but the problem of identification is aggravated by the syncretism between Maya and Toltec architecture during the subsequent Toltec occupation.

85 Southernmost of the Puuc sites is Etzná (or Edzná), best known for its five-storied structure which combines features of pyramids and palaces. Aerial reconnaissance has disclosed that Etzná is surrounded by a complex system of canals and reservoirs, and that a square, fortress-like structure is encompassed by a moat. Such a water-control system could have had multiple functions, such as communication, fishing, and provision of drinking water, and Ray Matheny suggests that the canals might have been connected with a raised-field system. While most of what one sees at Etzná is Late Classic in date, it is noteworthy that at least some of the canals go back to the Late Preclassic.

Art of the Late Classic

Late Classic Maya art evolves directly out of that of the early half of the period, but excepting the demonstrably late sculpture of the Puuc, there is very little outside influence still to be seen. Maya artists now were free to go their own way, developing a remarkably sophisticated style as introspective as that of Asia and almost as 'naturalistic' as that of Europe and the Mediterranean. But the Maya were not always interested in three-dimensionality, although they could when they wished give depth to a scene by foreshortening, and to figures by backlighting. Their art is essentially a painterly one, narrative and baroque, tremendously involved with ornament and grotesques but preserving what Proskouriakoff has called 'order in complexity'. Finally, the Late Classic Maya were, with their contemporaries the Moche of Peru, the only American Indians interested in rendering the uniqueness of individual characters through portraiture.

The Maya artists excelled in low relief carving, and that is what most Maya sculpture is, whether on stelae, lintels, or panels. By the eighth

86 Stone lintel from the Late Classic site of Kuná (Lacanhá), Mexico. The protagonist, a lord subordinate to the king of Bonampak, holds a 'ceremonial bar', a stylized, double-headed sky-serpent. In the text to the left is carved the *tun* ending 9.15.15.0.0. (4 June AD 746 in the Gregorian calendar). Ht 27¼ in. (68.8 cm).

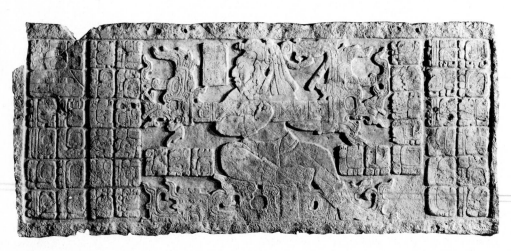

87 Detail from the Tablet of the Slaves, Palenque, dated to AD 730. Shown here is the head of Lord Chac Zutz, who sits cross-legged on the backs of two crouching captives. On either side of him are placed a man and woman carrying the symbols of rulership in their hands.

century AD, they had achieved a complete mastery of this medium, posing their figures in such a manner that in place of the rigid formality prevalent in earlier monuments, a kind of dynamic imbalance among the different parts of the composition was sought which leads the eye restlessly along. A lintel from Kuná, a site only a few miles from Bonampak, provides a magnificent example of artistic contraposition, the goateed Maya resting on one leg and leaning forward clasping a ceremonial bar; but surely the perfection of relief carving was attained on the Late Classic tablets from Palenque, particularly the Tablet of the Slaves which shows Lord Chac Zutz ('Great Bat') seated upon the backs of two barbaric-looking captives. Naturally, over such a wide area there were specializations, real schools of carvers at various sites. Copán, as has been mentioned, had a notable development of three-dimensional sculpture (as did Toniná in the Chiapas hills), while Palenque, at the other end of the Central Area, concentrated on reliefs

86

89
87

89 Stone tablet incised with the head of Chac Xib Chac, from the Late Classic period at Palenque.

carried out with extremely sophisticated use of carved and engraved lines.

Pottery objects of Late Classic manufacture run the gamut from crude, mold-made figurines and the ordinary pots and pans of everyday life to real works of art. Among the latter are the fantastic incense burners common at Palenque and in some of the Tabasco sites, consisting of tall, hollow tubes modeled with the figures or heads of gods, particularly the Jaguar God of the Underworld, sometimes placed one on top of the other like Alaskan totem poles. Vertical flanges were placed on either side, and the whole painted in reds, ochers, blue, and white, after firing.

Jaina, a small limestone island just off the coast of Campeche and separated from the mainland by a tidal inlet, is one of the most enigmatic archaeological sites in the Maya area. For some reason

88 (*opposite*) Large pottery censer, probably from a cave in Chiapas or Tabasco, Mexico. The main face is that of the Jaguar God of the Underworld, the guise of the Sun on his nightly journey beneath the earth. Censers of this form were especially popular at Palenque. Ht 23¾ in. (60.3 cm).

90 Pottery figurine of a woman sheltering a man, Jaina, Mexico. Ht 8 in. (20.3 cm).

known only to themselves, the ancients had used it as a necropolis, and it is close enough to the Puuc sites inland for it to have been their rulers and nobles who were buried there. Certainly the puniness of the temples constructed on the island is not in keeping with the great number of graves or with the magnificence of the offerings found in them. It is from these that archaeologists and looters have recovered the

90–92   delicate, sophisticated figurines for which Jaina is famous. All objects are hollow and fitted with whistles at their backs; the faces were usually made in molds, but these and other details were embellished by the fingers of the artist. At one level of comprehension the emphasis is upon portraiture of real persons, perhaps the occupants of the graves: haughty nobles and armed warriors, some with tattooed or scarified faces, beautiful young women and fat old matrons. But at another level, these might also represent deities. For example, of two common, rather

90   Freudian motifs, one depicts a mature woman sheltering a grown man as though he were her child, and might well be Ix Chel, the Mother Goddess; while the other, an ugly old man making advances to a handsome female must be an aged underworld divinity and his consort, Ix Chel, who is also the Moon Goddess. Another common supernatural

91   in Jaina collections is the Fat God, who seems to have been popular among the Maya of Campeche.

Maya potters achieved chromatic effects of great brilliance in their vessels by firing them at low temperatures, sacrificing durability for aesthetic effect. Late Classic polychromes, generally deep bowls, cylindrical vessels, or footed dishes, are sometimes painted with the same narrative skill as the wall paintings exhibit. One vessel (ill. 93) is a 10-inch-high (25-cm) vase from an otherwise run-of-the-mill grave at Altar de Sacrificios in the Central Area. Justifiably described as 'a ceramic masterpiece', six strange figures, all of them dead or wearing the attributes of death and darkness, are painted on its exterior along with glyphs including a Calendar Round date corresponding to AD 754. The figure of an old god with closed eyes apparently dancing with a sinister, grossly fat snake is so well done that it suggests the employment of artists of genius in decorating pottery. Vessels could also be carved when leather-hard, just before firing, some excellent vases in this style from Yucatán depicting God GI (Chac Xib Chac) seated among swirling volutes. Yucatán, though, had a greyish-brown pottery of its own called Slate ware, sometimes plain but often carved with geometric ornaments, glyphs, or the figures of seated lords.

It is natural that the Maya lavished upon jade, the most precious substance known to them, their full artistry. That these jades were traded over considerable distances is evident from Late Classic

91 Pottery figurine, probably from Jaina. The subject is the Fat God, wearing feathered war costume and carrying a shield. Ht 11½ in. (29.2 cm).

92 Pottery figurine from Jaina. A seated man holds an unidentified object, possibly a celt. Like all the finest pieces from Jaina, this figurine was made partly with a pottery mold and partly with the fingers, and was painted after firing. Ht 4½ in. (11.4 cm).

94

95

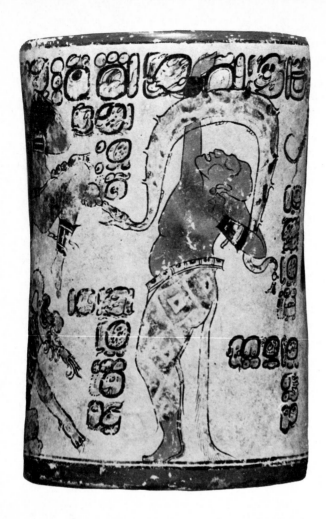

93 Polychrome pottery vase of the Tepeu culture from Altar de Sacrificios, Guatemala. This side shows an old man, perhaps God L, apparently dead, but dancing with a monstrous snake. Five other figures appear on the vase, all with death associations. In the text is a Calendar Round date probably corresponding to AD 754. Ht 10 in. (25.4 cm).

94 Black pottery jar, from Chocholá (southern Yucatán), Mexico. The vessel has been deeply carved with the figure of the rain deity, Chac Xib Chac, against a swirling background, and red pigment rubbed into the cut-away areas. Ht 5½ in. (14 cm).

95 Incised pottery bowl (Slate ware) from the Northern Area. The design, a modified step-and-fret pattern, is carried out in a negative smudging technique. Ht 4½ in. (11.4 cm).

96   This carved jade plaque from Nebaj, Guatemala, is emerald green with white clouding, and represents a Maya lord in conversation with a palace dwarf. W. 5¾ in. (14.6 cm).

97   Onyx bowl, said to be from the state of Campeche, Mexico. A row of incised glyphs encircles the rim. Below, on the fluted sides, are incised three seated profile figures, two men (one of whom is visible here) and a robed woman, with additional glyphs; each figure holds a symbolic object. Ht 4½ in. (11.4 cm).

Usumacinta-style pieces which were tossed into the Sacred Cenote at Chichén Itzá during the Post-Classic period, and some from the lowland Maya even found their way to Oaxaca and the Valley of Mexico. Most are very thin plaques with low relief carving on one face, probably executed by tubular drills of cane used with jade sand. A fine plaque from Nebaj in the Southern Area must be a product of a Central Area artist, and shows a recurrent theme, a richly dressed noble seated upon a throne, leaning forward to chat with a dwarf, perhaps a court buffoon.

96

Not only jade, but marble as well was worked by the lowland Maya lapidaries; but it must have been a rare substance, for objects made from it are infrequent. A fluted vase of translucent onyx marble, with incising in Late Classic style, is a fine example of the genre. It is somewhat doubtful if the well-known marble vessels from the Ulua region of western Honduras are to be considered as Maya at all, but fragments from them have been found in deposits assigned to the ultimate phase of the Late Classic in Belize and Petén sites. That the Maya could impose their artistic conventions on any medium is apparent in the 'eccentric' flint blades chipped to include divine faces in profile, and small blades of obsidian incised with the gods of the Maya pantheon; these were favorite objects for placing in caches under stelae or beneath temple floors in Central Area sites. Along the coast of Campeche, above all at Jaina, art in carved shell reached a high level, the Maya typically painting the lily by inlaying these lovely objects with small pieces of apple-green jade.

97

98
100

99

The end of Classic Maya civilization

As Professor Robert Sharer puts it, the downfall of the Classic Maya civilization was 'one of the most profound cultural failures in human history'. Almost the only fact surely known about it is that it really happened. Scholarly imaginations have run rife in coming up with explanations, and have included just about everything from epidemic diseases, invasion by foreigners from Mexico, social revolution (championed by Eric Thompson and still a plausible hypothesis), and even earthquakes and hurricanes. Unfortunately, the latest Classic inscriptions will throw little light on the problem, since their parsimonious texts never deal with mundane matters as censuses or agricultural production figures.

Basing himself on the assumption that cessation of monument erection at a particular city means its abandonment, John W. G. Lowe has recently performed a systems simulation of the Classic collapse and the processes that might have induced it. As summarized by Sharer, the basic scenario runs something like this. Between AD 672 and 751 (considered by many to mark the civilization's florescence), the number of communities carving new monuments continued to increase, but new construction took place only in already-established cities: Maya civilization had ceased to expand geographically. From 751 to about 790, long-standing alliances began to break down, interstate trade declined, and conflicts between neighboring city-states increased (the battle of 792 commemorated by the Bonampak murals illustrates this

98 The profiles of two gods can be seen facing left in this tour-de-force of the Tepeu flint chipper's art from Quiriguá, Guatemala. Ht 10 in. (25.4 cm).

99 Carved shell pendant, probably from Jaina. A young man with the flattened head so highly esteemed by the Maya appears above a fantastic fish, the body of which is covered with unreadable glyphs. The cut-away areas were once inlaid with jade. Ht $3\frac{1}{8}$ in. (7.9 cm).

100 Incised obsidians from an offering placed beneath a stela at Tikal (Tepeu culture). The flat side of a crude flake has in each instance been engraved with the figure of a deity or with a simplified mat design. L. of longest piece $2\frac{3}{4}$ in. (7 cm).

situation). From 790 to 830, the death rate of cities outstripped the birth rate, while after 830 construction stopped throughout the Central Area, with the exception of peripherally located sites like Lamanai. The katun ending date 10.3.0.0.0 (AD 889) was celebrated by inscriptions at only three sites. And the very last Long Count date to be recorded anywhere was the katun ending 10.4.0.0.0 (AD 909), incised on a jade from a site in southern Quintana Roo.

According to Lowe, this 'apocalypse' as he calls it, was brought about by the mutually enforcing interaction of several factors, set in motion by population growth, particularly among the élite, and by food shortages. Paradoxically, agricultural intensification (for instance, raised fields) would have led to declining per capita production through stress on the soil and through a labor shortage caused by the diversion of field hands to the élite centers to satisfy the cultural demands of the burgeoning upper class.

This explanation, although at present almost impossible to document archaeologically, is one that many Mayanists find plausible.

It was not just the 'stela cult' – the inscribed glorification of royal lineages and their achievements – that disappeared, but an entire world of esoteric knowledge, mythology, and ritual. Much of the élite cultural behavior to be described in Chapter 8, such as the complex Underworld mythology and iconography found on Classic Maya funerary ceramics, failed to re-emerge with the advent of the Post-Classic era, and one can only conclude that the royalty and nobility, including the scribes who were the repository of so much sacred and scientific knowledge, had 'gone with the wind'. They may well have been massacred by an enraged populace, and their screenfold books consumed in a holocaust similar to that carried out centuries later by Bishop Landa.

New investigations have shown that at least some of the Central Area population survived the debacle, for instance in the valleys of the Belize and New Rivers, finally to succumb to diseases introduced by the Spanish invaders of the sixteenth and seventeenth centuries. But these dwindling groups would have known little about the glories of the Classic past, and some would have been wanderers among the now-empty centers, camping out like savages, or archaeologists, in the rooms of forgotten palaces – peoples like the Lacandón, burning copal incense before the strange depictions of mortal men and women who had now become gods.

The Putun Maya

We have much to learn about the ninth century in the southern Maya lowlands, but surely Eric Thompson was right in thinking that the Putun or Chontal Maya of the Tabasco and southern Campeche plains had begun taking over some of the more important sites in the southern Petén, such as Seibal, perhaps moving into a power vacuum. These somewhat Mexicanized merchant-warriors controlled the great entrepôt of Xicallanco where Mexican and Maya traders met, and were known to the later Aztecs as 'Olmeca-Xicallanca'. There is now incontrovertible evidence that the Putun had not only penetrated into the lowland Maya 'heartland', they had reached the central highlands of Mexico. In recent years, excavations at the hilltop site of Cacaxtla, traditionally ascribed to the Olmeca-Xicallanca, have uncovered a ninth-century palace with brilliant polychrome murals in Maya style. Among other things, these show dignitaries in Maya costume bearing Maya 'ceremonial bars', which are in the style of the Putun-influenced stelae of Seibal, and a great war going on between two contending factions, which immediately recalls the battle scene of Bonampak.

The question remains, what were these Olmeca-Xicallanca or Putun Maya doing there, almost 500 miles from their homeland? For that matter, why are there bas-reliefs showing seated figures in Maya style on the ninth-century Temple of the Feathered Serpent at Xochicalco in Morelos, just south of the Valley of Mexico? It is now evident that the ninth century was a time of turmoil over much of Mesoamerica, with the power of Teotihuacan long since gone, and the old order in the Maya lowlands breaking down. In this power vacuum, the Putun, seasoned businessmen with strong contacts ranging from central Mexico to the Caribbean coast of Honduras, must have played a very aggressive role in a time of troubles, and their presence in the Mexican highlands may have played a formative role in what was to become the Toltec state.

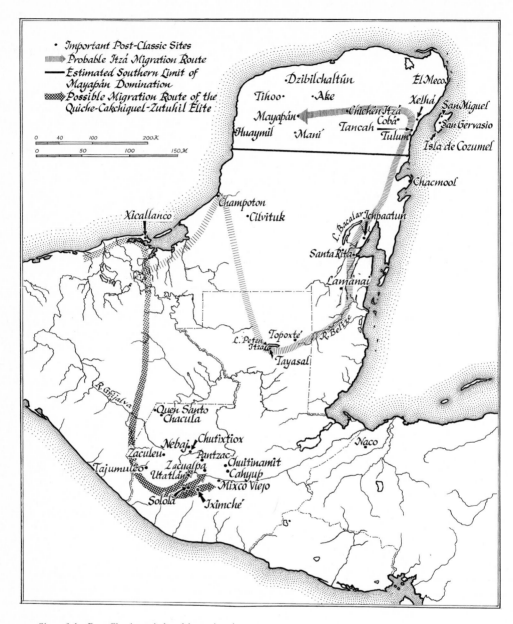

Legend

- Important Post-Classic Sites
- Probable Itzá Migration Route
- Estimated Southern Limit of Mayapán Domination
- Possible Migration Route of the Quiche-Cakchiquel-Zutuhil Élite

```
0    40     100           200 K
0      50        100        150 M
```

Dzibilchaltún · El Meco

Tihoo · ·Ake · Xelhá · San Miguel

Mayapán · Chichen Itzá · Cobá · San Gervasio

Huaymil · Mani · Tancah · Tulum · Isla de Cozumel

Chacmool

Champoton

·Cilvituk · L. Bacalar Ichpaatun

Xicallanco · Santa Rita

Lamanai

L. Petén Itzá · Topoxte · R. Belize

Tayasal

R. Gijalva · Quen Santo · Chacula · Naco

Nebaj · Chutixtiox

Zaculeu · Pantzac

Tajumulco · Zacualpa · Chuitinamit

Utatlán · Cahyup

Solola · Mixco Viejo

Iximche

101 Sites of the Post-Classic period and late migration routes.

By the close of the tenth century the destiny of the once proud and independent Maya had fallen into the hands of grim militarists from the highlands of central Mexico, where a new order of men had replaced the intellectual rulers of Classic times. About the events that led to the conquest of Yucatán by these foreigners, and the subsequent replacement of their state by a resurgent but already decadent Maya culture, we know a good deal, for we have entered rather shakily into what might be called history. The traditional annals of the peoples of Yucatán, and also of the Guatemalan highlanders, which were transcribed into Spanish letters early in Colonial times apparently reach back as far as the beginning of our Post-Classic era and are very important sources.

But they should be used with much caution, whether they come to us from Bishop Landa himself, from statements made by the native nobility, or from native lawsuits and land claims. These are often confused and often self-contradictory, above all since native lineages seem to have deliberately falsified their own history for political reasons. Our richest and most treacherous sources are the Katun Prophecies of Yucatán, contained in the so-called Books of Chilam Balam which derive their name from a Maya savant said to have predicted the arrival of the Spaniards from the east. The 'history' which they contain is based upon the Short Count, a cycle of 13 katuns ($13 \times 7,200$ days or $256\frac{1}{4}$ years), each katun of which was named from the last day, always Ahau, on which it ended. Unfortunately, the Post-Classic Maya thought in purely cyclic terms, so that if certain events had happened in a Katun 13 Ahau, they would recur in the next of the same name. The result is that prophecy and history are almost inextricably entwined in these documents that sometimes read like divine revelation; one such history, for example, begins:

> This is the record of how the one and only god, the 13 gods, the 8,000 gods descended, according to the words of the priests, prophets, Chilam Balam, Ah Xupan, Napuc Tun, the priest Nahau Pech, and Ah Kauil Ch'el. Then was interpreted the command to them, the measured words which were given to them.

The Toltec invasion and Toltec Chichén Itzá

Into the vacuum created by the collapse of the older civilizations of central Mexico moved a new people, the Nahua-speaking Toltec, whose northern origins are proclaimed by their kinship with the nonagricultural barbarians called the Chichimec. Shortly after AD 900 they had settled themselves at the key site of Tula under the leadership of a king named Topiltzin, who also claimed the title of Quetzalcoatl or 'Feathered Serpent' (the culture hero of Mexican theology). Prominent among these people were the military orders that were to play such a significant role in later Mexican history – the Eagles, the Jaguars, and the Coyotes – and which paid homage to the war god Tezcatlipoca ('Smoking Mirror') rather than to the more peaceable Quetzalcoatl. According to a number of quasi-historical accounts of great poetic merit, a struggle ensued between Topiltzin Quetzalcoatl and his adherents on the one hand, and the warrior faction on the other. Defeated by the evil magic of his adversary Tezcatlipoca, the king was forced to leave Tula with his followers, most probably in AD 987. In one version well known to all the ancient Mexicans, he made his way to the Gulf Coast and from there set across on a raft of serpents for Tlapallan ('Red Land'), some day to return for the redemption of his people.

Wracked by further internal dissentions and deserted by most of its inhabitants, the Toltec capital was finally destroyed by violence in AD 1156 or 1168, but its memory was forever glorious in the minds of the Mexicans, and there was hardly a ruling dynasty in Mesoamerica in later days which did not claim descent from the Toltec of Tula. The city, which was certainly the administrative center of an empire spanning central Mexico from the Atlantic to the Pacific, has been securely identified as an archaeological site in the state of Hidalgo, some 50 miles northwest of Mexico City, so that a good deal is known about Toltec art and architecture in its place of origin. Everywhere the Toltec went, they carried with them their own very unsympathetic style, in which there is an obsession with the image of the Toltec warrior, complete with pillbox-like headdress with a down-flying bird in front, a stylized bird or butterfly on the chest, and carrying a feather-decorated *atlatl* in one hand and a bunch of darts in the other. Left arms were protected by quilted padding, and the back by a small shield. Prowling jaguars and coyotes, and eagles eating hearts dominate the reliefs which covered their principal temple-pyramid, a testimony to the importance of the knightly orders among these militarists.

Now, it so happens that the Maya historical sources speak of the arrival from the west of a man calling himself Kukulcan (*kukul*, 'feathered', and *can* 'serpent') in a Katun 4 Ahau which ended in AD 987, who wrested Yucatán from its rightful owners and established his capital at Chichén Itzá. Unfortunately, as the Maya scholar Ralph Roys has shown, the accounts of this great event are seriously confused with the history of a later people called the Itzá, who moved into the peninsula during the next Katun 4 Ahau, in the thirteenth century, and gave their name to the formerly Toltec site of Chichén. In any case, the Maya credited Kukulcan and his retinue with the introduction of idolatry, but the impressions left by him were generally good, for Bishop Landa states:

They say he was favorably disposed, and had no wife or children, and that after his return he was regarded in Mexico as one of their gods and called Quetzalcoatl; and they also considered him a god in Yucatán on account of his being a just statesman.

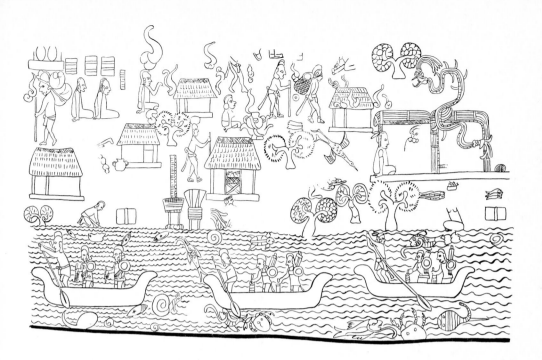

102 Wall painting from the Temple of the Warriors, Chichén Itzá. Canoe-borne Toltec warriors reconnoiter the Maya coast.

103 Repoussé gold disk from the Sacred Cenote, Chichén Itzá. Two Toltec men-at-arms attack a pair of fleeing Maya. Diam. $8\frac{3}{4}$ in. (22.2 cm).

104   View of the Toltec part of Chichén Itzá, looking northeast from the Nunnery. In the foreground is the Caracol; beyond it to the left, the Castillo or Temple of Kukulcan; and to the right, the Temple of the Warriors.

The goodwill contained in these words is almost certainly due to most of the ruling houses of later times being of Mexican rather than Maya descent, for surely the archaeological record tells us that the conquest of Yucatán by the supposedly peaceful Topiltzin Quetzalcoatl and his Toltec armies was violent and brutal in the extreme. The murals found in the Temple of the Warriors at Chichén Itzá, and the relief scenes on some golden disks fished up from the Sacred Cenote at the same site, tell the same story. The drama opens with the arrival of the Toltec forces by sea, most likely along the Campeche shore, where they reconnoiter a coastal Maya town with whitewashed houses. In a marine engagement in which the Maya come out in rafts to meet the Toltec war canoes, the former suffer the first of their defeats. Then the scene moves to the land, where in a great pitched battle (commemorated in the frescoes of the Temple of the Jaguars) fought within a major Maya settlement the natives are again beaten. The final act ends with the heart sacrifice of the Maya leaders, while the Feathered Serpent himself hovers above to receive the bloody offering.

The Yucatán taken over by the Toltec exiles was then in its Puuc phase, but following the invasion, Uxmal and most other important Puuc centers must have been abandoned under duress. Chichén Itzá, which in those days seems to have been called Uucil-abnal ('Seven Bushes'), became, under the rule of Topiltzin Quetzalcoatl, the supreme metropolis of a united kingdom, a kind of splendid recreation

102

103

104

of the Tula which he had lost. New architectural techniques and motifs were imported from Toltec Mexico and synthesized with Puuc Maya forms. For instance, columns were now used in place of walls to divide rooms, giving an air of spaciousness to halls; a sloping batter was placed at the base of outside walls and platforms; colonnades of pure Tula type were built, which included low masonry banquettes covered with processions of tough Toltec warriors and undulating feathered serpents; and walls were decorated with murals in bands. And everywhere the old Maya masks of the long-nosed sky-serpent were incorporated in these new buildings.

For not only was there a synthesis of styles at Chichén Itzá, but also a 105 hybridization of Toltec and Maya religion and society. Jaguar and Eagle knights rub elbows with men in traditional Maya costume and Mexican astral deities coexist with Maya gods. The old Maya order had been overthrown, but it is obvious that many of the native princes were incorporated into the new power structure.

At the hub of Toltec Chichén stands its most important structure, the so-called 'Castillo', a great four-sided temple-pyramid which Landa tells us was dedicated to the cult of Kukulcan. The corbel-vaulted temple at the summit of the four breathtaking stairways is a curious mixture of indigenous and foreign, sky-god masks embellishing the exterior, reliefs of tall war captains from Tula being carved upon the jambs of its doors. Inside the Castillo has been discovered an earlier Toltec-Maya pyramid, with beautifully preserved details, such as the chambers of the superstructure which contain a stone throne in the form of a snarling jaguar, painted red, with eyes and spots of jade and fangs of shell. Before it is one of the sculptures called 'chacmools', reclining figures with hands grasping plate-like receptacles held over the belly, perhaps for receiving the hearts of sacrificed victims. 'Chacmools' are ubiquitous at Tula and at Chichén, and are a purely Toltec invention.

From the Castillo may be seen the Temple of the Warriors, a 107 splendid building resting upon a stepped platform, surrounded by colonnaded halls. It is closely planned after Pyramid 'B' at Tula, but its far greater size and the excellence of the workmanship lavished upon it suggest that the Toltec intruders were better off in Yucatán, where they could call upon the skills of Maya architects and craftsmen. The building is approached on the northwest through impressive files of square columns, which are decorated on all four faces with reliefs of Toltec officers. At the top of the stairs a 'chacmool' gazes stonily out 106 upon the main plaza, while the entrance to the temple itself is flanked by a pair of feathered serpents, heads at the ground and tails in the air. Beyond them can be seen the principal sanctuary with its table or altar supported by little Atlantean Toltec warriors. All interior walls had been frescoed with lively scenes related to the Toltec conquest of Yucatán (ill. 102).

In 1926, just as restoration of the Temple of the Warriors by the Carnegie Institution staff was near completion, another such structure came to light underneath it, and from this, the Temple of the Chacmool, were recovered relief-carved columns still bearing the bright pigments with which they were painted. Two benches in the

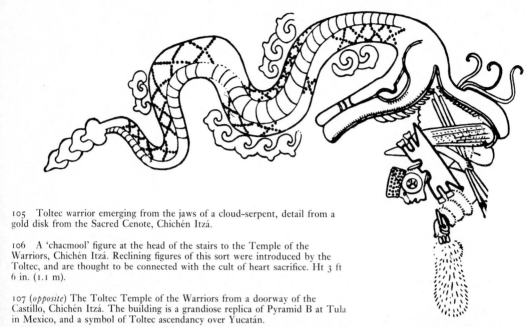

105   Toltec warrior emerging from the jaws of a cloud-serpent, detail from a
gold disk from the Sacred Cenote, Chichén Itzá.

106   A 'chacmool' figure at the head of the stairs to the Temple of the
Warriors, Chichén Itzá. Reclining figures of this sort were introduced by the
Toltec, and are thought to be connected with the cult of heart sacrifice. Ht 3 ft
6 in. (1.1 m).

107 (*opposite*) The Toltec Temple of the Warriors from a doorway of the
Castillo, Chichén Itzá. The building is a grandiose replica of Pyramid B at Tula
in Mexico, and a symbol of Toltec ascendancy over Yucatán.

108 The Toltec Ball Court
at Chichén Itzá. With walls
27 ft (8.2 m) high, and an
overall length of about 490 ft
(149 m), this is the largest
court in Mesoamerica. The
rings set high on either wall
were used in scoring the
game.

temple interior had been painted in a most interesting fashion, one with
a row of Toltec leaders seated upon jaguar thrones identical to that in
the interior of the Castillo, but the other with Maya nobles seated upon
stools covered with jaguar skin, bearing manikin scepters in Maya
fashion. Could these have been quisling princes?

The splendid Ball Court of Toltec Chichén is the largest and finest in
all Mesoamerica. Its two parallel, upright walls measure 272 ft long and
27 ft high (82.6 by 8.2 m), and are 99 ft (30 m) apart. At either end of the
I-shaped playing field is a small temple, the one at the north containing
extensive bas-reliefs of Toltec life. That the game was played Mexican-
style is shown by the two stone rings set high on the sides of the walls,
for a Spanish chronicler tells us that among the Aztec whichever team
managed to get the ball through one of these not only won the game and
the wager but the clothing of the onlookers. Above the east wall of the
109   court is placed the important Temple of the Jaguars, whose inner walls
are beautifully frescoed with Toltec battle scenes, so detailed and
convincing that the artist must have been a witness to the Toltec
invasion.

Landa describes 'two small stages of hewn stone' at Chichén, 'with
four staircases, paved on the top, where they say that farces were
represented, and comedies for the pleasure of the public,' surely to be
identified with the two Dance Platforms which have their facings
covered with themes directly imported from Tula, such as eagles and
110   jaguars eating hearts. Human sacrifice on a large scale must have been

another gift of the Toltec, for near the Ball Court is a long platform carved on all sides with human skulls skewered on stakes. The Aztec name given to it, Tzompantli, is certainly apt, for in Post-Classic Mexico such platforms supported the great racks upon which the heads of victims were displayed. Each of the six Ball Court reliefs depicts the decapitation of a ball player, and it is entirely possible that the game was played 'for keeps', the losers ending up on the Tzompantli.

Finally, the unlovely Caracol must be mentioned. This building which is actually in the Puuc section of Chichén, has been stigmatized by Eric Thompson as a 'two-decker wedding cake on the square carton in which it came'; it seems to date from very early Toltec times, but there are many Puuc architectural features (such as sky-serpent masks) incorporated in it. Most certainly it was an observatory, the snail-like spiral stairway in the interior giving access to exterior openings from which sights could have been made on the sun, moon, and Venus, as well as the cardinal directions, but it could also have been dedicated to the Kukulcan-Quetzalcoatl cult since circular temples were usually sacred to that god.

Chichén Itzá is most renowned not for its architecture, but for its Sacred Cenote, or Well of Sacrifice, reached by a 900-ft-long (274-m) causeway leading north from the Great Plaza. From Landa's pen comes the following:

> Into this well they have had, and then had, the custom of throwing men alive as a sacrifice to the gods, in times of drought, and they

109 Doorway of the Toltec Temple of the Jaguars, overlooking the Ball Court, Chichén Itzá. Shown here are one of two Feathered Serpent columns which support the lintel, and a door jamb with a relief figure of a Toltec warrior.

104

110 Toltec relief panel of a
jaguar eating a heart, from
the Dance Platform of The
Eagles, Chichén Itzá. Such a
theme is also known at Tula
in the Toltec homeland, and
is symbolic of the military
order of the Jaguars.

believed that they did not die though they never saw them again.
They also threw into it a great many other things, like precious
stones and things which they prized.

Shortly before the Spanish Conquest, one of our Colonial sources tells
us that the victims were 'Indian women belonging to each of the lords',
but in the popular imagination the notion has taken hold that only
lovely young virgins were tossed down to the Rain God lurking below
its greenish-black waters. The late Dr Hooton, who examined a
collection of some fifty skeletons fished up from the Sacred Cenote,
commented that 'all of the individuals involved (or rather immersed)
may have been virgins, but the osteological evidence does not permit a
determination of this nice point'. A goodly number of the skulls turned
out to be from adult males, and many from children, while pathology
showed that 'three of the ladies who fell or were pushed into the Cenote
had received, at some previous time, good bangs on various parts of the
head . . . and one female had suffered a fracture of the nose'!

As the great Mayanists Ralph Roys and A. M. Tozzer have stressed,
the peak of the sacrificial cult at the Sacred Cenote was reached after the
decline of Toltec Chichén, and continued into Colonial times and even
later. One crude rubber doll from the well has been recently shown to
have wrappings of rayon cloth! None the less, many of the objects
dredged from the muck at the bottom of the Cenote are of Toltec

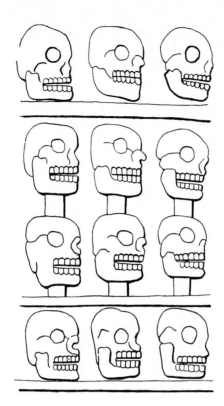

111 Bas-relief of skulls skewered on a rack, from the Tzompantli, Chichén Itzá.

manufacture, including some marvellously fine jades and the gold disks already mentioned. For metals had now appeared in the Maya area, 103, 105 although probably all casting and most working was done elsewhere and imported, the many copper bells and other objects from the well being of Mexican workmanship. From places as far afield as Panama the local lords brought treasures of gold to offer to their Rain God.

The Rain God's cult is also strikingly evident in the underground cavern of Balankanché, located $2\frac{1}{2}$ miles east of Chichén Itzá. In a deep, 112 hot, and humid chamber which they later sealed, the Toltec priests had placed almost 100 incense burners of pottery and stone, most of them at the base of an enormous stalagmitic formation in the center of the chamber. Twenty-six of these are hour-glass in shape, and had been modeled with the goggle-eyed visage of the Mexican Rain God, Tlaloc, and polychromed. Off to one side they had made an offering of 252 miniature *metates* with their *manos*, and it is tempting to speculate whether there might once have been 260 of these, the number of days in the sacred calendar.

This Toltec occupation has been detected at other places in the Yucatán Peninsula, and is everywhere marked by the presence of the glazed pottery called Plumbate ware, produced in kilns along the 113, 115 Guatemala-Chiapas border area near the Pacific shore. Plumbate vessels must have been made to Toltec taste, for they often take the

112 Chamber in the cave of Balankanché, Yucatán. In the center, stalactite and stalagmite have united in an immense pillar; around it were placed Toltec incense burners of pottery and stone.

form of Toltec warriors, but many are simple, pear-shaped vases supported on hollow legs, very much like the carved painted vessels also associated with the Toltec period in Yucatán. 114

What finally happened to the Toltec? All indications are that their mighty capital, Chichén Itzá, was abandoned in a Katun 6 Ahau which ended in AD 1224, and they are heard of no more. Another people now take the stage for a brief moment and Maya culture lives a little while longer.

A word of caution should be inserted here. The version of Toltec-Maya history given above is that worked out by the late Ralph Roys, the leading student of Maya ethnohistory of his time, but it is by no means accepted by all Mayanists. The basic problem of dealing with the Short Count chronological system has already been described; this means that other interpretations are possible, but not necessarily probable. A dissenting view which has often cropped up in recent years is that the Toltec of Tula, and the Toltec-Maya of Chichén Itzá, at least in part were contemporary with the terminal Late Classic Maya of the southern lowlands prior to their collapse, and that Tula was more influenced by the Maya than the reverse. Only modern excavations at Chichén Itzá, a site which – despite years of excavations – is still poorly known, will tell us whether this view is tenable, or, more likely, ill-founded.

113 A Toltec effigy jar
(Plumbate ware) in the form
of the god Itzamná, from
Guatemala. Ht 6 in.
(15.2 cm).

114 Hands are depicted in
black paint on this X-Fine
Orange ware jar from coastal
Campeche. Together with
Plumbate ware, pottery of
this kind is a marker for the
Toltec presence in the Maya
area. Ht *c.* 7 in. (17.8 cm).

115 A Toltec tripod jar
(Plumbate ware) from coastal
Campeche, Mexico.
Produced on the Pacific
slopes of Chiapas and
Guatemala in Toltec style,
this glazed ware was widely
traded over much of
southern Mesoamerica. Ht
7½ in. (19 cm).

The Itzá and the city of Mayapán

The Toltec may finally have been accepted by the natives of Yucatán, but the Itzá were always despised. Epithets such as 'foreigners', 'tricksters and rascals', 'the lewd ones', and 'people without fathers or mothers' are applied to them by the Maya chronicles, and the phrase 'those who speak our language brokenly' shows that they could not have been Yucatec in origin. Several scholars have suggested that at the beginning of their history the Itzá were a group of Mexicanized Chontal-Maya (that is, Putun) living in Tabasco, where commercial connections with central Mexico were deep-rooted. At any rate while the Toltec lorded it over Yucatán, the Itzá were settled in a place called Chakanputun ('savannah of the Putun'), probably Champoton on the coast of Campeche. About AD 1200 they were driven from this town and wandered east across the land, 'beneath the trees, beneath the bushes, beneath the vines, to their misfortune', migrating through the empty jungles to the region of Lake Petén Itzá, and to the eastern shores of Belize. Finally, this wretched band of warriors found their way up the coast and across to Chichén Itzá, where they settled as squatters in the desolate city, in Katun 4 Ahau (AD 1224–44).

Leading the Itzá diaspora to northern Yucatán was a man who also claimed the title of Kukulcan, like his great Toltec predecessor of the tenth century, and he must have consciously imitated Toltec ideas, such as the cult of the Sacred Cenote, which now reached a peak of intensity. And yet another cult was initiated, that of the Goddess of Medicine, one of the several aspects of Ix Chel, with pilgrims from all over the Northern Area voyaging to her shrine on the island of Cozumel.

In Katun 13 Ahau (AD 1263–83) the Itzá founded Mayapán, some of the tribe remaining behind at Chichén Itzá, which now had lost its old name of Uucil-abnal and taken on its present one (meaning 'mouth of the well of Itzá'). The wily Kukulcan II populated his city with provincial rulers and their families, thus ensuring a dominion over much of the peninsula. However, after his death (or departure), troubles increased, and it was not until about 1283 that Mayapán actually became the capital of Yucatán, after a revolt in which an Itzá lineage named Cocom had seized power, aided by Mexican mercenaries from Tabasco, the Canul ('guardians'). It may have been this sinister Praetorian Guard which introduced the bow-and-arrow to Yucatán.

Mayapán, which is situated in the west central portion of the peninsula, is a residential metropolis covering about $2\frac{1}{2}$ square miles and completely surrounded by a defensive wall testifying to the unrest of those days. There are over 2,000 dwellings within the wall, and it is estimated that between 11,000 and 12,000 persons lived in the city. At the center of Mayapán is the Temple of Kukulcan, a pitifully shoddy imitation of the Castillo at Chichén Itzá. The colonnaded masonry dwellings of important persons were near this, just as Landa tells us, but dwellings become poorer and poorer as one moves away from the center. Each group of thatched-roof houses probably sheltered a family and is surrounded by a low property wall. The city 'pattern' is completely haphazard: there are no streets, no arrangement to be discerned at all, and it seems as if the basically dispersed Maya had been forced by the Itzá to live jam-packed together within the walls in a kind of urban anarchy. No city like it had ever been seen before in the Maya area. On what did the population live? The answer is tribute, for Father Cogolludo tells us that luxury and subsistence goods streamed into the city from the vassals of the native princes whom the Cocom were holding hostage in their capital.

116 Pottery incense burner from a shrine at Mayapán. This effigy of God B, the Rain God Chac, carries a small bowl in one hand and a ball of flaming incense in the other. The censer was painted after firing with blue, green, black, red, white, and yellow pigments. Ht 21½ in. (54.6 cm).

117 Upper part of pottery incense burner from Mayapán, Mexico. God M, Ek Chuah, who was the patron of merchants, is shown here, identifiable from his partly broken, Pinnochio-like nose. Red, blue, and yellow paint had been applied to the censer. Ht 9½ in. (24.1 cm).

By this time, the Maya were thorough-going idolaters, and the excavators of Mayapán found a proliferation of shrines and family oratories, in which were placed brightly painted pottery incense burners of little artistic merit, representing Mexican gods such as Quetzalcoatl, Xipe Totec (the God of Spring), and the Old Fire God, side-by-side with Maya deities such as Chac the Rain God, the Maize God, and Itzamná (the Maya version of the Old Fire God).

116, 117

In an ill-omened era, Katun 8 Ahau (1441–61), fate began to close in upon the Itzá. Hunac Ceel was then ruler of Mayapán, an unusual figure who achieved prominence by offering himself as a sacrifice to be flung into the Sacred Cenote at Chichén, and living to deliver the Rain God's prophecy given him there. The ruler of Chichén Itzá was a man named Chac Xib Chac. According to one story, by means of sorcery Hunac Ceel drove Chac Xib Chac to abduct the bride of the ruler of Izamal, whereupon the expected retribution took place and the Itzá were forced to leave Chichén. Next it was the turn of the Cocom, and a revolt broke out within the walls of Mayapán, stirred up by an upstart Mexican lineage named Xiu which had settled near the ruins of Uxmal. The Maya nobles of Mayapán joined the Xiu, and the Cocom game was up; they were put to death and the once great city was destroyed and abandoned for all time.

Those Itzá who were driven from Chichén Itzá were to be in evidence for several centuries more, however. Once again they found themselves as outcasts in the deserted forests, this time wandering back to the Lake Petén Itzá which they had seen in a previous Katun 8 Ahau. 101 On an island in the midst of its waters they established a new capital, Tayasal, now covered by the city of Flores, chief town of northern Guatemala. Safe in the fastness of an almost impenetrable wilderness, their island stronghold was bypassed by history. Tayasal was first encountered by Hernán Cortés in 1524, while that intrepid conqueror was journeying across the Petén with his army to punish a rebellious insubordinate in Honduras, and he was kindly received by King Canek, whose name was borne by a long line of Itzá rulers. It was not until the seventeenth century that the Spaniards decided something must be done about this last, untamed Maya kingdom, and several missionaries were sent to convert Canek and his people – to no avail. It seems almost beyond belief that Tayasal fell to the Spaniards only in 1697, and that while students at Harvard College had been scratching their heads over Cotton Mather's theology, Maya priests 2,000 miles away were still chanting rituals from hieroglyphic books.

The independent states of Yucatán

With Mayapán gone, the whole peninsula fell into a condition of feudal anarchy. In place of a single, united kingdom were now sixteen rival statelets, each jealous of the power and lands of the other, and only too 118 eager to go to war in asserting its claims. Yet it is also true that the culture of the times, for whatever it was worth, was Maya, for much of what the Mexicans had brought was already forgotten and traditional Maya ways of doing things were substituted for imported habits.

There are few archaeological sites which can be assigned to this final phase, although the life of the times is well described by Landa and other early post-Conquest writers who were able to question natives who had actually participated in that culture. We are sure that there were one or more major towns within each province, but these were chosen by the Spaniards for their settlements and most are buried under centuries of Colonial and more recent constructions.

One site which was untouched, however, is Tulum, a small town in 119 the province of Ecab founded in the Mayapán period. Spectacularly placed on a cliff above the blue-green waters of the Caribbean, Tulum is surrounded by a defensive wall on three sides and by the sea on the fourth. Probably no more than five or six hundred persons lived there, in houses concentrated on artificial platforms arranged along a sort of 'street'. The principal temple, a miserable structure called the Castillo, and other important buildings are clustered together near the sea. On the upper façades of many of these dwarfish structures, which are of strikingly slipshod workmanship, are plaster figures of winged gods descending from above. Wall paintings have been found on both the interiors and outer surfaces of some temples, but the best preserved are in the two-storied Temple of the Frescoes. Like the murals of the Late 120 Post-Classic center of Santa Rita in northern Belize (discovered by Dr Thomas Gann in 1894 and subsequently destroyed), the style of these

147

118 The independent states of the Northern Area on the eve of the Spanish Conquest.

121

is less Maya than Mixtec, undoubtedly influenced by the pictorial manuscripts of that gifted people from the hilly country of Oaxaca. Yet the content of the Tulum frescoes is native Maya, with scenes of gods such as Chac and various female divinities performing rites among bean-like vegetation. In one, the Rain God sits astride a four-legged beast, for which there can be but one explanation: they had seen, or heard tell of, Spaniards riding on horseback. Not only Tayasal, then, but also Tulum must have lived for a while beyond the Conquest, protected by the dense forests of Quintana Roo.

The Central Area in the Post-Classic

As was mentioned in the last chapter, not all of the lowland Maya centers and populated regions suffered total decline and abandonment with the Classic collapse, although most certainly did. In fact, Cobá in

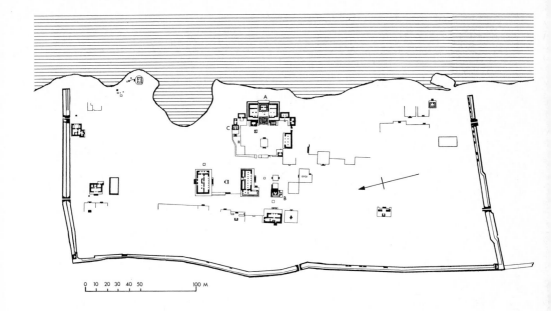

the northeast had a virtual renaissance in the Post-Classic, as Tulum-style superstructures were built on top of Classic pyramids. In the Central Area certain towns, including Tayasal, were founded and flourished after AD 1200 on islands in the chain of lakes that extends across the eastern Petén almost to the Belize border. Lamanai, the ancient port town on the New River, saw much construction during the Post-Classic, and was occupied well into the Colonial era as a church built in the sixteenth century (and abandoned in the next) testifies.

119 Plan of the walled town of Tulum, on the Caribbean coast of the Yucatán Peninsula. *A*, Castillo; *B*, Temple of the Frescoes; *C*, Temple of the Diving God.

Maya-Mexican dynasties in the Southern Area

In the mountain valleys of highland Guatemala, there were numerous independent nations on the eve of the Conquest, but the Quiché and Cakchiquel were the greatest of these. All indications are that they and their lesser neighbors, the Tzutuhil and Pokomam, had been there since very early times. And yet they claimed in their own histories that they had come from the west, from Mexico. As the Annals of the Cakchiquels relate:

> From the setting sun we came, from Tula, from beyond the sea; and it was at Tula that arriving we were brought forth, coming we were produced, by our mothers and fathers, as they say.

This claim may have been pure wishful thinking, similar to that of many Americans who would have liked their forebears to have stepped off the 'Mayflower' in 1620. The great authority on Quiché Maya culture and history, Dr Robert Carmack, traces the *actual* origin of the Quiché élite not to the Toltec diaspora of the late tenth and eleventh centuries, but to a much later incursion of Toltecized Chontal-Nahua

120 Temple of the Frescoes, Tulum, from the west, a photograph taken prior to 1923, before the walled site had been cleared. The temple is noted for its wall paintings carried out in a hybrid Mixtec-Maya style. Inset panels over the doorways contain stucco 'diving god' figures, while stuccoed faces at the corners of the lower story suggest its dedication to the god Itzamná.

121 Detail of a wall painting in the Temple of the Frescoes at Tulum. An aged goddess, probably Ix Chel, carries two images of the god Chac.

speakers (in other words, Putun Maya) from the Gulf Coast border region of Veracruz and Tabasco. These 'forefathers' would have arrived as small but very formidable military bands similar to the Japanese samurai, and terrorized the native Quiché-Cakchiquel highlanders. Gradually they established an epi-Toltec state, complete with a ruling line claiming descent from Quetzalcoatl. Many of the élite's personal names, as well as names of early places, objects, and institutions, seem to be Chontal rather than Quiché; and they introduced into the Guatemalan highlands many Nahua words for military and ritual matters.

101

The *conquistadores* have described the splendor of their towns, such as Utatlán, the Quiché capital which was burned to the ground by the terrible Pedro de Alvarado, or the Cakchiquel center Iximché. These sites were placed in defensive positions atop hills surrounded by deep ravines, and are completely Mexican down to the last architectural detail. Typically, the principal building is a large double temple with two frontal stairways, much like the Great Temple of the Aztec in Tenochtitlan, and there usually is a well-made ball court near by, for we know from the Popol Vuh that the highlanders were fond of that game. Lastly, all buildings are covered in Mexican fashion with flat beam-and-mortar roofs, the corbel principle being unknown here.

122 Group C, Chuitinamit, Guatemala, looking west; restoration drawing by Tatiana Proskouriakoff. The Quiché built an impressive stronghold here after driving out the Pokomam Maya. A typically Mexican feature of the late highland centers is the double pyramid in the middle of the group. In the background can be seen a ball court.

123 Group B, Mixco Viejo, Guatemala, looking east. The ruins of the Pokomam capital are surrounded on all sides by tremendously precipitous ravines. To take the town from its defenders, Alvarado's Spanish army had to advance up a steep path along which only two abreast could move, under a hail of rocks and poisoned arrows. This is the main group of the site, dominated by the usual double temple.

Best preserved of these late highland centers is Mixco Viejo, capital of the brave Pokomam nation; the almost impregnable site, surrounded by steep gorges, fell to Alvarado and two companies of Spanish infantry only through treachery.

Utatlán is the best known of these highland capitals, both archaeologically and ethnohistorically. In it, there was a fundamental social cleavage between the lords and their vassals: these were castes, in the strictest sense of the term. The former were the patrilineal descendants of the original warlords; they were sacred, and surrounded by royal emblems. The vassals served as foot-soldiers to the lords, and while they could and did receive military titles through their battlefield prowess, they were still subject to sumptuary laws. Merchants had a privileged status, but they had to pay tribute. In addition, the free population included artisans and serfs (a growing class of rural laborers). Slaves comprised both sentenced criminals and vassal war captives; in general, only captive lords were considered fit for sacrifice, or for consumption in cannibalistic rites.

There were twenty-four 'principal' lineages in Utatlán, closely identified with the buildings or 'Big Houses' in which they (the lords) carried out their affairs. The functions carried out in them were ceremonial lecturing; the giving of bride-price; and eating and drinking associated with marriages between the lineages. The Quiché state was headed by a king, a king-elect, and two 'captains', but there was also a kind of quadripartite rule (known also in Yucatán) embodied in four chiefs, one from each of the four major Utatlán lineages.

Documentary evidence unique for the ancient Maya enables us to associate specific ruined temples at Utatlán with gods revered by the Quiché. The major cult structures faced each other across a plaza, and were dominated by the Temple of Tojil, a Jaguar deity connected with the sun and with rain. In the same plaza was the circular temple dedicated to the Feathered Serpent, while the Ball Court of Utatlán represented the Underworld. There was a palace elaborating the idea of the Big Houses in honor of Utatlán's ruling lineage, the Cawek ('Rain') dynasty; other Big Houses can be identified as the range structures so typical of highland towns. Perhaps we have a clue here to the functions played by the 'palaces' in Classic sites of the southern lowlands.

The Spanish Conquest

'The raised wooden standard shall come!' cried the Maya prophet Chilam Balam, 'Our lord comes, Itzá! Our elder brother comes, oh men of Tantun! Receive your guests, the bearded men, the men of the east, the bearers of the sign of God, lord!'

The prediction came true in 1517, when Yucatán was discovered by Hernández de Córdoba, who died of wounds inflicted by Maya warriors at Champoton. The year 1518 saw the exploratory expedition of Grijalva, and that of the great Hernán Cortés in 1519, but Yucatán was for a while spared as the cupidity of the Spaniards drew them to the gold-rich Mexico. The Spanish Conquest of the northern Maya began only in 1528 under Francisco de Montejo, on whom the Crown bestowed the title of Adelantado. But this was no easy task, for unlike the mighty Aztec, there was no overall native authority which could be toppled, bringing an empire with it. Nor did the Maya fight in the accepted fashion. Attacking the Spaniards at night, plotting ambushes and traps, they were jungle guerrillas in a familiar modern tradition. Accordingly, it was not until 1542 that the hated foreigners managed to establish a capital, Mérida; even so revolt continued to plague the Spaniards throughout the sixteenth century.

The reduction of the Southern Area was largely the accomplishment of the resourceful but cruel Pedro de Alvarado, who arrived in Guatemala in 1523 fresh from his Mexican triumphs with cavalry, footsoldiers, and native auxiliaries. By 1541, the year of his death, the Quiché and Cakchiquel kingdoms had fallen under the Spanish yoke, and indigenous resistance was largely at an end.

But the Maya are, for all their apparent docility, the toughest Indians of Mesoamerica, and the struggle against European civilization never once halted. In 1847 and again in 1860 the Yucatec Maya rose against their white oppressors, coming very close the first time to taking the entire peninsula. As late as 1910 the independent chiefs of Quintana Roo were in rebellion against the dictatorial regime of Porfirio Díaz, and only in the last few decades have these remote Maya villagers begun to accept the rule of Mexico. Likewise the Tzeltal of highland Chiapas have repeatedly risen, most notably in 1712 and 1868. The

Cholan-speaking regions west of Lake Izabal in Guatemala were feared by missionaries and soldiers alike as 'The Land of War', and the pacification of these Maya took centuries. The survival of the Itzá on their island Tayasal is a case in point; another is that of the wild and still independent Lacandón. No, the Maya were never completely conquered, but their civilization and spirit were broken. As a poem from one of the books of Chilam Balam puts it:

> Eat, eat, thou hast bread;
> Drink, drink, thou hast water;
> On that day, dust possesses the earth;
> On that day, a blight is on the face of the earth,
> On that day, a cloud rises,
> On that day, a mountain rises,
> On that day, a strong man seizes the land,
> On that day, things fall to ruin,
> On that day, the tender leaf is destroyed,
> On that day, the dying eyes are closed,
> On that day, three signs are on the tree,
> On that day, three generations hang there,
> On that day, the battle flag is raised,
> And they are scattered afar in the forests.

7
Maya life on the eve of the Conquest

While we have until this moment been dealing mainly with the pots, jades, and ruins of a once-great people, we actually know a good deal more than this about the daily life of the Maya, particularly of the natives of Yucatán on the eve of the Conquest. For it is our good fortune that the early Spanish missionaries were accomplished scholars, and that owing to their eagerness to understand the nations they wished to convert to the Cross they have left us with first-class anthropological accounts of native culture as it was just before they came. So it is upon this foundation that we must interpret the archaeological remains of the Post-Classic Maya – and the Maya of the Classic as well.

The farm and the chase

Maya agriculture, which has been described in some detail in Chapter 1, was the foundation of their civilization. Maize, beans, squashes, chili peppers, cotton, and various kinds of root crops and fruit trees were cultivated. That the pre-Conquest lowlanders usually prepared their plots by the slash-and-burn method is certain, but exactly how trees were felled prior to the adoption of copper axes in the Post-Classic (and of steel ones in Colonial days) is unclear; perhaps they were merely ringed and left to die. The times of planting were under the control of a kind of farmer's almanac of which we apparently have examples in the codices. According to Landa, fields were communally owned and jointly worked by groups of twenty men, but this may not be very close to the real picture, as we shall see.

In Yucatán, the Maya stored their crops in above-ground cribs of wood, but also in 'fine underground places' which might well be the *chultuns* so common in Classic sites. The Spanish sources consistently fail to mention tortillas or flat cakes (*pek wah*) for the lowland Maya; while a few clay griddles have been found in Post-Classic occupations in sites like Lamanai, these may have been used to toast cacao beans rather than tortillas. However, other ways of preparing maize are mentioned in the sources. These include *saka'*, a corn-meal gruel which was taken with chili pepper as the first meal of the day; *k'eyen*, a mixture of water and sour dough carried in gourds to the fields for sustenance during the day; and the well-known tamales (*keehel wah*), which turn up in food offerings found painted on Late Classic ceramics. The

4

124

124 Woman grinding maize on a *metate*, from a Late Classic figurine from Lubaantún, Belize.

125 Huntsman slaying deer, on a Late Classic figurine from Lubaantún, Belize.

peasant cuisine (we know little of that current among the élite class) was largely confined to such simple foods and to stews compounded from meat and vegetables, to which were added squash seeds and peppers.

'Cash crops' were of prime importance to Yucatán. Cotton was widely grown, for the province was famed for its textiles which were exported over a very large area. Along river drainages in southern Campeche, Tabasco, and Belize and on the Pacific slope of Guatemala groves of cacao trees were planted, but in the north these were restricted to the bottoms of filled-in *cenotes* and other natural depressions. The cacao bean from this tree provided chocolate, the preferred drink of the Mesoamerican ruling classes, but well into Colonial times the beans served as a form of money in regional markets; so precious were they that the Maya traders encountered off the coast of Honduras by Columbus were said to have snatched up any that had dropped as though it was their own eyes that had fallen to the canoe bottom.

Every Maya household had its own kitchen garden in which vegetables and fruit trees were raised, and fruit groves were scattered near settlements as well. Papaya, avocado, custard apple, sapodilla, and the breadnut tree were all cultivated, but many kinds of wild fruits were also eaten, especially in times of famine.

There were several breeds of dogs current among the Maya, each with its own name. One such strain was barkless; males were castrated and fattened on corn, and either eaten or sacrificed. Another was used in the hunt. Both wild and domestic turkeys were known, but only the former used as sacrificial victims in ceremonies. As he still does today, the Maya farmer raised the native stingless bees, which are kept in small, hollow logs closed with mud plaster at either end and stacked up in A-frames, but wild honey was also much appreciated.

125   The larger mammals, such as deer and peccary, were hunted with the bow-and-arrow in drives (though in Classic times the *atlatl*-and-dart must have been the principal weapon), aided by packs of dogs. Birds like the wild turkey, partridge, wild pigeon, quail, and wild duck were taken with pellets shot from blowguns. A variety of snare and deadfalls are shown in the Madrid Codex, especially a trap for armadillo.

In Yucatán, fishing was generally of the offshore kind, by means of sweep and drag nets and hook-and-line, but fish were also shot with bow-and-arrow in lagoons. Inland, especially in the highland streams, stupefying drugs were pounded in the water, and the fish taken by hand once they had floated into artificial dams; one of the beautifully incised bones from Late Classic Tikal shows that this was also the practice in 66 the Petén. Along the coasts the catch was salted and dried or roasted over a fire for use in commerce.

Among wild products of the lowland forests of great cultural importance to the Maya was the resin of the copal tree, which (along with rubber and chewing gum!) was used as incense – so holy was this that one native source describes it as the 'odor of the center of heaven'. Another tree produced a bark for flavoring *balche*, a 'strong and stinking' mead imbibed in vast amounts during festivals.

Industry and commerce

Yucatán was the greatest producer of salt in Mesoamerica. The beds extended along the coast from Campeche, along the lagoons on the north side of the peninsula, and over to Isla Mujeres on the east. The salt, which Landa praised as the 'best . . . which I have ever seen in my life', was collected at the end of the dry season by the coastal peoples who held a virtual monopoly over the industry, although at one time it was entirely in the hands of the overlord of Mayapán. A few localities inland also had salt wells, such as the Chixoy valley of Guatemala, but it was sea salt that was in most demand and this was carried widely all over the Maya area. Other valuable Yucatecan exports were honey, cotton mantles, and slaves, and one suspects that it was such industrial specialization which supported the economy, not maize agriculture.

Further regional products involved in native trade were cacao, which could only be raised in a few well-watered places, quetzal feathers from the Alta Verapaz, flint and chert from deposits in the Central Area, obsidian from the highlands northeast of Guatemala City, and colored shells (particularly the thorny oyster) from both coasts. Jade and a host of lesser stones of green color were also traded, most originating in the beds of the Motagua River, but some which appeared on the market could well have been looted from ancient graves.

The great majority of goods traveled by sea since roads were but poor trails and cargoes heavy. This kind of commerce was cornered by the Chontal Maya, or Putun, such good seafarers that Thompson calls them 'the Phoenicians of Middle America'. Their route skirted the coast from the Aztec port of trade in Campeche, Xicallanco, around the peninsula and down to Nito near Lake Izabal, where their great canoes put in to exchange goods with the inland Maya. However, a special group of traders traveled the perilous overland trails, guided by the North Star and under the protection of their own deity, Ek Chuah, the Black God. Markets (*k'iwik*) are rarely mentioned where the lowland Maya are concerned, in contrast with Mexico where they were so large that the Spaniards were astonished, and it is probable that they were unimportant since there was little cause for heavy subsistence to change hands in this very uniform land. But we are told by one source that highland Guatemalan markets were 'great and celebrated and very rich', and these have persisted to this very day.

It was this trade that linked Mexico and the Maya, for they had much to exchange – especially cacao and the feathers of tropical birds for copper tools and ornaments – and it was probably the smooth business operations conducted by the Chontal that spared the Maya from the Aztec onslaught that had overwhelmed less cooperative peoples in Mesoamerica.

The life cycle

cf.87

Immediately after birth, Yucatecan mothers washed their infants and then fastened them to a cradle, their little heads compressed between two boards in such a way that after two days a permanent fore-and-aft flattening had taken place which the Maya considered a mark of beauty. As soon as possible, the anxious parents went to consult with a priest so as to learn the destiny of their offspring, and the name which he or she was to bear until baptism.

The Spanish Fathers were quite astounded that the Maya had a baptismal rite, which took place at an auspicious time when there were a number of boys and girls between the ages of three and twelve in the settlement. The ceremony took place in the house of a town elder, in the presence of their parents who had observed various abstinences in honor of the occasion. The children and their fathers remained inside a cord held by four old and venerable men representing the Chacs or Rain Gods, while the priest performed various acts of purification and blessed the candidates with incense, tobacco, and holy water. From that time on the elder girls, at least, were marriageable.

In both highlands and lowlands, boys and young men stayed apart from their families in special communal houses where they presumably learned the arts of war, and other things as well, for Landa says that the prostitutes were frequent visitors. Other youthful diversions were gambling and the ball game. The double standard was present among the Maya, for girls were strictly brought up by their mothers and suffered grievous punishments for lapses of chastity. Marriage was arranged by go-betweens and, as among all peoples with exogamous clans or lineages, there were strict rules about those with whom alliances could or could not be made – particularly taboo was marriage with those of the same paternal name. Monogamy was the general custom, but important men who could afford it took more wives. Adultery was punished by death, as among the Mexicans.

Ideas of personal comeliness were quite different from ours, although the friars were much impressed with the beauty of the Maya women. Both sexes had their frontal teeth filed in various patterns, and we have many ancient Maya skulls in which the teeth have been inlaid with small plaques of jade. Until marriage, young men painted themselves black (and so did warriors at all times); tattooing and decorative scarification began after wedlock, both men and women being richly elaborated from the waist up by these means. Slightly crossed eyes were held in great esteem, and parents attempted to induce the condition by hanging small beads over the noses of their children.

Death was greatly dreaded by all, the more so since the deceased did not automatically go to any paradise. Ordinary folk were buried beneath the floors of their houses, their mouths filled with food and a jade bead, accompanied by idols and the things which they had used while alive. Into the graves of priests they are said to have placed books. Great nobles, however, were cremated, a practice probably of Mexican origin, and funerary temples were placed above their urns; in earlier days, of course, inhumation in sepulchers beneath such mausoleums was the rule. To the Cocom dynasty of Mayapán was reserved the practice of mummifying the heads of their defunct lords, these being kept in the family oratories and fed at regular intervals.

126 Person of high rank in a palanquin, from a graffito incised on a wall at Tikal.

Society and politics

The ancient Maya realm was no theocracy or primitive democracy, but a class society with strong political power in the hands of an hereditary élite. To understand the basis of the state in sixteenth-century Yucatán, we have to go right to the heart of the matter, to the people themselves.

In Yucatán, every adult Maya had two names. The first came to him from his mother, but could only be transmitted from women to their offspring, that is, in the female line. The second derived from the father, and similarly was exclusively passed on in the male line. There is now abundant evidence that these two kinds of name represented two different kinds of cross-cutting and coexistent descent groups: the matrilineage and the patrilineage. There were approximately 250 patrilineages in Yucatán at the time of the Conquest, and we know from Landa how important they were. For instance, they were strictly exogamous, all inheritance of property was patrilineal, and they were self-protection societies, all members of which had the obligation to help each other. Titles deriving from early Colonial times show that they had their own lands as well, which is probably what Landa meant when he said that all fields were held 'in common'. As for the matrilineage, it probably acted principally within the marriage regulation system, in which matrimony with the father's sister's or mother's brother's daughter was encouraged, but certain other kinds forbidden.

Now, while among many more primitive people such kin groups are theoretically equal, among the Maya this was not so, and both kinds of lineage were strictly ranked; to be able to trace one's genealogy in both lines to an ancient ancestry was an important matter. For there were strongly marked classes. At the top were the nobles (*almehen*, meaning he whose descent is known on both sides), who had private lands and held the more important political offices, as well as filling the roles of high-ranking warriors, wealthy farmers and merchants, and clergy. The commoners were the free workers of the population, probably, like their Aztec cousins, holding in usufruct from their patrilineage a stretch of forest in which to make their *milpas*; but in all likelihood even these persons were graded into rich and poor. There is some indication of serfs, who worked the private lands of the nobles. And at the bottom were the slaves who were mostly plebeians taken in war, prisoners of

126

127 Standing captive, incised on a bone from the Temple I tomb, Tikal (Late Classic period).

159

higher rank being subjected to the knife. Slavery was hereditary, but these menials could be redeemed by payments made by fellow members of one's patrilineage.

By the time the Spaniards arrived, political power over much of the inhabited Maya area was in the hands of ruling castes of Mexican or Mexican-influenced origin. Yucatecan politics was controlled by such a group, which of course claimed to have come from Tula and Zuyuá, a legendary home in the west. In fact, any candidate for high office had to pass an occult catechism known as the 'Language of Zuyuá'. At the head of each statelet in Yucatán was the *halach uinic* ('real man'), the territorial ruler who had inherited his post in the male line, although in an earlier epoch and among the highland Maya there were real kings (*ahau*) who held sway over wider areas. The *halach uinic* resided in a capital town and was supported by the products of his own lands, such as cacao groves worked by slaves, and by tribute.

The minor provincial towns were headed by the *batabs*, appointed by the *halach uinic* from a noble patrilineage related to his own. These ruled through local town councils made up of rich, old men, led by an important commoner chosen anew each year among the four quarters which made up the settlement. Besides his administrative and magisterial duties, the *batab* was a war leader, but his command was shared by a *nacom*, a highly tabooed individual who held office for three years.

The Maya were obsessed with war. The Annals of the Cakchiquels and the Popol Vuh speak of little but intertribal conflict among the highlanders, while the sixteen states of Yucatán were constantly battling with each other over boundaries and lineage honor. To this sanguinary record we must add the testimony of the Classic monuments and their inscriptions. From these and from the eye-witness descriptions of the *conquistadores* we can see how Maya warfare was waged. The *holcan* or 'braves' were the footsoldiers; they wore cuirasses of quilted cotton or of tapir hide and carried thrusting spears with flint points, darts-with-*atlatl*, and in late Post-Classic times, the bow-and-arrow. Hostilities typically began with an unannounced guerrilla raid into the enemy camp to take captives, but more formal battle opened with the dreadful din of drums, whistles, shell trumpets, and war cries. On either side of the war leaders and the idols carried into the combat under the care of the priests were the two flanks of infantry, from which rained darts, arrows, and stones flung from slings. Once the enemy had penetrated into home territory however, irregular warfare was substituted, with ambuscades and all kinds of traps. Lesser captives ended up as slaves, but the nobles and war leaders either had their hearts torn out on the sacrificial stone, or else were beheaded, a form of sacrifice favored by the Classic Maya.

8
Maya thought and culture

As in almost all the early civilizations of which we have record, it is extremely difficult to separate primitive scientific knowledge from its ritual context, but this should not lead one to suppose that a people like the Maya or the Sumerians had not evolved a considerable body of empirically derived information about the natural world. As we shall see, arithmetic and astronomy had reached a level comparable to that achieved by the ancient Babylonians and surpassing in some respects that of the Egyptians; but one should not exaggerate. Science in the modern sense was not present. In its place we find, as with the Mesopotamian civilizations, a combination of fairly accurate astronomical data with what can only be called numerology, developed by Maya intellectuals for religious purposes.

None the less, our knowledge of ancient Maya thought must represent only a tiny fraction of the whole picture, for of the thousands of books in which the full extent of their learning and ritual was recorded, only four have survived to modern times (as though all that posterity knew of ourselves were to be based upon three prayer books and *Pilgrim's Progress*). These are written on long strips of bark paper, folded like screens and covered with gesso. Pictorial representations on Classic Maya funerary pottery show that in Classic times the codices had jaguar-skin covers, and were painted by scribes using brush or turkey-feather pens dipped in black or red paint contained in cut conch-shell inkpots.   130

According to the early sources, the Maya books contained histories, prophecies, songs, 'sciences', and genealogies, but our four examples are completely ritual, or ritual-astronomical, works compiled in the Northern Area during the Post-Classic. The Dresden Codex is the   128
finest, and measures 8 inches high and $11\frac{3}{4}$ ft long (20.3 by 358.2 cm);
on internal evidence, some believe it to have been written in Campeche,   136
but the Soviet scholar Knorosov considers that it belongs to the Toltec-Maya period at Chichén Itzá. The Madrid and the very fragmentary Paris codices are much poorer in execution than the Dresden and somewhat later in date. Thompson has even suggested that a Spanish priest might have obtained the Madrid Codex at Tayasal.

In 1971 there was exhibited at the Grolier Club in New York a fourth Maya book which has since been labeled the 'Grolier Codex'; it once   129
belonged to a private collector in Mexico and on circumstantial evidence seems to have been found in a wooden box in a cave near

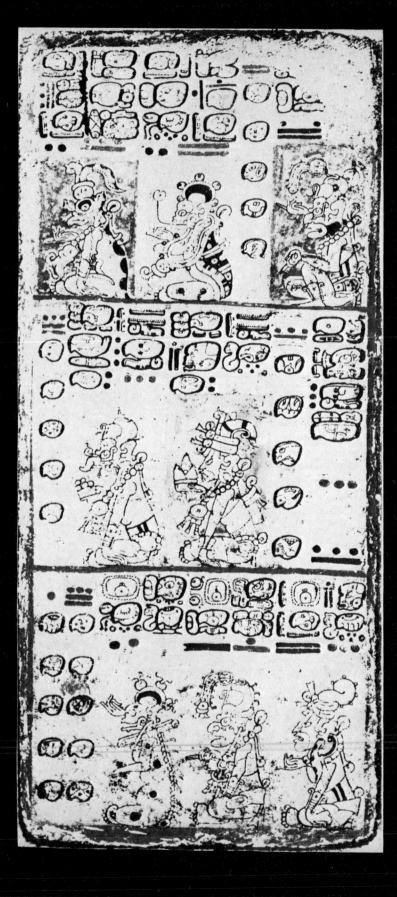

Tortuguero, Chiapas, within the past two decades. Unfortunately in very bad condition, it comprises about one half of a twenty-page table concerned with the Venus cycle. Although its authenticity has been vigorously disputed by Thompson, the radiocarbon date of AD 1230 from its paper is fully consistent with the Toltec-Maya style in which the glyphs and associated deities are drawn.

To these must be added the Classic Maya inscriptions. And then we have a great deal of very valuable information on Maya ritual in the early post-Conquest accounts, and in various esoteric texts like the Books of Chilam Balam, written in Maya but transcribed into Spanish letters. From all these documents it can readily be seen that Maya life was deeply imbued with religious feeling, and that ritual behavior gave meaning and a sense of security to all strata of Maya society.

129   Pages from the Grolier Codex, a Toltec-Maya book dealing with the planet Venus.

128 (*opposite*) The Dresden Codex is the earliest and most beautiful of the surviving folding-screen books of the Maya. Written on a long strip of bark paper, each page coated with fine stucco, much of it is concerned with 260-day ritual counts divided up in various ways, the divisions being associated with specific gods. The texts immediately above each deity contain their names and epithets. Ht 8 in. (20.3 cm).

130   Rabbit God writing in a folding-screen codex with jaguar-skin covers. Detail from a Late Classic cylindrical vase in codex style, northern Petén or southern Campeche. Eighth century AD.

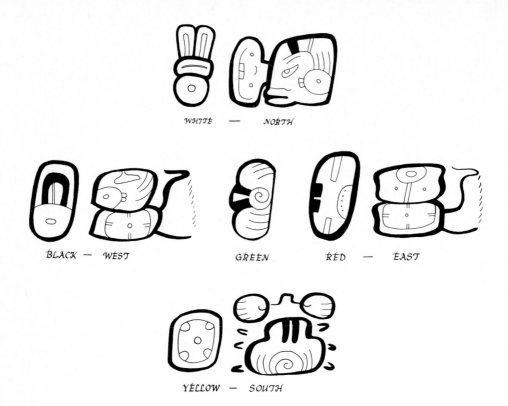

WHITE — NORTH

BLACK — WEST   GREEN   RED — EAST

YELLOW — SOUTH

The universe and the gods

131 Glyphs for the world directions and associated colors.

The idea of cyclical creations and destructions is a typical feature of Mesoamerican religions, as it is of Oriental. The Aztec, for instance, thought that the universe had passed through four such ages, and that we were now in the fifth, to be destroyed by earthquakes. The Maya thought along the same lines, in terms of eras of great length, like the Hindu *kalpas*. There is a suggestion that each of these measured 13 baktuns, or something less than 5,200 years, and that Armageddon would overtake the degenerate peoples of the world and all creation on the final day of the thirteenth. Thus, following the Thompson correlation, our present universe would have been created in 3114 BC, to be annihilated on 23 December AD 2012, when the Great Cycle of the Long Count reaches completion.

Maya cosmology is by no means simple to reconstruct from our very uneven data, but apparently they conceived of the earth as flat and four-cornered, each angle at a cardinal point which had a color value: red for east, white for north, black for west, and yellow for south, with green at the center. The sky was multi-tiered, and supported at the corners by four Bacabs, Atlantean gods with the appropriate color associations. Alternatively, the sky was held up by four trees of different colors and species, with the green ceiba or silk-cotton tree at the center. Each of the thirteen layers of heaven had its own god, that of the uppermost being the *muan* bird, a kind of screech-owl. The underworld was nine-layered with nine corresponding 'Lords of the Night'; this cold, unhappy place was the final destination of most Maya after death, and through it passed the heavenly bodies such as the sun and moon after they had disappeared below the horizon.

Classic art and the Post-Classic codices suggest that the flat earth was thought of as the back of a monstrous crocodile resting in a pool filled with water-lilies. Its counterpart in the sky was a double-headed serpent, a concept probably stemming from the fact that the word for sky, *caan*, is a homonym of the word for snake. On the body of the sky-serpent are marked not only its own sign, crossed bands, but also those of the sun, moon, Venus, and other celestial bodies.

Exceedingly little is known about the Maya pantheon. That their Olympus was peopled with a bewildering number of gods can be seen in the eighteenth-century manuscript, 'Ritual of the Bacabs', in which 166 deities are mentioned by name, or in the pre-Conquest codices where more than thirty can be distinguished. This theogonic multiplicity results in part from the gods having many aspects. Firstly, each was not only one but four individuals, separately assigned to the color-directions. Secondly, a number seem to have had a counterpart of the opposite sex as consort, a reflection of the Mesoamerican philosophy of dualism, the unity of opposite principles. And lastly, every astronomical god had an underworld avatar, as he died and passed beneath the earth to reappear once more in the heavens.

132 Some gods of the Maya pantheon with their name glyphs, from the Dresden Codex. *a*, Death God; *b*, Chac, the Rain God; *c*, North Star God; *d*, Itzamná; *e*, Maize God; *f*, Sun God; *g*, Young Moon Goddess; *h*, Bolon Dzacab; *i*, Ek Chuah, the Merchant God; *j*, Ix Chel, Old Moon Goddess and Goddess of Medicine.

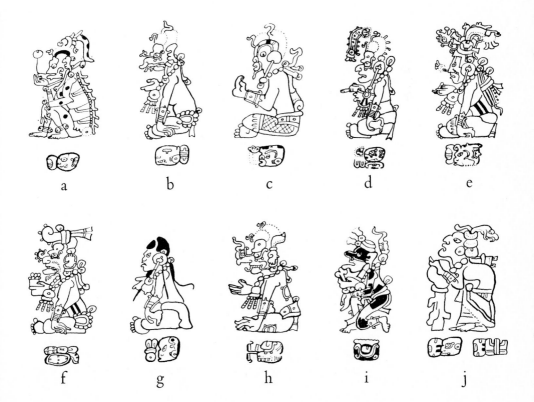

a   b   c   d   e

f   g   h   i   j

While some Maya sources speak of a one-and-only god (Hunab Ku) who was incorporeal and omnipotent, the supreme deity was surely Itzamná ('Lizard House'), pictured as an aged man with Roman nose in the codices, the inventor of writing and patron of learning and the sciences. His wife was Ix Chel, 'Lady Rainbow', the old goddess of weaving, medicine, and childbirth; she was also the old Moon Goddess, and the snakes in her hair and the claws with which her feet and hands are tipped prove her the equivalent of Coatlicue, the Aztec mother of gods and men. All the other gods, including the Bacabs, were apparently the progeny of this pair.

132*d*

132*j*

The Sun God, Ah Kinchil, is very similar to Itzamná in the codices, and may have been one of his aspects. On his night journey beneath the earth, he becomes the Jaguar God of the Underworld of fearsome aspect, often pictured on Classic monuments. It is believed that a young, half-naked lady prominent in the Dresden Codex represents the Moon Goddess, a younger variant of Ix Chel known as Ix Ch'up ('The Woman'), perhaps the consort of Ah Kinchil. Other celestial deities were the North Star, and various guises of Venus.

At the corners of the world were the benevolent Chacs, the Rain Gods, each of different color but all deeply venerated by the Maya who saw them as manifested in thunder and lightning bolts. There were also the quadruple Bacabs, each of whom presided over one quarter of the 260-day period in turn.

Further, there were patrons of the classes and professions. Heading this list is Kukulcan, god of the ruling caste; introduced after the Classic collapse, his cult reached a peak in Toltec times. Several war gods were venerated by the soldiers, some of them clearly deified heroes famed for their conquests. For the merchants and cacao growers there was Ek Chuah, with black face and Pinocchio nose, but there were also patron deities of hunters, fishers, beekeepers, tattoo artists, comedians, singers and poets, dancers, lovers, and even suicides. Less easy to deal with are gods who may have been connected with the idea of lineage and descent; one of these is God K or Bolon Dzacab ('Many Matrilineages'), whose face with baroquely branching nose can be seen on the ceremonial bars and manikin scepters brandished by persons of high rank on Classic monuments. On God K's forehead is a mirror with a tube in it which emits smoke, and one leg has in place of a foot the head and body of a dragon-like serpent; he is thus cognate with the snake-footed Tezcatlipoca ('Smoking Mirror') of the Aztecs. Since the latter was the chief god of the royal house, so must God K have been the patron of the Maya lords.

132*i*

132*h*

The Classic Maya Underworld

It is now clear that Classic Maya pictorial ceramics, whether painted or carved, had a funerary function, which is hardly surprising considering that their final destination was the tombs and graves of the honored dead. The Maya Underworld, which is the subject matter dealt with in these remarkable scenes, was known as Xibalbá, 'Place of Fright'. Part of a very complex mythology concerning it and its dread denizens has been miraculously preserved in the Popol Vuh manuscript, discovered among the Quiché Maya in the nineteenth century. This great Underworld epic was probably formulated during the Late Preclassic. It centers upon the doings of two sets of twins, young lords who are summoned in turn to Xibalbá by its horrible rulers (these bear the names of mortal diseases). The first pair, Hun Hunahpu and Vucub Hunahpu (1 Ahau and 7 Ahau in the lowland calendar), are forced to endure various houses of torture, and are finally defeated in a ball game, to suffer death by decapitation.

The Xibalbans hang up Hun Hunahpu's head in a calabash tree. One day, a young Underworld princess named Lady Blood happens by and holds up her hand to the head, which spits into it. She becomes pregnant, and is banished in disgrace to the earth's surface, where she enters the house of the malevolent old mother of Hun Hunahpu (surely Ix Chel, the old moon and ancestress). There Lady Blood gives birth to Hunahpu and Xbalanque, the glorious Hero Twins. These grow up to be great ballplayers and blowgunners, as well as tricksters. Through skill and subterfuge they defeat not only a monstrous and arrogant anthropomorphic bird named Vucub Caquix (a theme celebrated on several Classic ceramics), but also their jealous half-brothers Hun Batz and Hun Chuen, whom they turn into Monkey-men. These latter become the patrons of scribes, artists, musicians, and dancers for all the Maya, including those of Post-Classic Yucatán.

The Hero Twins are also summoned, like their father and uncle, to the Underworld to play ball with the angry Xibalbans. In a virtual 'Harrowing of Hell', they turn the tables on the rulers and defeat them, eventually rising up through the surface of the earth to the sky, where they reach apotheosis as the sun and the moon (or, as Thompson believed, the sun and Venus). This was the sacred paradigm for the rulers of the Maya realm, who must have believed that like Hunahpu and Xbalanque, they would never suffer total extinction in Xibalbá. As for the Twins' father, Hun Hunahpu, iconographic research by Karl Taube has shown that he was none other than the Maize God, his severed head symbolizing the harvested ear of corn, and the maize seed planted beneath the surface arising from Xibalbá in resurrection, to reach fruition in the fields of our own world. 133

It is thus no surprise to find incredibly explicit pictorial references to the Underworld epic on Classic Maya pottery. The entire epic, of which the Popol Vuh preserves only a fragment, must have been written in codices which would have been the equivalent of the Egyptian Book of the Dead.

The iconography of Xibalbá is rich and complex. Heading the pantheon are three aged divinities – God L, who wears an owl headdress and smokes a cigar; God N, ruler of the year 's end, who can be identified with the quadruple Pauahtuns, directional divinities who stood at the four corners of the Underworld and held up the earth; and God D or Itzamná, here in his role as a chthonic deity. Also present in Xibalbá are the Jaguar God of the Underworld, whose face was emblazoned on Maya war shields, and Chac Xib Chac or GI, whose chief role seems to have been the sacrifice of gods and men by decapitation. 134

Hunahpu and Xbalanque often appear in ceramic scenes, the former marked by the black spots of death and the latter by patches of jaguar skin over face and body; there are wonderful representations of Vucub Caquix being shot with blowguns by one or both Twins. These youths were considered divine rulers of the dead right into the Colonial era, and Professor David Kelley has even suggested that the very name 'Palenque', the great Maya site which is significantly located in the west, region of death, might be a corruption of 'Xbalanque'. It may be significant that the known Emblem Glyphs of Palenque feature a bone or one of two animal skulls as their main element.

Funerary ceramics tell of an even stranger obsession of the Classic élite. This was the taking of ceremonial enemas by means of a leather or rubber syringe-bag fitted with a bone tube. The aged Pauahtun himself was often the recipient, administered at the hands of a beautiful young consort. The exact substance injected remains in doubt, but the vases show the liquid was kept in wide-mouthed jars and had froth on top. This suggests the intoxicating *balche* mead, and we do know from Aztec accounts of the Huastec, linguistic relatives of the Maya, that those people habitually intoxicated themselves by means of 'wine' enemas. On the other hand, Dr Peter Furst has pointed to the widespread custom in lowland South America of administering powerful hallucinogens in enemas, and has documented the custom among the contemporary Huichol of western Mexico (who use the potent *peyote* or spineless cactus buttons for the infusion). Incidentally, the otherwise

133 Plate in codex style, from northern Guatemala or southern Campeche. Eighth century AD. In the center, the Maize God (Hun Hunahpu) emerges from the split surface of the earth, depicted as a turtle carapace, as he is resurrected by his Hero Twin sons, Hunahpu (left) and Xbalanque (right). The latter pours water from a jar to ensure the sprouting of the corn.

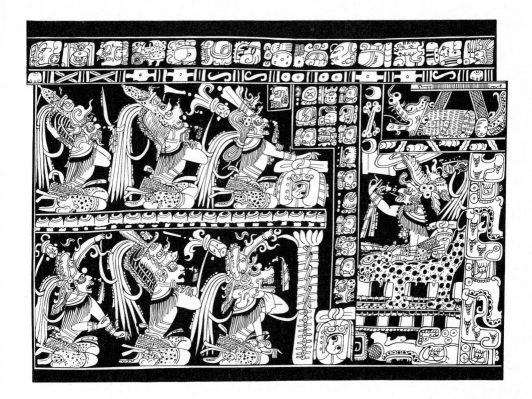

unexplained bone tubes found in Classic Maya tombs and graves probably represented the surviving remains of the enema apparatus.

135   Deep caverns have always been conceptual entrances to Xibalbá for past and present Maya. One such cave, now named Naj Tunich, was discovered in 1979 by local residents in karst terrain near Poptun, in the southeastern Petén. The cave is huge, measuring 2,790 ft (850 m) deep along its longest passage. It has ancient walls, Late Classic burials, and terminal Late Preclassic pottery, but it was apparently extensively looted before archaeologists could get to it. The importance of Naj Tunich lies in its extensive hieroglyphic texts (altogether comprising about 400 glyphs) and scenes, all executed in carbon black on the cave walls. The latter include depictions of the ball game, amorous activities which are probably of a homosexual nature, and Maya deities, which not unexpectedly include the Hero Twins, Hunahpu and Xbalanque. The style of the writing and painting is closely related to Late Classic vases in 'codex style', and must have been carried out by one or more artists or scribes skilled in the production of Maya books.

134   Rollout of a Late Classic cylindrical vase, probably from Naranjo, Guatemala. This is a night scene of God L (right) in his Underworld palace, at the creation of our present era. Facing him are six major lords of Xibalbá, including the Jaguar God of the Underworld and GI (Chac Xib Chac).

Rites and ritual practitioners

In contrast to that of the Aztec, the late Post-Classic Maya clergy was not celibate. Sons succeeded their fathers to the office, although some were second sons of lords. Their title, Ah Kin ('He of the Sun') suggests a close connection with the calendar and astronomy, and the list of duties outlined by Landa makes it clear that Maya learning as well as ritual was in their hands. Among them were 'computation of the years, months, and days, the festivals and ceremonies, the administration of the sacraments, the fateful days and seasons, their methods of divination and their prophecies, events and the cures for diseases, and their antiquities and how to read and write with the letters and characters . . .', but they also kept the all-important genealogies. During the prosperity of Mayapán, an hereditary Chief Priest resided in that city whose main function seems to have been the overseeing of an academy for the training of candidates for the priesthood, but in no source do we find his authority or that of the priests superseding civil power.

The priest was assisted in human sacrifices by four old men, called Chacs in honor of the Rain God (recalling the sacrificial role of the Classic rain deity Chac Xib Chac), who held the arms and legs of the victim, while the breast was opened up by another individual who bore the title of Nacom (like the war leader). Another religious functionary was the Chilam, a kind of visionary shaman who received messages from the gods while in a state of trance, his prophecies being interpreted by the assembled priests.

Every single Maya ritual act was dictated by the calendar, above all by the 260-day count. These sacred performances were imbued with symbolic meaning. For instance, the numbers 4, 9, and 13 and the color-directions appear repeatedly. Before and during rituals food taboos and sexual abstinence were rigidly observed, and self-mutilation was carried out by jabbing needles and sting-ray spines through ears,

135 Section of paintings and hieroglyphic texts from the walls of Naj Tunich cave, Guatemala. The figure at top left may be a musician, seated near his conch-shell trumpet. At bottom left is a ballplayer, complete with protective belt and knee-pad; this is probably Hunahpu, one of the Hero Twins in the Popol Vuh story. Late Classic, eighth century AD.

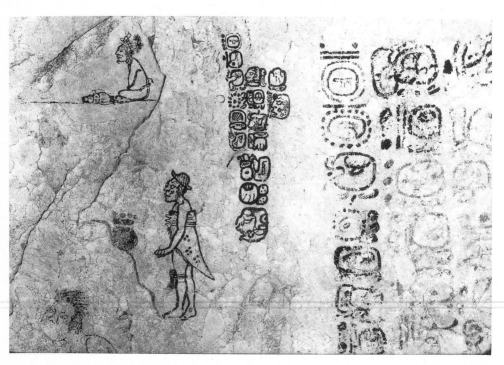

136 New Year ceremonies in the Dresden Codex. Below, the Death God sacrifices before the New Year image; middle, the idol of Itzamná in the temple; above, the Opossum God carries out the image of the Maize God to a shrine at the entrance of the town.

cheeks, lips, tongue, and the penis, the blood being spattered on paper or used to anoint the idols. On the eve of the Conquest such idols were censed with copal and rubber as well as ritually fed. Human sacrifice was perpetrated on prisoners, slaves, and above all on children (bastards or orphans bought for the occasion). Nevertheless, before the Toltec era, animals rather than people may have been the more common victims, and we know that such creatures as wild turkeys, dogs, squirrels, quail, and iguanas were considered fit offerings for the Maya gods.

Our understanding of the Yucatecan ritual round is crippled by Landa's sporadic inability to distinguish between what he called 'movable feasts', *i.e.* rites determined by the 260-day count, and those geared to the nineteen months of the 365-day Vague Year. But apparently the greatest ceremonies had to do with the inauguration of the New Year. These took place in every community within the Uayeb, the five unnamed and unlucky days at the close of the previous year, and involved the construction of a special road (perhaps like the Classic 'causeways') to idols placed at a certain cardinal point just outside the town limits; a new direction was chosen each year in a four-year counterclockwise circuit. There were all sorts of omens, good or bad, for every year, but an inauspicious augury could be offset by expiatory rites, such as the well-known fire-walking ceremony in which priests ran barefoot over a bed of red-hot coals.

Throughout the year, there were agricultural rites and ceremonies for such important economic groups as hunters, beekeepers, fishermen, and artisans, probably geared to the 260-day count if we may rely on the testimony of the Madrid Codex, which seems mainly devoted to such matters. Increase of game, abundance of honey and wax, and so forth were the purpose of these activities, which so often take the form of the 'sympathetic magic' defined by Sir James Frazer, for instance compelling the rain to fall by having the Chacs empty water from pots onto a fire.

Despite past claims that Classic Maya societies were organized as theocracies, that is, as states ruled by priests, there is not the slightest evidence for the existence of priests in Classic times! That role was seemingly played by the élite – the rulers and nobility – and by the scribes. David Stuart has recently isolated in Classic ceramic texts the title for scribe (*ah dzib*) and has demonstrated that on one vase ascribed to Naranjo, the scribe/artist had signed his name as a royal prince from

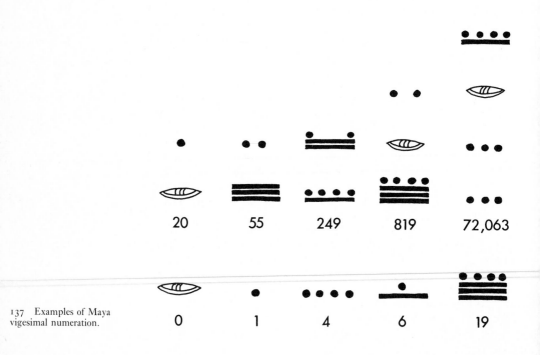

137 Examples of Maya vigesimal numeration.

that city. And the discovery at Copán of a magnificent scribal palace, complete with Monkey-man God sculptures, shows the exalted status that these devotees of Hun Batz and Hun Chuen occupied in ancient times. Probably all knowledge of writing, the calendar, astronomy, and the esoteric world of the supernatural was in their hands. The institution of priesthood must therefore have been introduced to the Maya by the Toltec.

The Classic élite were obsessed with blood, both their own and that spilled by high-ranking captives. Hieroglyphic and iconographic studies, particularly by David Joralemon and David Stuart, have shown the supreme significance of ritually shed blood by the Classic Maya rulers and their families. This was drawn at calendrically important intervals by men from the penis, and from the tongue by their wives. The penis-perforator was usually a stingray spine or bone 'awl' and seems to have been ritually adorned and deified. Scenes on stelae once thought to have been concerned with water or maize kernels cascading from the lowered hands of rulers are now known to portray blood dripping from their mutilated members. Further, Stuart has demonstrated that the so-called 'water prefix', a constant element in Emblem Glyphs, also stands for blood. Thus, 'blood' signified noble lineage and descent, as it traditionally did in Europe.

Numbers and the calendar

Otto Neugebauer, the historian of science, considers positional, or place-value, numeration as 'one of the most fertile inventions of humanity', comparable in a way with the invention of the alphabet. Instead of the clumsy, additive numbers used by the Roman and so many other cultures of the world, a few peoples have adopted ' a system whereby the position of a number symbol determines its value and consequently a limited number of symbols suffices to express numbers, however large, without the need for repetitions or creation of higher new symbols.'

The Maya, and probably the Olmec and Zapotec before them, operated with only three such symbols: the dot for one, the bar for five 137 and a stylized shell for nought. Unlike our system adopted from the Hindus, which is decimal and increasing in value from right to left, the Maya was vigesimal and increased from bottom to top in vertical columns. Thus, the first and lowest place has a value of one; the next above it the value of twenty; then 400; and so on. It is immediately apparent that 'twenty' would be written with a nought in the first place and a dot in the second, although it also had a symbol of its own. Professor Sánchez has demonstrated the ease with which calculations like addition and subtraction could be carried out in the system, but has also suggested in contradiction to others that multiplication and division, although not mentioned in the sources, would also have been possible.

And what kind of calculations were made, and for what purposes? Landa says that the purely vigesimal notation was used by merchants, especially those dealing in cacao, and he mentions that computations were performed 'on the ground or on a flat surface' by means of

a   b   c   d   e   f

138   Glyphs for the cycles of the Long Count. *a*, Introducing Glyph; *b*, baktun; *c*, katun; *d*, tun; *e*, uinal; *f*, kin.

counters, presumably cacao beans, maize grains and the like. But the major use to which Maya arithmetic was put was calendrical, for which a modification was introduced: when days were counted, the values of the places were those of the Long Count, so that while the first two places had values of one and twenty respectively, the third was thought of as a *tun* of 360 days (18 × 20), and so on up the line. For operating within their incredibly involved calendar, which among other things included the permutation of the Long Count with the 52-year Calendar Round, the Maya scribes found it necessary to construct tables of multiples; in the Dresden Codex, such tables include multiples of 13, 52, 65, 78, and 91 (the nearest whole number approximating one quarter of a year). Fractions find no place in their system – they were always trying to reach equations of cycles in which all numbers are integers, *e.g.* 73 × 260 days equals 52 × 365 days.

138   There are several kinds of dates expressed on the Classic Maya monuments and in the Dresden manuscript. Leading off a typical Classic inscription is the Initial Series, a Long Count date preceded by an Introductory Glyph with one of the nineteen month-gods infixed. This is immediately followed by the day reached in the 260-day count, and, after an interval filled by several other glyphs, the day of the month (365-day count). The intervening glyphs indicated which of the nine gods of the underworld is ruling over that day (in a cycle of nine days), and lunar calculations which will be considered later.

However, this is not the whole story, for there are usually a number of other dates on the same monument. These are reached by Distance Numbers, which tell one to count forwards or backwards by so many days from the base date, and while the intervals are usually of modest length, in a few examples these span millions of years. And then there are Period Ending Dates in the inscriptions, which commemorate the completion of a katun, half-katun ('lahuntun', that is, ten tuns), quarter-katun ('hotun'), or tun. As an example one might cite the katun ending 9.18.0.0.0, which was celebrated all over the Central Area. 'Anniversaries' also dot the Classic inscriptions; these are Calendar Round dates falling at intervals of so many katuns or tuns from some date other than the above-mentioned Period Ending Dates.

Why this apparent obsession with dating and the calendar? What do all the dates on the Classic monuments mean? They were formerly explained as the work of priests working out the positions of calendrical and celestial cycles in a religion which was essentially the worship of time itself. As we shall see, an utterly different explanation is not only possible, but probable.

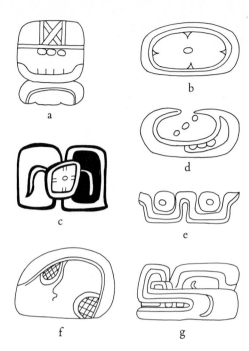

139 Glyphs for the earth and the heavenly bodies in the codices. *a, Caan*, the Sky; *b, Kin*, the Sun; *c*, solar eclipse; *d, U*, the Moon; *e, Nohoch Ek*, Venus; *f, Cab*, the Earth; *g*, believed to be Mars.

The sun and the moon

To the Maya the round of 365 days – 18 months of 20 days plus the 5 extra days of the Uayeb – was as close to the solar year as they cared to get. This 'Vague Year' began among the Yucatec of Landa's time on 16 July (Julian calendar). Yet the earth actually takes about $365\frac{1}{4}$ days to complete its journey about the sun, so that the Vague Year must have continually advanced on the solar year, gradually putting the months out of phase with the seasons. We know that none of the Maya intercalated days on Leap Years or the like, as we do, and it has been shown that more sophisticated corrections thought to have been made by them are a figment of the imagination. Yet their lunar inscriptions show that they must have had an unusually accurate idea of the real length of the Tropical Year.

Curiously, the Maya went to far greater trouble with the erratic moon. In the inscriptions, Initial Series dates are followed by the so-called Lunar Series, which contains up to eight glyphs dealing with the cycles of that body. One of these records whether the current lunar month was of 29 or 30 days, and another tells the age of the moon on that particular Long Count date. Naturally, the Maya, like all civilized peoples, were faced with the problem of coordinating their lunar calendar with the solar, but there is slight indication that they used the 19-year Metonic cycle (on which the 'Golden Number' in the Book of Common Prayer is based). Instead, from the mid-fourth century AD each center made its own correction to correlate the two. However, in AD 682 the scribes of Copán began calculating with the formula 149 moons = 4,400 days, a system which was eventually adopted by almost

139d

all the Maya centers. In our terms, they figured a lunation to average 29.53020 days, remarkably close to the actual value 29.53059!

Of great interest to Mayanists and astronomers alike have been the eclipse tables recorded on seven pages of the Dresden Codex. These cover a cycle of 405 lunations or 11,960 days, which conveniently enough equals 46 × 260 days – a kind of formula with which the Maya were deeply concerned, for such equations enabled them to coordinate the movements of the heavenly bodies with their most sacred ritual period. The ancients had found out, at least by the mid-eighth century AD but possibly much earlier, that lunar and solar eclipses could only occur within plus or minus 18 days of the node (when the moon's path crosses the apparent path of the sun); and this is what the tables are, a statement of when such events were likely. They also seem to have been aware of the recession of the node (or at least of its effect over long periods of time), and Eric Thompson suggested that the tables were constructed anew every half-century or so.

139*c*

The celestial wanderers and the stars

Venus is the only one of the planets for which we can be absolutely sure the Maya made calculations. Unlike the Greeks of the Homeric age, they knew that with the Evening and Morning Stars they were dealing with the same object. For the apparent, or synodical, Venus year they used the figure of 584 days (the actual value is 583.92, but they were close enough!), divided into four periods of varying length – Venus as Morning Star, disappearance at superior conjunction, appearance as Evening Star, and disappearance at inferior conjunction. After five Venus 'years' its cycle met with the solar round, for 5 × 584 = 8 × 365 = 2,920 days. Such an eight-year table can be found in the Dresden Codex and in the recently discovered Grolier Codex.

Some have questioned whether the movements of planets other than Venus were observed by the Maya, but it is hard to believe that one of the Dresden tables, listing multiples of 78, can be anything other than a table for Mars, which has a synodic year of 780 days; or that the Maya intellectuals could have overlooked the fact that 117, the product of the magic numbers 9 and 13, approximates the length of the Mercury 'year' (116 days). It has even been suggested that Jupiter was of interest to them. They were, of course, astrologers not astronomers, and all these bodies which were seen to wander against the background of the stars must have influenced the destiny of prince and pauper among the Maya.

Potentially the most significant new breakthrough along these lines has been the confirmation by Floyd Lounsbury of Yale University of the exact correlation between the Maya and Christian calendars, long a bone of contention. Any valid correlation has to fit two historical facts: one is that Bishop Landa stated that 16 July, AD 1553 (Julian) was the Calendar Round day 12 Kan 1 Pop in the late Yucatecan Maya calendar (this would have been 11 Akbal 1 Pop in the Classic system); the other is that the Spanish Conquest of Yucatán began in a katun which ended on a day 13 Ahau. The two currently rival correlations are one which would have this correspond to the Long Count date 11.3.0.0.0 13 Ahau

– espoused by some archaeologists working in Yucatán, but impossible since it violates the Landa equation – and one corresponding to 11.16.0.0.0 13 Ahau, long championed by Eric Thompson.

That Thompson was correct is demonstrated not only by this and other historical information from Post-Classic Yucatán, but also by the Dresden Codex itself. The eclipse predictions tables of this book forecast a solar eclipse on 9.16.4.10.8 12 Lamat 1 Muan; given the first Thompson correlation (he successively advocated three during his lifetime, each a day apart from the other), this would be 8 November AD 755 in the Julian calendar – the precise date of a lunar-solar conjunction! No other correlation satisfies this requirement. Furthermore, Lounsbury has shown that the base number of the Venus Table as given in the Dresden Codex (9.9.9.16.0 1 Ahau 18 Kayab) is contrived; as usual with such carefully chosen dates, it contains many integral multiples of important calendrical components. 1 Ahau was important throughout Mesoamerica as the conceptual heliacal rising of the deified Venus (that is, its rising just ahead of the sun on the eastern horizon following its disappearance in inferior conjunction).

This contrived base date had been projected backwards in time from the *real* base of the Dresden Venus Table, namely 10.18.9.15.0. Using the first Thompson correlation again, this was 20 November, AD 934, a red-letter day on which *both* Venus and Mars rose heliacally with each other in the east, on a day 1 Ahau 18 Kayab. Such an extraordinarily rare celestial event must have seared itself into the Maya astronomical mind.

With the correlation now fixed, it should be possible, by consulting modern astronomical tables, to test the hypothesis, long held by David Kelley, that the Classic Maya inscriptions contain references to the heavenly bodies, above and beyond the lunar data which customarily follow initial Long Count dates on Maya stelae. Lounsbury has found confirmation of this hypothesis at the famous site of Bonampak, renowned for its murals. The Long Count position of the date associated with the great battle scene corresponds to 2 August, AD 792 (Julian); the tables tell us that this date was marked by the Inferior Conjunction of Venus, by a zenith passage of the sun (as it passes directly overhead on its way to its winter 'home'), and by the conjunction of Venus with the star Regulus.

That Venus played a sanguinary role among the Maya similar to that of Mars in the western Old World can be seen in the glyph for war: a Venus sign over another element, sometimes the Emblem Glyph of the site attacked. The date selected by the Bonampak astronomers for this martial action was, in the words of Professor Lounsbury, 'apparently seen as a propitious date for the undertaking, the outcome of which was such as to confirm the opinion'. Likewise, the first visibility of Venus as Evening Star on 29 November, AD 735, set off an attack on the southern Petén site of Seibal by two of its rivals, leading to the capture of its ruler the next day. This unfortunate was kept alive for another twelve years, finally being sacrificed at a ritual ball game timed for an inferior conjunction of Venus. 'Star Wars' indeed!

Jupiter was also taken into account by the Classic Maya: the accession, at age forty-nine, and apotheosis twenty-one years later of the great Palenque ruler Chan-Bahlum was set by the planet's second station (the end of its retrograde or east-to-west movement against the background of the stars).

The astronomer Anthony Aveni and the architect Horst Hartung have determined that the ancient Maya used buildings and doorways and windows within them for astronomical sightings, especially of Venus. At Uxmal, for instance, all buildings are aligned in the same direction, except the House of the Governor. A perpendicular taken from the central doorway of this structure reaches a solitary mound about $3\frac{1}{2}$ miles away; Venus would have risen precisely above the mound when the planet reached its southerly extreme in AD 750. In collaboration with Sharon Gibbs, they have shown that in the case of the Caracol at Chichén Itzá, the whole building is aligned to the northerly extremes of Venus at about AD 1000, as is a diagonal sightline in one of the windows of the tower top; another diagonal sightline matched the planet's setting position when it attained its maximum southerly declination.

The Chaldean and Egyptian astrologers divided up the sky in various ways, each sector corresponding to a supposed figure of stars, so as to check the march of the sun as it retrogrades from sector to sector through the year, and to provide a star clock for the night hours. The zodiac of Mesopotamia is the best known of such systems. Did the Maya have anything like it? On this subject there is little agreement, but some have seen an indication of a partial zodiac on a damaged page of the Paris Codex, which shows a scorpion, turtle, and rattlesnake pendant from a celestial band. Very little is known of star lore among the Maya, but they did have constellations called *tzab* ('rattlesnake rattle', the Pleiades) and *ac* ('turtle', made up of stars in Gemini), with which they could tell the time of night; so a 'zodiac' is quite probable.

The nature of Maya writing

Notable advances have been made in epigraphy, and it is probably not exaggerating to say that as much as 85 per cent of the total body of Classic Maya inscriptions can now be 'read' – 'read' in the sense that we understand their meaning with some precision if not always how they were pronounced in Maya. This means that the ancient Maya are now the only truly historical civilization in the New World, with records going back to the third century after Christ.

Thirty years ago, however, it could truly be said that few studies had made such little advancement with so much effort as the decipherment of the Maya script. This is not to say that a great deal was not understood, but there is a difference between unraveling a meaning for a sign, and matching it with a word in the Maya tongue. Progress was most rapid on those glyphs which were of mainly calendrical or astronomical significance. For instance, by the mid-nineteenth century the Abbé Brasseur de Bourbourg had discovered Landa's *Relación*, from which he was able to recognize day glyphs and interpret the bar-and-dot numeration in the codices. It was quickly discovered that Maya writing was to be read in double columns from left to right, and top to bottom. At the turn of the century all of the following had been

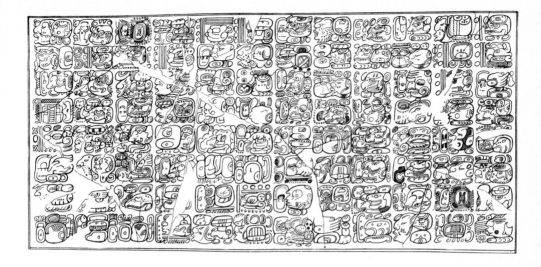

correctly deciphered by scholars in Europe and America: the zero and 'twenty' signs, the world directions and the colors, Venus, the months (also in Landa), and the Long Count. In a remarkable collaboration between astronomers and epigraphers, the mysteries of the Lunar Series had been unveiled by the early 1930s. But after these intellectual triumphs, fewer and fewer successes were scored, leading a few pessimists such as Sylvanus Morley and Eric Thompson to the quite unfounded claim that there was little else in these texts but calendrical and astronomical mumbo-jumbo.

140   Tablet of the 96 Hieroglyphs, from Palenque. A very long text of the Late Classic period, marking the first katun anniversary of the accession to the throne by Lord Kuk ('Quetzal') in AD 764. The text is completely historical, containing Kuk's pedigree.

If we accept as a basic premise that there is some kind of system in the glyphs used in the non-calendrical texts, then there are a limited number of possibilities as to what this might be. In a system of pictographs, every sign is but a picture of the thing referred to; for some primitive peoples of the world, this suffices. However, one cannot draw a picture of everything which one might wish to communicate over long distances and through time. Accordingly, as Professor Lounsbury points out, every known script which is not merely pictographic has proceeded in two ways, that is, has moved in the semantic and the phonetic dimensions.

Moving semantically, to express a concept not easily visualized, one would picture something related to it, for instance a representation of a fire to express the word 'hot'; almost all the world's scripts have adopted this principle at some time in their evolution. In its purest form, such a system could be called ideographic, and could be 'read' without reference to any particular language. Numbers such as our own Arabic ones are also ideographs for which all sorts of people have separate terms; so were the bars and dots of the Mesoamericans.

However, completely ideographic writing systems are virtually unknown, since most literate peoples have attempted to reduce the ambiguities which would be proliferated in them. Instead, there have been many developments along the phonetic dimension. Rebus or puzzle writing is the simplest form of this, in which an ideograph is now employed for its sound value, as the sign for 'fire' could be utilized in English as a sign meaning to 'fire' or sack a subordinate. As children we have all run across such examples of rebus writing as 'I saw Aunt Rose,' all expressed in pictographs, and for peoples like the Mixtec and Aztec, this was apparently the only script they knew.

However, there yet remain many uncertainties in even a rebus system. Most ancient scripts, like the Chinese, Sumerian, and Egyptian, are properly called 'logographic', in that each hieroglyph usually expresses a whole word which may be an ideograph or rebus sign, but which more often combines *both* semantic and phonetic components into a single compound sign. One of these compound types is a phonetic rebus to which a semantic determinant is added. The other is a semantic (that is, ideographic) sign linked to a phonetic complement. In time, as the language changes, the phonetic side of the script becomes less and less obvious, as with Chinese. But the real trouble with logographic systems (to Western eyes, at least) is their sheer unwieldiness – to be literate in Chinese one must memorize at least 7,000 'characters'. The process of simplification necessarily concentrates on phoneticism, generally deriving something like a syllabary from the phonetic signs; since the phonemes, the smallest units for distinctive sound speech, are very much limited in any tongue, so are the number of signs in the syllabary. And finally, the alphabet arises as all the phonemes become separately distinguished, instead of appearing as syllables of the consonant-vowel sort. This is the ultimate step in the reduction of a writing system.

With these preliminary remarks, what kind of a system do we then find in the Maya script? Bishop Landa has given to us his famous 'alphabet' in which some twenty-nine signs are presented. Several extremely distinguished Maya scholars have stumbled badly in trying to read the codices and the inscriptions with Landa's treacherous 'ABC', while some have gone so far as to declare it a complete fraud. A more careful examination suggests that this is really not an alphabet in the usual sense. For instance, there are three signs for 'A', two for 'B', two for 'L'. Secondly, several signs are quite clearly glossed as syllables of the consonant-vowel sort, i.e. *ma*, *ca*, and *cu*. We shall consider this important point later.

After the almost complete failure of decipherments along the strictly phonetic lines suggested by the Landa 'alphabet', a diametrically opposite line was taken by many authorities, namely that the script was purely ideographic, with perhaps a few rebus signs imbedded in the texts from time to time. That is to say, any one sign could have as many referents or associations as the priests could think up, and that only they could read the holy signs, which in general character were more ritualistic than linguistic. There is a striking resemblance between this position and that of the would-be decipherers of the Egyptian script before the great discoveries of Champollion.

This resemblance was not lost upon the Soviet epigrapher Yuri Knorosov, a student of Egyptian hieroglyphic writing. In 1952, he began publishing a series of studies which has re-opened the question of the Landa 'alphabet' and the possibility of phoneticism in the Maya script. About 287 signs, not including variants, appear in the codices. If

141

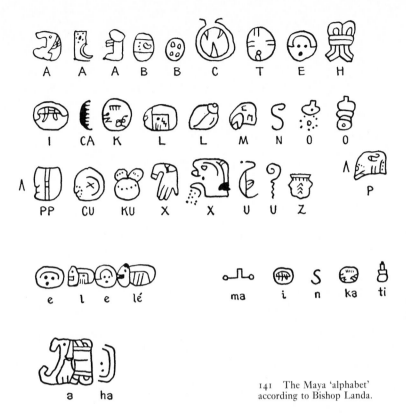

141 The Maya 'alphabet' according to Bishop Landa.

the system were completely alphabetic, then the language of the texts would have contained this many phonemes; if purely syllabic, then there would have been about half this number of phonemes. Both are linguistic impossibilities. On the other hand, if all signs were ideograms – representing units of meaning only – then the script represented an incredibly small number of ideas, certainly not enough for civilized communication. With this in mind, Knorosov presented convincing evidence that the Maya were writing in a mixed, logographic system in which phonetic and semantic elements were combined as in Sumerian or Chinese, but that they also had a fairly complete syllabary.

Knorosov's starting point was Landa's 'ABC'. Thompson had already demonstrated that the bishop's native informant had mistaken his instructions, that is, he gave the Maya sign not for the letter itself, but for the names of the letters; see, for instance, the first 'B', which shows a footprint on a road – 'road' is *be* in Yucatec, and this is exactly what the Spaniards call that letter. But the point is that this is really a partial and much flawed syllabary, not an alphabet, and Knorosov was able to show that words of the very frequent consonant-vowel-consonant (CVC) sort were written with two syllabic signs standing for CV-CV, the final vowel (usually the same as the first) not being pronounced. The proof of phonetic-syllabic writing is, of course, in the reading, and a number of Knorosov's readings have been confirmed by 142

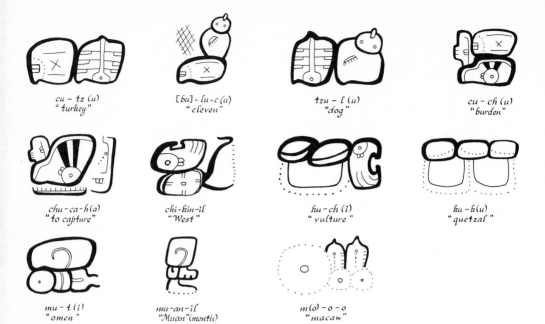

cu – tz (u) "turkey"	[bu] – lu – c (u) "eleven"	tzu – l (u) "dog"	cu – ch (u) "burden"
chu – ca – h (a) "to capture"	chi – kin – il "West"	ku – ch (i) "vulture"	ku – k (u) "quetzal"
mu – t (i) "omen"	mu – an – il "Muan" (month)	m (o) – o – o "macaw"	

142 Phonetic-syllabic readings of Maya signs given by Y. V. Knorosov.

the contexts in which the signs appear in the codices, especially by the pictures which accompany various passages of text.

If this were all that needed to be done, it would be a simple job to read the Maya hieroglyphs, but the semantic dimension is very much there. There is a strong hint that phonetic complements were often attached to ideograms to help in their reading, either prefixed as a representation of the initial sound of the sign, or postfixed as the final consonant; these, if recognized, would notably advance the process of decipherment. Phonetic redundancy of this sort was already being practiced in the Classic; for example, David Kelley was the first to notice that the name of the great Palenque ruler Pacal ('Hand-shield') could be written either as a picture of a hand-shield, or phonetically as *pa-ca-l(a)*, or both.

Although ridiculed by Thompson and his followers, Knorosov's phonetic approach is now almost universally utilized by Maya epigraphers. Since the initial work of Knorosov and Kelley, the recognition of phonetic construction in the script has proceeded at such a pace that participants in a conference held in Albany in 1979 were able to draw up a list of almost 100 signs that had phonetic value (some of them, of course, allographs for one and the same syllable). It is also now recognized that in Maya, as in many ancient scripts, a number of signs are polyvalent, that is, a particular sign may have more than one phonetic reading, and it may also be read for its ideographic value.

The content of Maya writing

All four codices deal exclusively with religious and astronomical matters, as is quite obvious from the pictures of gods associated with the texts, from the tables, and from the high frequency of passages geared to the 260-day count. Thus, we have in these texts little more than short phrases of esoteric significance, surely to be read in an archaic Yucatec, which often seem to match passages in the Books of Chilam Balam.

What, then, of the subject matter of the inscriptions? Until quite recently, the prevailing opinion was that this was in no way different from that of the books; and further, that all those dates recorded on the monuments were witnesses to some sort of cult in which the time periods themselves were deified. The great John Lloyd Stephens was of a different mind, writing about Copán:

> One thing I believe, that its history is graven on its monuments. No Champollion has yet brought to them the energies of his enquiring mind. Who shall read them?

The discovery within the last few decades of the historical nature of the monumental inscriptions has been one of the most exciting chapters in the story of New World archaeology.

It began in 1958, when Heinrich Berlin published evidence that there was a special kind of sign, the so-called 'Emblem Glyph', associated with specific archaeological sites, and recognizable from the same kind of glyphic elements which appear affixed to each. Thus far, the Emblem Glyphs for a number of Classic centers – including Tikal, Piedras Negras, Copán, Quiriguá, Seibal, Naranjo, Palenque, and Yaxchilán – have been surely identified. Berlin suggested that these were either the names of the 'cities' themselves or of the dynasties which ruled over them, and proposed that on the stelae and other monuments of these sites their histories might be recorded.

The next breakthrough was by Tatiana Proskouriakoff of the Carnegie Institution, who analyzed thirty-five dated monuments from Piedras Negras. The arrangement of stelae before structures she found was not random; rather, they fell into seven groups. Within a single such group, the time span covered by all the dates on the stelae is never longer than an average lifetime, which immediately raised the possibility that each group was the record of a single reign. This has

143 Some Emblem Glyphs from the Classic monuments. *a*, Tikal; *b*, Naranjo; *c*, Yaxchilán; *d*, Piedras Negras; *e*, Palenque; *f*, Seibal; *g*, Copán; *h*, Quiriguá.

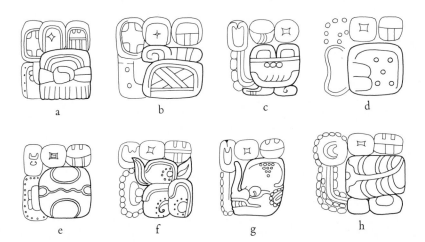

a   b   c   d

e   f   g   h

a   b   c

144 Historical glyphs in the
monumental texts. *a*,
Birthday Glyph; *b*, Accession
Glyph; *c*, 'Shield Jaguar'; *d*,
'Bird Jaguar'; *e*, prefix for
female names and titles.

d   e

now proved to be so. The first monument in a series shows a figure,
usually a young man, seated in a niche above a platform or plinth; on
this stela two important dates are inscribed. One is associated with a
glyph like an animal's head with a toothache, and has been shown to
record the accession to power of the young man; the other appears with
the 'up-ended frog' glyph and is that same person's date of birth. Later
monuments in a particular group celebrate marriages and the birth of
offspring, and Proskouriakoff has been able to identify the signs for
personal names and titles, particularly of women who are quite
prominent in Classic Maya sculpture. Military victories were also
marked with great frequency, especially if an important enemy
happened to have been taken captive by the ruler.

Thus, the figures which appear in Classic reliefs are not gods and
priests but dynastic autocrats and their spouses, children, and
subordinates. As the records for one reign come to an end, the next
begin with the usual accession motif. Among the more complete
documents which we have for the temporal dynasties which ran the
ancient Maya centers are the inscriptions carved on the many stone
lintels of Yaxchilán; from these Proskouriakoff has reconstructed the
history of the extremely militant 'Jaguar' dynasty, which ruled the site
in the eighth century AD. The record begins with the exploits of a lord
called 'Shield Jaguar'; he was succeeded in AD 752 by 'Bird Jaguar'
(both these names recall the double names of the Yucatec – matronymic
followed by patronymic), who was probably his son. As an example of
how much of the writing that accompanies the reliefs celebrating the
victories of this ruler can now be read or at least interpreted, we have
Lintel 8 of Yaxchilán, which begins with a Calendar Round date falling
in AD 755. Below this is Knorosov's *chucah* or 'capture' glyph, then a
glyph resembling a jeweled skull, which is obviously the name of the
prisoner on the right. Above right, the second glyph is that of the Bird
Jaguar himself (the figure with spear), beneath which is the Emblem
Glyph of Yaxchilán.

Of special interest are those inscriptions which indicate the
interference of some centers with the destinies of others. For instance,

68

144*b*

144*e*

72

145
142

143*c*

the Yaxchilán Emblem Glyph appears with one of the most prominent women in the Bonampak frescoes, and, thanks to a royal marriage, the glyph for Tikal appears quite frequently on monuments at Naranjo. Piedras Negras is not far downstream from Yaxchilán, and the famous Lintel 3 from that site is now believed to show a Yaxchilán ruler presiding over a council called in the late eighth century to choose a successor to the Piedras Negras throne.

In 1973, Linda Schele and Peter Mathews were able to announce at a conference in Palenque that they had worked out the dynastic record of all the Palenque rulers going back to AD 465; this record has later been refined by them and Floyd Lounsbury. Thanks to their research, we can now place such important figures as Pacal and Chan-Bahlum in relation to the stupendous art and architecture that was created for them. Palenque, like Yaxchilán, had entered into the realm of history.

Important glyphs now known to relate to dynastic affairs include the signs for events such as battles (the 'star-shell' glyph), taking of office, inauguration or 'seating' in office, ritual blood-letting, and death, in addition to the birth and accession glyphs. As one would expect with ruling families obsessed with noble lineage and marriage affiliation, there are a number of relationship glyphs which have recently been recognized, such as 'child of father', 'child of mother', 'child of parent', and 'wife' (*atan* in Maya), as well as a sign expressing the relationship (unpleasant in the extreme) between a local dynast and an important captive whom he had taken.

Thanks to advances in Maya dynastic history, scholars are now gaining some idea of how the Central Area was governed in Classic

145 Lintel 8, Yaxchilán. A record of the capture of 'Jeweled Skull' and one other enemy by 'Bird Jaguar' and a companion.

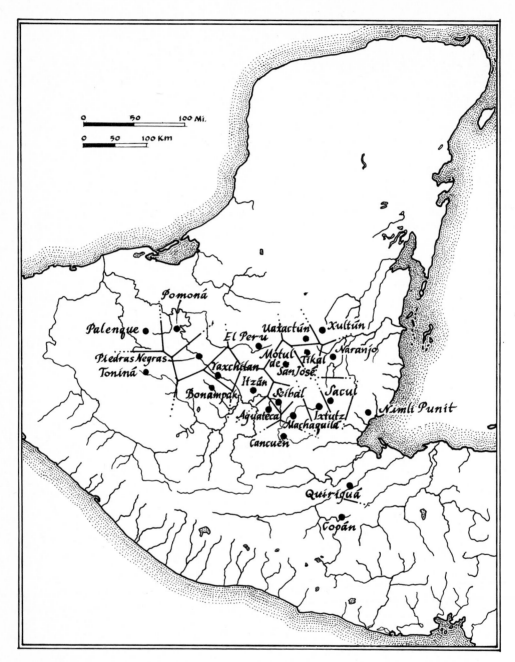

146 Political geography of the Central Maya Area at AD 790, based on the distribution of cities with Emblem Glyphs. Boundaries are only approximate. The southern lowlands were characterized by rival city-states, with none having hegemony over the rest.

times. From earliest times until the Classic downfall and the coming of the Toltec to Yucatán, there was never any overall authority among the ancient Maya. Based upon the analysis of sites with Emblem Glyphs, the epigrapher Peter Mathews has drawn a political geography of the 146 Central Area during the Classic which bears a striking resemblance to post-Mayapan Yucatán: this was no 'Old Empire', to use Morley's outdated phrase, but a series of city-states with constantly shifting alliances and hostilities. By the last centuries of the Classic, the highest goal of these lineage-proud dynasts was to capture the ruler of a rival city-state in battle, to torture and humiliate him (sometimes for years), and then to subject him to decapitation following a ball game which the prisoner was always destined to lose.

If this is all history, then why the Lunar Series and the calculations far into the past and future? Because the Classic Maya élite believed in astrology, and must have consulted their scribes for lunar and other cosmic auguries at every important civil event, as did the Babylonians, Etruscans, Egyptians, and many other peoples of the Old World. There is a logic to astrology which not only the ancients have found compelling – Kepler and Newton did likewise – so we need not condemn the Maya for their beliefs. Another Maya concern was with lineage, and we find figures and dates on some monuments which can only refer to distant ancestors.

Thus, Berlin showed that the dates in inscriptions of the Temple of 75 the Cross at Palenque fall into three groups. The first are so ancient that they could only be referring back to deified ancestors of a legendary epoch; the next may have to do with distant progenitors of a more intermediate time; and the third are connected with contemporary historical events.

It will be remembered that the tablet of the Temple of the Cross celebrates the accession to the throne by Lord Chan-Bahlum following the death of his predecessor, Lord Pacal, in AD 683. Now, Pacal was born on a day 8 Ahau in the 260-day count. The very earliest date on the tablet is 3,722 years earlier, and also falls on a day 8 Ahau, which in itself is suspicious. Professor Lounsbury has demonstrated that on this initial date, a mythical ancestress was born, but in addition the interval between her birth and that of Pacal – 1,359,540 days – is an integral multiple of seven different important Maya periods, including the synodic period of Mars! It is inescapable that the initial date was thus contrived to fit the needs of numerology and astrology, thus intertwining religion, genealogy, and history in the characteristic Maya style.

So far, no Champollion has appeared who could read the Maya inscriptions *in toto*. But it should be remembered that it was the identification of personal names and titles in the Egyptian script that enabled that great scholar to do what he did. Indeed, the recognition of the real subject matter of the Maya monumental texts has opened the way to their complete decipherment.

Select bibliography

For an early but comprehensive list of works on Maya archaeology, the reader is referred to 'Bibliografía de Arqueología y Etnografía: Mesoamérica y Norte de México, 1514–1960' by Ignacio Bernal (*Instituto Nacional de Antropología e Historia, Memorias*, VII, Mexico 1962), which contains over 3,800 titles on the subject. I have tried to concentrate on those articles and volumes which I have found most useful in the preparation of this book, and which might be of interest to those wishing to follow certain topics further.

Chapter 1
General works on Mesoamerica and the Maya

BAUDEZ, CLAUDE-FRANÇOIS, and PIERRE BECQUELIN. *Les Mayas*. Paris 1984.
BENSON, ELIZABETH P. *The Maya World*. Revised edition. New York 1977.
BLOM, FRANS, and OLIVER LA FARGE. *Tribes and Temples*, 2 vols. New Orleans 1926.
COVARRUBIAS, MIGUEL. *Indian Art of Mexico and Central America*. New York 1957.
FERGUSON, WILLIAM M., and JOHN Q. ROYCE. *Maya Ruins of Mexico in Color*. Norman, Oklahoma 1977.
—, *Maya Ruins in Central America in Color*. Albuquerque 1984.
HAMMOND, NORMAN. *Ancient Maya Civilization*. New Brunswick and Cambridge, England 1982.
—, (ed.). *Social Process in Maya Prehistory*. London and New York 1977. (Contains 25 essays, including three on the Maya collapse.)
HENDERSON, JOHN S. *The World of the Ancient Maya*. Ithaca 1981.
HOLMES, WILLIAM H. *Archaeological Studies Among the Ancient Cities of Mexico*, 2 vols. Chicago 1895–7.
KIRCHHOFF, PAUL. 'Meso-America', in *Heritage of Conquest*, ed. Sol Tax, 17–30. Glencoe, Illinois 1952.
MARQUINA, IGNACIO. *Arquitectura Prehispánica*. Mexico 1951.
MAUDSLAY, ALFRED P. *Biología Centrali-Americana, Archaeology*. Text and 4 vols. of plates. London 1889–1902.
MILLER, MARY ELLEN. *The Art of Mesoamerica from Olmec to Aztec*. London and New York 1986.

MORLEY, SYLVANUS G., and GEORGE W. BRAINERD. *The Ancient Maya*. Fourth edition, revised by Robert J. Sharer. Stanford 1983.
PROSKOURIAKOFF, TATIANA. 'An album of Maya architecture', *Carnegie Institution of Washington*, publ. 558. Washington 1946.
RIESE, BERTHOLD. *Geschichte der Maya*. Stuttgart.
SCHELE, LINDA, and MARY E. MILLER. *The Blood of Kings: Dynasty and Ritual in Maya Art*. Fort Worth 1986. (The definitive statement of what is now known about Maya art and culture.)
SPINDEN, HERBERT J. 'A study of Maya art', *Memoirs of the Peabody Museum of Archaeology and Ethnology, Harvard University*, vol. 6. Cambridge 1913.
STEPHENS, JOHN L. *Incidents of Travel in Central America, Chiapas, and Yucatán*, 2 vols. New York 1841.
—, *Incidents of Travel in Yucatán*, 2 vols. New York 1843.
STIERLIN, HENRI. *Maya: Guatemala, Honduras et Yucatán*. Fribourg 1964.
STUART, GEORGE C. and GENE S. STUART. *The Mysterious Maya*. Washington 1977.
THE MAYA AND THEIR NEIGHBORS. Dedicated to Alfred M. Tozzer. New York 1941.
THOMPSON, J. ERIC S. *The Rise and Fall of Maya Civilization*. Norman 1954.
TOZZER, ALFRED M. (ed.). 'Landa's Relación de las Cosas de Yucatán', *Papers of the Peabody Museum of Archaeology and Ethnology, Harvard University*, vol. 18. Cambridge 1941. (Thanks to the extensive notes which accompany Landa's text, this is virtually an encyclopedia of ancient Maya life.)

The setting

FLANNERY, KENT V. (ed.). *Maya Subsistence*. New York 1982.
HARRISON, PETER D., and B. L. TURNER II (eds.). *Pre-Hispanic Maya Agriculture*. Albuquerque 1978.
MCBRYDE, FELIX W. 'Cultural and historical geography of southwest Guatemala', *Smithsonian Institution, Institute of Social Anthropology*, publ. no. 4. Washington 1945.
WRIGHT, A. C. S., *et al*. *Land in British Honduras*. London 1959.

Maya linguistic distributions

JUSTESON, JOHN S., *et al. The Foreign Impact on Lowland Mayan Language and Script.* New Orleans 1985.

MCQUOWN, NORMAN A. 'The classification of the Maya languages', *International Journal of American Linguistics*, vol. 22 (1956), 191–5.

SWADESH, MAURICE. 'Interrelaciones de las lenguas mayenses', *Anales del Instituto Nacional de Antropología e Historia*, XIII, 231–67. Mexico 1961.

Chapter 2

BRAINERD, GEORGE W. 'The archaeological ceramics of Yucatán', *Anthropological Records*, 19. Berkeley and Los Angeles 1958.

COE, MICHAEL D. 'A fluted point from highland Guatemala', *American Antiquity*, vol. 25, no. 3 (1960), 412–13.

—, 'La Victoria, an early site on the Pacific coast of Guatemala', *Papers of the Peabody Museum of Archaeology and Ethnology, Harvard University*, vol. 53. Cambridge 1961.

COE, MICHAEL D., and RICHARD A. DIEHL. *In the Land of the Olmec*, 2 vols. Austin 1980.

COE, MICHAEL D., and KENT V. FLANNERY. *Early Cultures and Human Ecology in South Coastal Guatemala.* Washington 1967.

MACNEISH, RICHARD S. 'The origins of New World civilization', *Scientific American*, vol. 211, no. 5 (1964), 29–37.

MACNEISH, RICHARD S. and FREDRICK A. PETERSON, 'The Santa Marta Rock Shelter, Ocozocoautla, Chiapas, Mexico', *Papers of the New World Archaeological Foundation*, no. 14. Provo 1962.

MACNEISH, RICHARD S., S. J. K. WILKERSON, and A. NELKEN-TURNER. *First Annual Report of the Belize Archaic Archaeological Reconnaissance.* Andover 1980.

SHOOK, EDWIN M. 'The present status of research on the Pre-Classic horizons in Guatemala', in *The Civilizations of Ancient America.* ed. Sol Tax, 93–100. Chicago 1951.

SMITH, ROBERT E. 'Ceramic sequence at Uaxactún, Guatemala', *Middle American Research Institute*, publ. 20, 2 vols. New Orleans 1955.

WEAVER, MURIEL PORTER. *The Aztecs, Maya, and Their Predecessors.* Second edition. New York 1981.

Chapter 3

ADAMS, RICHARD E. W. (ed.). *The Origins of Maya Civilization.* Albuquerque 1977. (Fifteen essays, including one on the Swasey phase of Belize.)

BRAINERD, GEORGE W. 'Early ceramic horizons in Yucatán', in *The Civilizations of Ancient America*, ed. Sol Tax, 72–8. Chicago 1951.

COE, MICHAEL D. 'Early steps in the evolution of Maya writing', in *Origins of Religious Art and Iconography in Preclassic Mesoamerica*, ed. H. B. Nicholson, 107–22. Los Angeles 1976.

COE, WILLIAM R. 'Tikal, Guatemala, and emergent Maya civilization', *Science*, vol. 147, no. 3664 (1965), 1401–19.

FREIDEL, DAVID A. 'Culture areas and interaction spheres: contrasting approaches to the emergence of civilization in the Maya lowlands', *American Antiquity*, vol. 44, no. 1 (1979), 36–54. (Contains a description of the Cerros stucco masks.)

ICHON, ALAIN. 'Les sculptures de la Lagunita, El Quiché, Guatemala', *Centre National de la Recherche Scientifique, R.C.P.* 294. Paris 1977.

LOWE, GARETH W., THOMAS A. LEE, and EDUARDO E. MARTÍNEZ. 'Izapa: an introduction to the ruins and monuments', *Papers of the New World Archaeological Foundation*, no. 31. Provo 1973.

MATHENY, RAY T. (ed.). 'El Mirador, Petén, Guatemala: an interim report', *Papers of the New World Archaeological Foundation*, no. 45. Provo 1980.

MORLEY, SYLVANUS G. and FRANCES R. 'The age and provenance of the Leiden Plate', *Carnegie Institution of Washington, Contributions to American Anthropology and History*, no. 24. Washington 1939.

NORMAN, V. GARTH. 'Izapa sculpture, part I: album'. *Papers of the New World Archaeological Foundation*, no. 30. Provo 1973.

PARSONS, LEE A. 'The origins of Maya art: monumental stone sculpture of Kaminaljuyú, Guatemala, and the southern Pacific coast', *Dumbarton Oaks Studies in Pre-Columbian Art and Archaeology*, no. 28. Washington 1986.

PENDERGAST, DAVID M. 'Lamanai, Belize: summary of excavation results, 1974–1980', *Journal of Field Archaeology*, vol. 8, no. 1 (1981), 29–53.

RICKETSON, OLIVER G. and EDITH B. 'Uaxactún, Guatemala, Group E – 1926–1931', *Carnegie Institution of Washington*, publ. 477. Washington 1937.

SHOOK, EDWIN M. and ALFRED V. KIDDER. 'Mound E-III-3, Kaminaljuyú, Guatemala', *Carnegie Institution of Washington, Contributions to American Anthropology and History*, no. 53. Washington 1952.

STIRLING, MATTHEW W. 'Stone monuments of southern Mexico', *Bureau of American*

Ethnology, bulletin 138. Washington 1943. (Contains a description of the monuments at Izapa.)

WILLEY, GORDON R. and JAMES C. GIFFORD. 'Pottery of the Holmul I style from Barton Ramie, British Honduras', in *Essays in Pre-Columbian Art and Archaeology* by Samuel K. Lothrop *et al.*, 152–70. Cambridge, Mass., 1961.

Chapters 4 and 5
There are a great many publications on the Classic Maya civilization. Only a few of the most relevant can be listed here.

General survey
PROSKOURIAKOFF, TATIANA, 'A Study of Classic Maya Sculpture', *Carnegie Institution of Washington*, Publication 593. Washington 1950.

The Southern Maya Area
BORHEGYI, STEPHAN F. 'Aqualung archaeology', *Natural History*, vol. 67, no. 3 (1958), 120–5. (Describes underwater finds in Lake Amatitlán.)

KIDDER, ALFRED V., JESSE L. JENNINGS, and EDWIN M. SHOOK. 'Excavations at Kaminaljuyú, Guatemala', *Carnegie Institution of Washington*, publ. 561. Washington 1946.

PARSONS, LEE A. *Bilbao, Guatemala*, 2 vols. Milwaukee 1967–9.

SMITH, A. LEDYARD, and ALFRED V. KIDDER. 'Excavations at Nebaj, Guatemala', *Carnegie Institution of Washington*, publ. 594. Washington 1951.

THOMPSON, J. ERIC S. 'An archaeological reconnaissance in the Cotzumalhuapa region, Escuintla, Guatemala', *Carnegie Institution of Washington, Contributions to American Anthropology and History*, no. 44. Washington 1948.

WAUCHOPE, ROBERT. 'Excavations at Zacualpa, Guatemala', *Middle American Research Institute*, publ. no. 14. New Orleans 1948.

The Central Maya Area
BULLARD, WILLIAM R., Jr., 'Maya settlement pattern in northeastern Petén, Guatemala', *American Antiquity*, vol. 25, no. 3 (1960), 355–72.

CARR, ROBERT F. and JAMES E. HAZARD. 'Map of the ruins of Tikal, El Petén, Guatemala', *Tikal Reports*, no. 11. Philadelphia 1961.

COE, WILLIAM R. *Piedras Negras Archaeology: Artifacts, Caches, and Burials*. Philadelphia 1959.

—, *Tikal, a Handbook of the Ancient Maya Ruins*. Philadelphia 1967.

CULBERT, T. PATRICK (ed.). *The Classic Maya Collapse*. Albuquerque 1973. (Contains all the old and new theories about the downfall of the Classic Maya civilization.)

GORDON, GEORGE B. 'Prehistoric ruins of Copán, Honduras', *Memoirs of the Peabody Museum of Archaeology and Ethnology, Harvard University*, vol. 1, no. 1. Cambridge, Mass., 1896.

HARTUNG, HORST. *Die Zeremonialzentren der Maya*. Graz 1971.

HELLMUTH, NICHOLAS M. *Tikal, Copán Travel Guide*. St Louis 1978. (A well-illustrated introduction to Maya ruins in Guatemala and Honduras.)

KIDDER, ALFRED V. 'The artifacts of Uaxactún, Guatemala', *Carnegie Institution of Washington*, publ. 576. Washington 1947.

LONGYEAR, JOHN M. 'Copán ceramics', *Carnegie Institution of Washington*, publ. 597. Washington 1952.

MALER, TEOBERT. 'Researches in the central portion of the Usumatsintla Valley', *Memoirs of the Peabody Museum of Archaeology and Ethnology, Harvard University*, vol. 2 (no. 1, 1901; no. 2, 1903). Cambridge, Mass.

—, 'Explorations in the Department of Petén, Guatemala', *Memoirs of the Peabody Museum of Archaeology and Ethnology, Harvard University*, vol. 5, no. 1. Cambridge, Mass., 1911.

MILLER, MARY E. *The Murals of Bonampak*. Princeton, 1986.

MORLEY, SYLVANUS G. 'The inscriptions of Copán', *Carnegie Institution of Washington*, publ. 219. Washington 1920.

—, 'Guide book to the ruins of Quiriguá', *Carnegie Institution of Washington*, supplementary publ. no. 15. Washington 1935.

—, 'The inscriptions of Petén', *Carnegie Institution of Washington*, publ. 437, 5 vols. Washington 1937–8.

ROBERTSON, MERLE GREENE. *The Sculpture of Palenque*. Vol. I, *The Temple of the Inscriptions*. Princeton 1983. Vol. II, *The Early Buildings of the Palace and the Wall Paintings*. Princeton 1985.

RUPPERT, KARL, J. ERIC S. THOMPSON, and TATIANA PROSKOURIAKOFF, 'Bonampak, Chiapas, Mexico', *Carnegie Institution of Washington*, publ. 602. Washington 1955.

RUZ, ALBERTO. 'Exploraciones en Palenque', in *Proceedings of the Thirtieth International Congress of Americanists*, 5–22. Cambridge, Mass., 1954.

—, 'Palenque', *Official Guide, Instituto Nacional de Antropología e Historia*. Mexico 1960.

—, *El Templo de las Inscripciones, Palenque*. Mexico City 1973.

SHARER, ROBERT J. (ed.). 'Quiriguá Project 1974–1979', *Expedition*, vol. 23, no. 1, 5–10.
—, (ed.). *Quiriguá Reports I, II*. Philadelphia 1979, 1983.
SIDRYS, RAYMOND, and RAINER BERGER. 'Lowland Maya radiocarbon dates and the Classic Maya collapse'. *Nature*, vol. 277, 269–277.
SMITH, A. LEDYARD. 'Uaxactún, Guatemala: excavations of 1931–7'. *Carnegie Institution of Washington*, publ. 588. Washington 1950.
SMITH, ROBERT E. 'Ceramic sequence at Uaxactún, Guatemala' (see under Chapter 2).
STROMSVIK, GUSTAV. 'Guide book to the ruins of Copán', *Carnegie Institution of Washington*, publ. 577. Washington 1947.
THOMPSON, J. ERIC S. 'Excavations at San José, British Honduras', *Carnegie Institution of Washington*, publ. 506. Washington 1939.
WILLEY, GORDON R. 'The structure of ancient Maya society: evidence from the southern lowlands', *American Anthropologist*, vol. 58, no. 5 (1956), 777–82.
—, 'The Altar de Sacrificios excavations: general summary and conclusions', *Papers of the Peabody Museum of Archaeology and Ethnology*, vol. 64, no. 3. Cambridge 1973.
WILLEY, GORDON R., *et al.* 'Prehistoric Maya settlements in the Belize Valley', *Papers of the Peabody Museum of Archaeology and Ethnology, Harvard University*, vol. 54. Cambridge, Mass., 1965.
WILLEY, GORDON R. (ed.). 'Excavations at Seibal, Department of Petén, Guatemala', *Memoirs of the Peabody Museum of Archaeology and Ethnology, Harvard University*, vols. 13–15. Cambridge, Mass., 1975–1982.
WILLEY, GORDON R., and PETER MATHEWS (eds.). 'A consideration of the early Classic Period in the Maya lowlands', *Institute for Mesoamerican Studies*, Publication no. 10. Albany 1985.

The Northern Maya Area
ANDREWS, E. WYLLYS IV. 'Excavations at Dzibilchaltún, northwestern Yucatán, Mexico', *Proceedings of the American Philosophical Society*, vol. 104, no. 3 (1960), 254–65.
ANDREWS, E. WYLLYS IV, and E. WYLLYS ANDREWS V. 'Excavations at Dzibilchaltún, Yucatán, Mexico', *Middle American Research Institute, Tulana University*, Publication 48. New Orleans 1980.
BRAINERD, GEORGE W. 'The archaeological ceramics of Yucatán', (see under Chapter 2).
GENDROP, PAUL. *Los estilos Río Bec, Chenes y Puuc en la arquitectura maya*. Mexico 1983.
GROTH-KIMBALL, IRMGARD. *Maya Terrakotten*.

Tübingen 1960. (Excellent photographs of Jaina figurines.)
HELLMUTH, NICHOLAS M. *The Escuintla Hoards: Teotihuacan Art in Guatemala*. St. Louis 1975.
MATHENY, RAY, *et al.* 'Investigations at Edzná, Campeche, Mexico', *Papers of the New World Archaeological Foundation*, no. 46. Provo 1980 and 1983.
POLLOCK, H. E. D. 'The Puuc: an Architectural survey of the hill country of Yucatán and northern Campeche, Mexico', *Memoirs of the Peabody Museum of Archaeology and Ethnology, Harvard University*, vol. 19. Cambridge, Mass., 1980.
RUPPERT, KARL, and J. H. DENNISON Jr. 'Archaeological Reconnaissance in Campeche, Quintana Roo, and Petén', *Carnegie Institution of Washington*, publ. 543. Washington 1943.
RUZ, ALBERTO. *Campeche en la Arqueología Maya*. Mexico 1945.
—, 'Uxmal', *Guía Official, Instituto Nacional de Antropología e Historia*, Mexico 1956.
STEPHENS, JOHN L. *Incidents of Travel in Yucatán* (see under Chapter 1; still the best guide to the Puuc sites).
THOMPSON, J. ERIC S., *et al.* 'A preliminary study of the ruins of Cobá, Quintana Roo, Mexico', *Carnegie Institution of Washington*, publ. 424. Washington 1932.

Chapter 6
BARRERA VÁSQUEZ, ALFREDO, and SYLVANUS G. MORLEY. 'The Maya chronicles', *Carnegie Institution of Washington, Contributions to American Anthropology and History*, no. 48. Washington 1949.
BRINTON, DANIEL G. *The Maya Chronicles*. Philadelphia 1882.
CARMACK, ROBERT M. *Quichean Civilization*. Berkeley and Los Angeles 1973.
—, *The Quiché Maya of Utatlán*. Norman 1981.
CHAMBERLAIN, ROBERT S. 'The conquest and colonization of Yucatán', *Carnegie Institution of Washington*, publ. 582. Washington 1948.
CHASE, ARLEN F., and PRUDENCE M. RICE (eds.). *The Lowland Maya Postclassic*. Austin 1985.
FOX, J. W. *Quiché Conquest*. Albuquerque 1978.
GANN, THOMAS. 'Mounds in northern Honduras', *Bureau of American Ethnology, 19th Annual Report*, part 2, 655–92. Washington 1900 (illustrates the Santa Rita frescoes).
LOTHROP SAMUEL K. 'Tulum, an archaeological study of the east coast of Yucatán', *Carnegie Institution of Washington*, publ. 335. Washington 1924.
—, 'Metals from the Cenote of Sacrifice,

Chichén Itzá, Yucatán', *Memoirs of the Peabody Museum of Archaeology and Ethnology, Harvard University*, vol. 10, no. 2. Cambridge, Mass., 1952.

MILLER, ARTHUR G. *On the Edge of the Sea: Mural Painting at Tancah-Tulum, Quintana Roo.* Washington 1982.

MORRIS, EARL H., *et al.* 'The Temple of the Warriors at Chichén Itzá, Yucatán', *Carnegie Institution of Washington*, publ. 406, 2 vols. Washington 1931.

POLLOCK, H. E. D., *et al.* 'Mayapán, Yucatán, Mexico', *Carnegie Institution of Washington*, publ. 619. Washington 1962. (The account of Itzá history in Chapter 6 is largely based upon the Roys eassay.)

PROSKOURIAKOFF, TATIANA. 'Jades from the Cenote of Sacrifice, Chichén Itzá, Yucatán, Mexico', *Memoirs of the Peabody Museum of Archaeology and Ethnology*, Vol. 10, no. 1. Cambridge, Mass., 1974.

RECINOS, ADRIAN. *Popul Vuh: the Sacred Book of the Ancient Quiché Maya.* Norman, Oklahoma 1950. (An early edition, still valuable for its scholarly footnotes.)

RECINOS, ADRIAN AND DELIA GOETZ. *The Annals of the Cakchiquels.* Norman, Oklahoma 1953.

ROYS, RALPH L. 'The Book of Chilam Balam of Chumayel', *Carnegie Institution of Washington*, publ. 438. Washington 1933.

—, 'The political geography of the Yucatán Maya', *Carnegie Institution of Washington*, publ. 613. Washington 1957.

RUPPERT, KARL. 'The Caracol at Chichén Itzá, Yucatán, Mexico', *Carnegie Institution of Washington*, publ. 454. Washington 1935.

SANDERS, WILLIAM T. 'Prehistoric ceramics and settlement patterns in Quintana Roo, Mexico', *Carnegie Institution of Washington*, publ. 606, 155–264. Washington 1960.

SHEPARD, ANNA O. 'Plumbate, a Mesoamerican trade ware', *Carnegie Institution of Washington*, publ. 573. Washington 1948.

SMITH, A. LEDYARD. 'Archaeological reconnaissance in central Guatemala', *Carnegie Institution of Washington*, publ. 608. Washington 1955.

THOMPSON, J. ERIC S. *Maya History and Religion.* Norman, Oklahoma 1970. (Contains first-class studies of Maya ethnohistory. Especially important for its treatment of the Putun Maya.)

TOZZER, ALFRED M. 'Chichén Itzá and its Cenote of Sacrifice', *Memoirs of the Peabody Museum of Archaeology and Ethnology, Harvard University*, vols. 11, 12. Cambridge, Mass., 1957.

WOODBURY, R.B., and A. TRIK. *The Ruins of Zacaleu, Guatemala*, 2 vols. Boston 1953.

Chapter 7

BLOM, FRANS. 'Commerce, trade, and monetary units of the Maya', *Middle American Research Series*, no. 4, 557–66. New Orleans 1932.

COE, MICHAEL D. 'A model of ancient community structure in the Maya Lowlands', *Southwestern Journal of Anthropology*, vol. 21, no. 2 (1965), 97–114.

FOLLETT, PRESCOTT H. F. 'War and weapons of the Maya', *Middle American Research Series*, publ. 4, 374–410. New Orleans 1932.

MILES, S. W. 'The sixteenth-century Pokom-Maya: a documentary analysis of social structure and archaeological setting', *Transactions of the American Philosophical Society*, vol. 47, pt. 4 (1957).

ROYS, RALPH L. 'The Indian background of Colonial Yucatán', *Carnegie Institution of Washington*, publ. 548. Washington 1943.

SCHOLES, FRANCE V. and RALPH L. ROYS. 'The Maya Chontal Indians of Acalan-Tixchel', *Carnegie Institution of Washington*, publ. 560. Washington 1948.

THOMPSON, J. ERIC S. 'Trade relations between the Maya highlands and lowlands', *Estudios de Cultura Maya*, vol. IV, 13–49. Mexico 1964.

TOZZER, ALFRED M. 'Landa's Relación de las Cosas de Yucatán (see under Chapter 1; this is the most important work on Maya life in the late pre-Conquest period).

Chapter 8

ANDERS, FERDINAND. *Das Pantheon der Maya.* Graz, Austria 1963.

AVENI, ANTHONY F. 'Venus and the Maya', *American Scientist*, vol. 67 (1979), 274–85.

—, *Skywatchers of Ancient Mexico.* Austin 1980.

BENSON, ELIZABETH P. (ed.). *Mesoamerican Writing Systems.* Washington 1973.

BERLIN, HEINRICH. 'El glifo "emblema" en las inscripciones mayas', *Journal de la Société des Américanistes*, vol. 47 (1958), 111–9.

COE, MICHAEL D. *The Maya Scribe and His World.* New York 1973.

—, *Lords of the Underworld: Masterpieces of Classic Maya Ceramics.* Princeton 1978.

FURST, PETER T., and MICHAEL D. COE. 'Ritual enemas', *Natural History*, vol. 86, no. 3 (1977), 88–91.

KELLEY, DAVID H. 'A history of the decipherment of Maya script', *Anthropological Linguistics*, vol. 4, no. 8 (1962).

—, 'Fonetismo en la escritura Maya', *Estudios de Cultura Maya*, vol. II, 277–318. Mexico 1962.

—, 'Glyphic evidence for a dynastic sequence at

Quiriguá, Guatemala', *American Antiquity*, vol. 27 (1962), 323–5.

—, *Deciphering the Maya Script*. Austin and London 1976. (Should be read as an update to Thompson's 1950 work.)

KNOROSOV, YURI V. 'The problem of the study of the Maya hieroglyphic writing', *American Antiquity*, vol. 23, no. 3 (1958), 284–91.

—, 'Selected chapters from "The Writing of the Maya Indians"', translated by Sophie D. Coe. *Russian Translation Series, Peabody Museum of Archaeology and Ethnology, Harvard University*, vol. 4. Cambridge, Mass., 1967.

LEÓN-PORTILLA, MIGUEL. *Time and Reality in the Thought of the Maya*. Boston 1973.

LOUNSBURY, FLOYD G. 'Maya numeration computation, and calendrical astronomy', in *Dictionary of Scientific Biography*, vol. 15, supplement I (1978), 759–818.

—, 'Astronomical knowledge and its uses at Bonampak, Mexico', in *Archaeoastronomy in the New World*, ed. A. F. Aveni, 143–68. Cambridge 1982.

MARCUS, JOYCE. *Emblem and State in the Classic Maya Lowlands*. Washington 1976.

MORLEY, SYLVANUS G. 'An introduction to the study of the Maya hieroglyphs', *Bureau of American Ethnology*, bulletin 57. Washington 1915.

PROSKOURIAKOFF, TATIANA. 'Historical implications of a pattern of dates at Piedras Negras, Guatemala', *American Antiquity*, vol. 25, no. 4 (1960), 454–75. (A now classic paper.)

—, 'The lords of the Maya realm', *Expedition*, vol. 4, no. 1 (1961), 14–21.

—, 'Portraits of women in Maya art', in *Essays in Pre-Columbian Art and Archaeology* by S. K. Lothrop and others, 81–99. Cambridge, Mass., 1961.

ROBICSEK, FRANCIS, and DONALD M. HALES. *The Maya Book of the Dead: the Ceramic Codex*. Charlottesville, Virginia 1981.

ROBERTSON, MERLE GREENE (ed.). *Palenque Round Table Series (Mesa Redonda de Palenque)*. Vols. 1–3, Pebble Beach, Calif., 1974–76. Vol. 4, Palenque 1979. Vol. 5, Austin 1980. (Much of the recent information on Maya iconography and epigraphy has appeared in this indispensable series.)

SÁNCHEZ, GEORGE I. *Arithmetic in Maya*. Austin, Texas 1961.

SATTERTHWAITE, LINTON, Jr. 'Concepts and structures of Maya calendrical arithmetics', *Joint Publications of the Museum of the University of Pennsylvania and the Philadelphia Anthropological Society*, no. 3. Philadelphia 1947.

SCHELE, LINDA. *Maya Glyphs; the Verbs*. Austin 1982.

—, 'Human sacrifice among the Classic Maya', in *Ritual Human Sacrifice in Mesoamerica*, ed. E. H. Boone, 7–45. Washington, D.C., 1984.

—, *Notebook for the Maya Hieroglyph Workshop*. Austin 1986.

SCHOCKEN, WOLFGANG A. *The Calendar of the Maya*. Boston 1986.

STUART, DAVID. 'Royal auto-sacrifice among the Maya: a study of image and meaning', *Res* 7/8, 6–20.

STUART, GEORGE E. 'Maya art treasures discovered in caves', *National Geographic*, vol. 160, no. 2 (1981), 220–36. (The cave drawings of Naj Tunich.)

TEDLOCK, DENNIS. *Popol Vuh*. New York 1985. (The definitive edition of the greatest piece of Native American literature, and the key source for the understanding of pre-Conquest Maya iconography and thought.)

TEEPLE, JOHN E. 'Maya astronomy', *Carnegie Institution of Washington, Contributions to American Archaeology*, no. 2. Washington 1930.

THOMPSON, J. ERIC S. 'Maya arithmetic', *Carnegie Institution of Washington, Contributions to American Anthropology and History*, no. 36. Washington 1942.

—, 'Maya hieroglyphic writing. Introduction', *Carnegie Institution of Washington*, publ. 589. Washington 1950. (A monumental survey of Maya calendrics, religion, and astronomy.)

—, *A Catalog of Maya Hieroglyphs*. Norman, Oklahoma 1962. (Covers glyphs of both the monuments and codices.)

VILLACORTA, J. ANTONIO and CARLOS A. *Códices mayas*. Guatemala 1930. (Three of the four Maya hieroglyphic books reproduced in a useful edition.)

ZIMMERMAN, GÜNTER. *Die Hieroglyphen der Maya-Handschriften*. Hamburg 1956. (A catalog of the glyphs in the codices.)

List of illustrations

All maps were drawn by Mrs Jean Zallinger and Mr Peter Zallinger. Other drawings are by the author, unless otherwise indicated.

Frontispiece: Detail of Maya lord shown fully in ill. 48. Photo Charles Uht, courtesy Museum of Primitive Art, New York.

1 Map of topographical features and cultural areas.

2 Lake Atitlán, Guatemala. Photo courtesy Frederick Church Collection, Olana, New York.

3 The Lacandón rain forest. Photo Dr T. C. Schneirla, courtesy American Museum of Natural History, New York.

4 Burning a lowland maize field. Photo courtesy Peabody Museum, Harvard University.

5 Prehistoric Maya raised field system. Photo Alfred H. Siemens.

6 Map of language groups in Maya area.

7 Map of sites of Early Hunters, Archaic, and Early and Middle Preclassic periods.

8 Fluted obsidian point, Early Hunters period.

9 Los Tapiales stone tools, Early Hunters period. Courtesy Ruth Gruhn and Alan L. Bryan.

10 Milling stones from Archaic sites in northern Belize. Photo Michael D. Coe.

11 Ocós culture figurines and vessels, Early Preclassic period.

12 Swasey phase plastered platform at Cuello, Early Preclassic period. Photo Norman Hammond.

13 Monument 52 at the Olmec site of San Lorenzo, Early Preclassic period. Photo Michael D. Coe.

14 Las Charcas pottery vessels, Middle Preclassic period. After Shook 1951.

15 Las Charcas female figurine, Middle Preclassic period. Courtesy Peabody Museum, Harvard University.

16 Map showing sites of the Late Preclassic period.

17 Schematic representation of the 260-day count.

18 Signs for the months in the 365-day count.

19 Part of the 52-year Calendar Round.

20 Stela 1 from El Baúl.

21 Monument 1 at Monte Alto, probably Late Preclassic period. Photo Milwaukee Public Museum.

22 View of Kaminaljuyú, from a photograph by A. P. Maudslay.

23 Plan of Tomb II, Mound E-III-3, at Kaminaljuyú. After Shook and Kidder 1952.

24 Effigy bowl from Tomb I, Mound E-III-3 at Kaminaljuyú. Courtesy Peabody Museum, Harvard University.

25 Soapstone jar from Tomb I, Mound E-III-3 at Kaminaljuyú. Courtesy Peabody Museum, Harvard University.

26 Incised bowl from Tomb I, Mound E-III-3 at Kaminaljuyú. Courtesy Peabody Museum, Harvard University.

27 Stela from Kaminaljuyú with man wearing masks of long-lipped gods.

28 Broken Miraflores stela from Kaminaljuyú. After R. Girard, *Los Mayas Eternos*, Mexico 1962, fig. 242.

29 Usulután ware bowl from Burial 85, Tikal. Courtesy University Museum, Philadelphia.

30 Pyramid E-VII-sub, Uaxactún. Photo courtesy Peabody Museum, Harvard University.

31 Greenstone mask, Tikal. Courtesy University Museum, Philadelphia.

32 Structure N10-43 at Lamanai, Belize, a Late Preclassic temple-pyramid. After David Pendergast.

33 Maps showing sites of the Classic period.

34 The Leiden Plate. After Kidder, Jennings and Shook 1946, fig. 108.

35 Structure A-7 at Kaminaljuyú. After S. G. and F. R. Morley 1939.

36 Carved jade bead from Kaminaljuyú. Courtesy University Museum, Philadelphia.

37 Thin Orange ware anthropomorphic vessel from Kaminaljuyú. Courtesy Peabody Museum, Harvard University.

38 Tripod vessel with cover from Kaminaljuyú. Courtesy Peabody Museum, Harvard University.

39 Pottery incense burner with heads of gods.

Courtesy Stephan F. Borhegyi and the Milwaukee Public Museum.

40 Pottery of the Tzakol phase at Uaxactún. After Smith 1955.

41 Tomb chamber of Burial 48, Tikal. Photo courtesy University Museum, Philadelphia.

42 Two-part ceramic effigy from Burial 10, Tikal. Courtesy University Museum, Philadelphia.

43 Stela 31 at Tikal. Courtesy University Museum, Philadelphia.

44 Fragmentary stela in Teotihuacan style, from Tikal. After H. Moholy-Nagy.

45 Lid of stuccoed bowl from Tikal. Courtesy Peabody Museum, Harvard University.

46 Jade plaque of the god Vucub Caquix, from Copán, Honduras. Photo Charles Uht, courtesy Museum of Primitive Art, New York.

47 Jade object from Pomona, Belize. Courtesy Peabody Museum, Harvard University.

48 Seated wooden figure from Tabasco, Mexico. Photo Charles Uht, courtesy Museum of Primitive Art, New York.

49 Double-chambered vessel, possibly from Campeche. Photo Charles Uht, courtesy Museum of Primitive Art, New York.

50 Upper façade of building at Acanceh, Mexico. Photo courtesy Peabody Museum, Harvard University.

51 Stone relief of the Crab God, from El Baúl. Courtesy Peabody Museum, Harvard University.

52 Monument 4, Sta Lucía Cotzumalhuapa.

53 Thin stone head from El Baúl. Courtesy Peabody Museum, Harvard University.

54 Plan of central Tikal. After Carr and Hazard 1961.

55 Room in the Five-Story Palace at Tikal.

56 Reconstruction drawing of Copán by Tatiana Proskouriakoff. Courtesy Peabody Museum, Harvard University.

57 Ball Court at Copán. Photo courtesy Peabody Museum, Harvard University.

58 Stela 4 from Machaquilá. Drawn by Ian Graham.

59 Stone head and torso of the Young Maize God from Copán. Courtesy American Museum of Natural History, New York.

60 Head of torchbearer at Copán. Photo G. Ekholm, courtesy American Museum of Natural History, New York.

61 Stela D and its 'altar', Copán. From a lithograph published by Frederick Catherwood in 1844.

62 Stela D at Quiriguá. From a photograph taken by A. P. Maudslay in 1855. Courtesy American Museum of Natural History, New York.

63 Altar of Zoomorph O at Quiriguá. Courtesy Peabody Museum, Harvard University.

64 Carved wooden lintel from Temple IV, Tikal. Courtesy Museum für Völkerkunde, Basel.

65 Temple I at Tikal. Photo courtesy University Museum, Philadelphia.

66 Two incised bones from Tikal. After A. Trik, 'The splendid tomb of Temple I, Tikal, Guatemala'.

67 Incised bone from Tikal. After Trik.

68 Stela 14 from Piedras Negras. Courtesy University Museum, Philadelphia.

69 Detail of wall painting, Room 1, Bonampak. Courtesy Peabody Museum, Harvard University.

70 Sculptured stone from Bonampak. Courtesy Peabody Museum, Harvard University.

71 Wall painting in Room 2, Bonampak. Courtesy Peabody Museum, Harvard University.

72 Relief from Yaxchilán. Courtesy Trustees of the British Museum.

73 Palace and Tower at Palenque.

74 Decorated pier on the Palace, Palenque. From a photograph by A. P. Maudslay. Courtesy American Museum of Natural History, New York.

75 Cross-section of the Temple of the Cross at Palenque. After Holmes 1895-7, fig. 64.

76 Temple of the Sun at Palenque. Photo courtesy American Museum of Natural History, New York.

77 Funerary Crypt in the Temple of the Inscriptions, Palenque. Photo Alberto Ruz L.

78 Jade mosaic mask from Palenque. Photo Alberto Ruz L.

79 North façade of Structure V at Hormiguero. Photo Karl Ruppert, courtesy Peabody Museum, Harvard University.

80 Reconstruction drawing of the Palace at Xpuhil by Tatiana Proskouriakoff. Courtesy Peabody Museum, Harvard University.

81 The Nunnery Quadrangle at Uxmal. After G. Kubler, *The Art and Architecture of Ancient America*, Harmondsworth 1962, fig. 47.

82 West wing of the Palace at Sayil. Photo

courtesy Peabody Museum, Harvard University.

83 Arch at Labná. From a view published by Frederick Catherwood in 1844.

84 East wing of the Nunnery at Chichén Itzá. From a lithograph by Frederick Catherwood.

85 Five-storied structure at Etzná. Photo Fred Nelson, courtesy Ray J. Matheny.

86 Stone lintel from Kuná (Lacanhá). Photo Nickolas Murray, courtesy Dumbarton Oaks, Washington, D.C.

87 Detail from the Tablet of the Slaves, Palenque. Photo Alberto Ruz L.

88 Pottery censer probably from Tabasco. Courtesy American Museum of Natural History, New York.

89 Stone-tablet incised with the head of Chac, from Palenque. After Ruz 1954, fig. 5.

90 Pottery figurine from Jaina. Courtesy American Museum of Natural History, New York.

91 Pottery figurine probably from Jaina. Photo Charles Uht, courtesy Museum of Primitive Art, New York.

92 Pottery figurine from Jaina. Courtesy Dumbarton Oaks, Washington, D.C.

93 Polychrome pottery from Altar de Sacrificios. Photo Ian Graham.

94 Black pottery jar from Chocholá. Courtesy Dumbarton Oaks, Washington, D.C.

95 Incised pottery bowl from the Northern Area. Courtesy American Museum of Natural History, New York (Erickson Collection).

96 Carved jade plaque from Nebaj. Courtesy Peabody Museum, Harvard University.

97 Onyx bowl said to be from Campeche. Courtesy Dumbarton Oaks, Washington, D.C.

98 Eccentric flint from Quiriguá. Courtesy Trustees of the British Museum.

99 Carved shell pendant from Jaina. Courtesy Dumbarton Oaks, Washington, D.C.

100 Incised obsidians from Tikal. Courtesy Trustees of the British Museum.

101 Map showing sites of the Post-Classic period and late migration routes.

102 Wall painting from the Temple of the Warriors, Chichén Itzá. After *The Art of the Maya*, Carnegie Institution of Washington.

103 Repoussé gold disk from the Sacred Cenote, Chichén Itzá. After Lothrop 1952.

104 View of the Toltec part of Chichén Itzá.

Photo courtesy Peabody Museum, Harvard University.

105 Detail from a gold disk from the Sacred Cenote, Chichén Itzá. After Lothrop 1952.

106 'Chacmool' figure, Temple of the Warriors, Chichén Itzá. Photo Charles R. Wicke.

107 Temple of the Warriors at Chichén Itzá. Photo courtesy Peabody Museum, Harvard University.

108 Ball Court at Chichén Itzá. Photo Charles R. Wicke.

109 Doorway of the Temple of the Jaguars at Chichén Itzá. Photo courtesy Peabody Museum, Harvard University.

110 Relief panel from the Dance Platform of the Eagles, Chichén Itzá. Courtesy American Museum of Natural History, New York.

111 Bas-relief of skulls from the Tzompantli, Chichén Itzá.

112 Chamber in the cave of Balankanché. Courtesy George E. Stuart and the Middle American Research Institute.

113 Toltec effigy jar from Guatemala. Courtesy Peabody Museum, Harvard University.

114 X-Fine Orange ware jar from coastal Campeche. Courtesy Peabody Museum, Harvard University.

115 Toltec tripod jar from coastal Campeche. Courtesy Peabody Museum, Harvard University.

116 Pottery incense burner from Mayapán. Courtesy Peabody Museum, Harvard University.

117 Upper part of pottery incense burner from Mayapán. Courtesy Peabody Museum, Harvard University.

118 Map showing the independent states of the Northern Area on the eve of the Spanish Conquest.

119 Plan of the walled town of Tulum. After Lothrop 1924, pl. 25.

120 Temple of the Frescoes at Tulum. Photo courtesy Peabody Museum, Harvard University.

121 Detail of a wall painting, Temple of the Frescoes, Tulum.

122 Reconstruction drawing of Group C at Chuitinamit by Tatiana Proskouriakoff. Courtesy Peabody Museum, Harvard University.

123 Group B at Mixco Viejo.

124 Figurine of a woman grinding maize on a *metate*. After T. A. Joyce, 'The pottery

whistle-figurines of Lubaantun'.

125 Figurine of a huntsman slaying deer. After Joyce, op. cit.

126 Graffito of a person in a palanquin from Tikal. After H. T. Webster, 'Tikal graffiti', fig. 12.

127 Incised bone showing standing captive, from Tikal.

128 Page from the Dresden Codex.

129 Pages from the Grolier Codex. Photo Michael D. Coe.

130 Detail from a Late Classic cylindrical vase in codex style, northern Petén or southern Campeche. Drawing by Diane Griffiths Peck.

131 Glyphs for the world directions and associated colors.

132 Gods of the Maya pantheon, from the Dresden Codex. After Zimmerman 1956, tables 6, 7.

133 Plate in codex style, from northern Guatemala or southern Campeche. Eighth century AD. Photo © Justin Kerr.

134 Rollout of a Late Classic cylindrical vase, probably from Naranjo, Guatemala. Drawing by Diane Griffiths Peck.

135 Section of paintings and hieroglyphic texts from the walls of Naj Tunich cave, Guatemala. Late Classic, eighth century AD. Courtesy National Geographic Magazine.

136 New Year ceremonies in the Dresden Codex. After T. A. Joyce, *Mexican Archaeology*, fig. 58.

137 Examples of Maya vigesimal numeration.

138 Glyphs for the cycles of the Long Count.

139 Glyphs for the earth and the heavenly bodies in the codices.

140 Tablet of the 96 Hieroglyphs from Palenque. After E. J. Palacios, 'Inscripción recientemente descubierta en Palenque', fig. 1.

141 The Maya 'alphabet' according to Bishop Landa.

142 Phonetic-syllabic readings of Maya signs given by Y. V. Knorosov.

143 Emblem Glyphs from the Classic monuments.

144 Historical glyphs in the monumental texts.

145 Lintel 8 at Yaxchilán. After T. Proskouriakoff, 'Historical data in the inscriptions of Yaxchilán', fig. 1.

146 Map showing the political geography of the Central Maya Area at AD 790, based on the distribution of cities with Emblem Glyphs. After Peter Mathews.

Index

Numerals in *italics* refer to illustration numbers

Abaj Takalik 52
Abejas culture 35
Acanceh 84, 89; *50*
Adams, Richard E. W. 20, 78
agriculture, highland 15; lowland 15, 17–20, 32–4, 61, 128, 155–6; *4, 5*
aguadas 16
Ah Kinchil *see* Sun God
Alexander, Herbert 30
Altar de Sacrificios 42, 123; *93*
Altun Ha 42, 100, 111
Alvarado, Pedro de 151, 152, 153
Annals of the Cakchiquels 149, 160
Archaic period 24, 25, 31–4

architecture, Acanceh 84; Chenes 113; Chicanel 61–2; Classic Maya 21, 92–4, 114; Puuc 114; Río Bec 112–3
Arévalo culture 37, 40
astronomy 24, 46, 139, 161, 169, 173, 175–80, 179, 182; *139*
atlatl 78, 132, 156, 160; *43*
Avendaño y Loyola, Fray Andrés de 98
Aveni, Anthony 178

Bacabs 164, 165, 166
bajos 6, 19, 98
baktun 49, 67, 114, 164
Baktun 7 dates 50, 51, 52
Baktun 8 dates 52
Balankanché 141; *112*
balche 157, 168
ball game 13, 85–7, 88, 94, 138,

139, 151, 158, 169, 177, 187; *52, 57, 108, 122*
baptism 158
batab 160
Batak 46
Becan 89
bee-keeping 156, 172
Belize River 16
Berlin, Heinrich 183, 187
Bird Jaguar 184; *144, 145*
Bolon Dzacab 51, 166; *132*
Bonampak 89, 104–5, 108, 119, 126, 129, 177, 185; *69–71*
Borhegyi, Stephan de 56
Brainerd, George W. 37, 114
Brasseur de Bourbourg, Charles Etienne 178
breadnut 17, 20, 43, 156
Bronson, Bennett 20
Bryan, Alan 30

burials 37, 43, 76, 122, 159; *see also* tombs
Butterfly Goddess 70

cacao 15, 87, 88, 155, 156, 157, 158, 160, 166, 173, 174; *see also* chocolate
Cacaxtla 129
Cakchiquel 25, 84, 149, 151, 153
calendar 13, 22, 27, 45, 47–51, 87, 131, 169, 170, 173–4, 179; *17–19, 138, 140*
Calendar Round 22, 47, 49, 50, 53, 123, 174, 176, 184; *19, 93*
Campbell, Lyle 24
Canek 147
Canul 144
Carmack, Robert 149
Catherwood, Frederick 22, 45
causeways 64, 93, 104, 114, 172
cenotes 15, 21, 37, 93, 156; *see also* Sacred Cenote
ceremonial bar 93, 118, 129, 166; *86*
ceremonial enemas 168–9
Cerros 63, 64
Chaan-muan 104
Chac 51, 79, 115, 146, 148, 157, 166, 170, 172; *66, 89, 116, 132*
'chacmool' 135; *106*
Chac Xib Chac 51, 123, 146, 167, 170; *89*
Chac Zutz 118; *87*
Chakanputun 144
Champollion, Jean François 180, 187
Champoton 153
Chan-Bahlum 108, 178, 185, 187
Chenes 113, 115
Chetumal Bay 63
Chiapa de Corzo 50
Chicanel culture 61–2, 64, 75; *30*
Chichén Itzá 20, 114, 115, 126, 131–42, 144, 146, 147, 161, 178; *84, 102–11*
Chichicastenango 60
chicle 112
Chilam Balam 131, 152
Chilam Balam, Books of 22, 131, 153, 155, 163, 183
Childe, V. Gordon 46
chili peppers 15, 32, 155
Chixoy Valley 60, 157
chocolate 52, 85, 156
Chol 25, 26
Cholan languages 25, 26, 153–4
Chontal 26, 128–9, 144, 149, 151, 157, 158
Chorti 26
Chuitinamit *122*
Chuj 25
chultun 42–3, 155
Ciudad Real, Fray Antonio de 21
Classic Veracruz civilization 72
climate 16, 31

Clovis 30
Coatlicue 166
Cobá 113–4, 148–9
Cocom 144, 145, 146, 159
Cogolludo, Diego López 145
Colomba 52
color-directions 13, 164, 165, 166, 170; *131*
Comitán 14
copal 27, 128, 156, 171
Copán 26, 88, 89, 94, 97, 119, 173, 175, 183; *56–7, 59–61*
copper 141, 155, 158
corbel vault 21, 62, 65, 93, 105, 115, 135
Córdoba, Francisco Hernández de 153
Cortés, Hernán 17, 147, 153
cotton 155, 156, 157, 160
Cotzumalhuapa culture 52, 84–8; *51–3*
Cozumel 144
Cuadros culture 35, 36
Cuello 37; *12*

Dahlin, Bruce 64
Danta pyramid 64
Death God 61, *132, 136*
Del Río, Antonio 22
Desert culture 32, 33
Díaz, Porfirio 153
Distance Numbers 174
dog 156
Dresden Codex 161, 166, 174, 176, 177; *128, 132, 136*
dynasties 115, 152, 159, 184, 185, 187
Dzibilchaltún 43, 89

Early Hunters period 24, 29–31
eclipses 45, 176, 177
Ehecatl 87
Ek Chuah 157, 166; *117, 132*
El Baúl 52, 54; *20, 51, 53*
El Mirador 62, 64
Emblem Glyphs 78, 168, 173, 177, 183, 184, 185, 187
enemas 168–9
Esperanza culture 69–74; *35–8*
Etzná 118; *85*

Fat God 54, 122; *91*
fauna, highland 15; lowland 17
Feathered Serpent 84, 87, 129, 132, 134, 153; *64, 109; see also* Gucumatz, Kukulcan, Quetzalcoatl
figurines 36, 38, 42, 73, 121, 122; *11, 15, 90–92*
fishing 35, 36, 156, 172
flora, highland 15; lowland 16; *3*
Flores 147
Formative *see* Preclassic
Förstemann, Ernst 22
Freidel, D. A. 63
Furst, Peter 168

Gann, Thomas 147
geology 14, 15, 29
Gibbs, Sharon 178
God B *see* Chac
God GI *see* Chac Xib Chac
God K *see* Bolon Dzacab
God L 108, 167; *93, 136*
God M *see* Ek Chuah
God N 167
Goddess of Medicine 144
gold 134, 141; *103, 105*
Great Cycle 50, 164
Grijalva Valley 50
Grolier Codex 161, 176; *129*
Gruhn, Ruth 30
Gucumatz 29

hachas 87
halach uinic 160
Hammond, Norman 37
harbor, Lamanai 63, 179
Hartung, Horst 178
Hauberg Stela 67
Healey, Giles 104
Hellmuth, Nicholas 74, 78
Hero Twins 167, 168, 169; *135*
holcan 160
Hooton, Earnest A. 140
Hormiguero 112; *79*
Huastec 11, 25, 168
Huehuetenango 30
Huehueteotl 87
human sacrifice 13, 56, 78, 88, 104, 108, 134, 135, 138–40, 152, 160, 167, 170, 171, 177; *111*
Hunab Ku 166
Hunac Ceel 146
Hunahpu 167, 169; *135*
hunting 11, 30, 31, 156, 172; *125*

Ichon, Alain 60
incense burners 59, 72, 121, 141, 146; *39, 112, 116–17*
'Indian Church' *see* Lamanai
Initial Series 174, 175
Introductory Glyph 52, 67, 174; *138*
Isla Mujeres 157
Itzá 17, 26, 132, 144–7, 154
Itzamná 146, 166, 167; *42, 113, 132, 136*
Ix Chel 122, 144, 166, 167; *121, 132*
Ix Ch'up 166
Ixil 25
Iximché 151
Izamal 146
Izapan civilization 51–2, 54, 56, 59, 60, 62, 65, 67, 68

Jaguar God 62, 108, 121, 166, 167; *88*
Jaina 121–2, 126; *90–2, 99*
Joralemon, David 173
Justeson, John 67

Kaminaljuyú 37, 40, 53, 54–60, 62, 69, 70, 73, 74, 78; *22–8, 35–7*
Kanjobalan language 25
katun 49, 128, 131, 132, 142, 144, 146, 147, 174
Katun Prophecies 131
Kaufman, Terence 24
Kekchi 25, 26
Kelley, David 45, 168, 177, 182
kin 49
Kirchhoff, Paul 11
Knorosov, Yuri V. 161, 180–2, 184; *142*
Kowalski, Jeff 115
Kukulcan 135, 139, 144, 166
Kukulcan I 132
Kukulcan II 144
Kuná 118; *86*

Labná *83*
Lacandón 16, 17, 25, 26, 104, 128, 154
Laguna de los Términos 26
Lake Amatitlán 74
Lake Atitlán 25, 74; *2*
Lake Izabal 25, 153, 157
Lake Petén Itzá 144, 147
Lake Petenxil 33
La Lagunita 60
Lamanai 63, 64, 128, 149, 155; *32*
Landa, Fray Diego de 18, 22, 114, 128, 131, 132, 135, 138, 139, 144, 147, 155, 157, 158, 159, 170, 171, 174, 175, 176, 177, 178, 179, 180, 181; *141*
Las Charcas culture 40, 42; *14–15*
La Venta 38
La Victoria 36
Leiden Plate 67, 78; *34*
lexicostatistics 26, 32
lineages 131, 144, 152–3, 159, 166, 170, 173, 185, 187
lintels 83, 98, 100, 118, 119, 184, 185; *64, 86*
Loltún cave 31, 65
Long Count 22, 24, 38, 43, 49–50, 52, 53, 65, 67, 68, 73, 78, 93, 97, 104, 114, 128, 164, 174, 175, 176, 177, 179; *34, 41, 138*
'Long-lipped' God 51; *27*
Los Tapiales 30
Lounsbury, Floyd G. 176, 177, 179, 185, 187
Lowe, John W. G. 126, 128
Lowe-Ha phase 31
Lunar Series 175, 179, 187

MacNeish, R. S. 31, 32, 34
Madrid Codex 156, 161, 172
maize 13, 15, 18, 20, 32, 33, 35, 42, 155, 157, 173, 174

Maize God 94, 146, 167; *132–3*
Mamean language 25
Mamóm culture 42–3, 62
Mangelsdorf, Paul C. 32
Maní 37
manikin scepter 93, 97, 138, 166; *58*
markets and trade 11, 13, 67, 73, 74, 78, 114, 128, 152, 157–8, 184, 185
Mars 176, 177, 187; *139*
Matheny, Ray 64, 118
Mathews, Peter 78, 185, 187
Maudslay, Alfred P. 22, 40
Maya Mountains 15
Mayan language family 24–7; *6*
Mayapán 144–5, 157, 159, 170, 187
Mercury 176
Mérida 22, 84, 153
Mesoamerica, defined 11, 13
military orders 132; *110*
Miller, Mary 104
Miraflores culture 54–60, 62, 69, 70; *22–8*
mirrors 72, 166
Mixco Viejo 152; *123*
Mixe-Zoquean 26, 27, 51
Mixtec 50, 148, 180
Moche 118
Monkey-man Scribes 97, 167, 173
Monte Alto 53–4; *21*
Montejo, Francisco de 153
moon 45, 51, 87, 139, 165, 175–6; *139; see also* Lunar Series
Moon Goddess 122, 166; *52, 132*
Mopán 26
Morley, Sylvanus G. 11, 32, 89, 105, 114, 179, 187
Motozintlec 25
'mushroom stones' 56

nacom 160, 170
Nahua 27, 131, 149, 151
Nahuat language 84, 88
Nahuatl language 26, 84
Naj Tunich 26, 169; *135*
Nakum 100
Nal-Tel 35
Naranjo 100, 172, 183, 185; *134*
Nebaj 25, 126; *96*
Needham, Joseph 45
Neugebauer, Otto 173
New River 16, 63, 128, 149
Nine Lords of the Night 108
Nito 157
North Star 157, 166; *132*
numeration 50, 88, 161, 173–4, 178, 179, 187; *137*

Oaxaca 27, 38, 50, 126, 148
Ocós culture 35, 36, 37; *11*
Old Fire God 87, 146

Olmec civilization 13, 27, 38, 50, 51, 52, 54, 65, 94, 173; *13*
Olmeca-Xicallanca 128, 129
Oxkintok 83

Pacal 108, 110, 182, 185, 187
Palenque 7, 22, 26, 51, 105–110, 118, 168, 177, 182, 183, 185, 187; *74–8, 87, 89*
paper, fig-bark 13, 46, 100, 161
Paris Codex 161, 178
Pauahtuns 167, 168
Pendergast, David M. 63, 111
penis-perforator 173
Period Ending Dates 174
Piedras Negras 100, 104, 183, 185; *68*
Pipil 26, 84, 85, 88
Pleistocene 29
Plumbate ware 141–2; *113, 115*
pochteca 73, 78, 88
Pokomam 149, 152; *123*
political organization 67, 83, 131, 147, 159, 160, 187
Popol Vuh 29, 51, 111, 151, 160, 166–7; *135*
Poptun 169
population 20, 26, 38, 67, 89, 91, 114, 128, 144, 147
Preclassic 19, 24, 34–43, 47, 50, 51, 52, 54, 56, 60, 61, 62, 63, 64, 65, 67, 111, 118
priests 67, 93, 131, 135, 158, 159, 160, 169–70, 172–3, 174, 180
prisoners 104, 107, 119, 160, 171, 173, 177, 185, 187; *71, 127*
Proskouriakoff, Tatiana 60, 112, 118, 183–4
Proto-Mayan 25
Puerto Barrios 67
Puleston, Dennis 19, 20, 31, 43
Purrón 35
Putun 128–9, 144, 151, 157
Puuc culture 113, 114–18, 134, 135, 139; *81–4*
Puuc Hills 15, 113, 114, 118

Quetzalcoatl 84, 87, 132, 139, 146, 151; *see also* Topiltzin Quetzalcoatl, Kukulcan, Feathered Serpent
Quetzaltenango 14
Quiché 25, 29, 60, 149, 151, 152, 166; *122*
Quichean languages 25
Quiriguá 88, 97, 183; *62–3, 98*

radiocarbon dating 22, 30, 37, 40, 42, 62, 163
Rain God 38, 52, 78, 79, 94, 140, 141, 146, 148, 157, 166, 170; *see also* Chac, Tlaloc
Regulus 177

reservoirs 93, 100, 118
Richmond Hill 31
Río Azul 78
Río Bec 20, 89, 112, 113; *79, 80*
Río Hondo 16
Río Lacanhá 104
Río Lacantún 42
Río Motagua 14, 21, 88, 94, 97, 157
Río Negro 14
Río Usumacinta 16, 25, 94, 100, 104, 105, 126
Robertson, Merle Greene 107
roof comb 21, 98, 107, 112; *75*
Roys, Ralph L. 132, 142
rubber 85, 156, 172
Ruz, Alberto 108, 140

sacbe, see causeways
Sacred Cenote 126, 134, 139–41, 144, 146; *103, 104*
salt 157
Sánchez, George I. 173
San Cristóbal de las Casas 25
San Lorenzo 38; *13*
San Rafael 30
Santa Lucía Cotzumalhuapa 85; *52*
Santa Marta rockshelter 32
Sayil *82*
Schele, Linda 67, 185
Seibal 42, 89, 128, 177, 183
settlement pattern 20, 21, 89–91, 93, 147
Sharer, Robert 126
Shield Jaguar 184; *72, 144*
Short Count 131, 142
Siemens, Alfred 19
sky-serpent 62, 112, 113, 114, 115, 135, 139, 165
Slate ware 123; *95*
slaves 18, 119, 152, 157, 159–60, 171
social organization 105, 128, 135, 152, 153, 159–60, 170, 172
soils 15, 18, 34
Spinden, Herbert J. 22
squashes 13, 15, 32, 155, 156
Stephens, John Lloyd 22, 45, 94, 183
Stuart, David 172, 173
sun 107, 139, 165, 167, 175–6, 177; *139*
Sun God 108, 111, 114, 166; *132*
Swadesh, Maurice 24
Swasey 37; *12*
sweat baths 43, 94, 100, 104

talud-tablero 70, 84
tamales 13, 155

Tamaulipas 33
Tapachula 51
Tapachulteco 51
Taube, Karl 167
Tayasal 17, 147, 148, 154, 161
tecomates 35, 36, 37, 40
Tehuacán Valley
Tenochtitlan 151
teosinte 32
Teotihuacan 68–9, 70, 72, 73, 74, 75, 79, 80, 83, 84, 88, 89, 94, 129; *37–8, 43–4, 50*
Tepeu 29; *93, 98, 100*
Tezcatlipoca 132, 166
Thin Orange ware 70, 79; *37*
Thompson, J. Eric S. 22, 24, 26, 50, 85, 114, 126, 128, 139, 157, 161, 163, 164, 167, 176, 177, 179, 181, 182
Tigre pyramid 64
Tikal 15, 42, 59, 62, 63, 64, 65, 67, 75, 78, 79, 80, 89, 91, 93, 98–100, 105, 112, 183, 185; *29, 31, 41–5, 54–5, 64–7, 100*
Tiquisate 74, 79
Tlalchitonatiuh 87
Tlaloc 78, 80, 87, 115, 141; *43–4*
Tlapallan 132
Tojil 153
Tojolabal 25
Tolstoy, Paul 46
Toltec 26, 114, 115, 118, 229, 131–43, 144, 149, 151, 161, 163, 166, 171, 173, 187; *102–15*
tombs 38, 54–6, 62, 65, 70, 76, 98, 99–100, 108–110, 111, 166; *41, 77*
Toniná 119
Topiltzin Quetzalcoatl 132, 134; *see also* Kukulcan I
tortillas 13, 155
Totonac 115
Tozzer, Alfred M. 140
Tres Zapotes 50, 51
Trik, Aubrey 99
Tripsacum 32
Tula 132, 135, 138, 142, 149, 160
Tulum 114, 147–8, 149; *119–21*
tun 9, 174
260-day count 45, 48, 166, 170, 171, 172, 174, 176, 182, 187; *17*
Tzakol culture 75–80; *40–2, 45, 47, 49*
Tzeltal 25, 153
Tzeltalan languages 25, 26
tzolkin 47
Tzotzil 25

Tzutuhil 25, 149

Uaxactún 42, 62, 63, 64, 68, 75, 80, 89, 100; *4, 30, 40*
Uayeb 172, 175
uinal 49
Usulután ware 56, 61; *29*
Usumacinta *see* Río Usumacinta
Utatlán 151, 152–3
Uucil-abnal 134, 144
Uxmal 21, 114–15, 134, 146, 178; *81*

Vague Year 47–9, 50, 172, 175; *18*
Valley of Mexico 68, 69, 79, 126, 129
Venus 13, 107, 139, 163, 165, 166, 167, 176, 177, 178, 179; *129, 139*
Vucub Caquix 51, 59, 61, 111, 167

wall paintings 47, 62, 69, 75–6, 104–5, 138, 185; *69, 71, 102, 121*
warfare 62, 83, 104–5, 123, 126, 129, 132, 134, 135, 138, 144, 147, 152, 160, 184, 185, 187
War gods 132, 166
Wind God 87
writing 13, 21, 22, 26, 27, 43, 46, 50, 59–60, 65, 94, 97, 100, 104, 108, 118, 161, 163, 178–85, 187; *97, 99, 128–44*

Xbalanque 167, 168, 169
Xe culture 40
Xibalbá 78, 166, 167, 169; *134*
Xicallanco 26, 128, 157
Xincan language 26
Xipe Totec 79, 87, 146; *39, 45*
Xiu family 114, 146
Xochicalco 129
Xpuhil 112; *80*

Yaxchilán 100, 104, 183, 184, 285
Yaxhá 80, 89
Yaxuná 65, 114
'yokes' 85, 87
Yucatec 25, 26, 33, 110, 153, 158, 160, 171, 175, 176, 183, 184

Zapotec 27, 38, 173
zodiac 45, 178
Zoquean languages 26
Zuyuá 160